Introduction to Neural Networks with Java

Introduction to Neural Networks with Java

by Jeff Heaton

Heaton Research, Inc.
St. Louis

Introduction to Neural Networks with Java, First Edition

Second printing

Publisher: Heaton Research, Inc

Author: Jeff Heaton

Editor: Mary McKinnis

Select Illustrations: Carrie Spear

```
ISBN's for all Editions:
0-9773206-0-X, Softcover
0-9773206-3-4, Adobe PDF e-book
```

SOFTWARE LICENSE AGREEMENT: TERMS AND CONDITIONS

WARRANTY

Heaton Research, Inc. warrants the enclosed media to be free of physical defects for a period of ninety (90) days after purchase. The Software is not available from Heaton Research, Inc. in any other form or media than that enclosed herein or posted to www.heatonresearch. com. If you discover a defect in the media during this warranty period, you may obtain a replacement of identical format at no charge by sending the defective media, postage prepaid, with proof of purchase to:

```
Heaton Research, Inc.
Customer Support Department
1734 Clarkson Rd #107
Chesterfield, MO 63017-4976

Web: www.heatonresearch.com
E-Mail: support@heatonresearch.com
```

After the 90-day period, you can obtain replacement media of identical format by sending us the defective disk, proof of purchase, and a check or money order for $10, payable to Heaton Research, Inc..

DISCLAIMER

Heaton Research, Inc. makes no warranty or representation, either expressed or implied, with respect to the Software or its contents, quality, performance, merchantability, or fitness for a particular purpose. In no event will Heaton Research, Inc., its distributors, or dealers be liable to you or any other party for direct, indirect, special, incidental, consequential, or other damages arising out of the use of or inability to use the Software or its contents even if advised of the possibility of such damage. In the event that the Software includes an online update feature, Heaton Research, Inc. further disclaims any obligation to provide this feature for any specific duration other than the initial posting.

The exclusion of implied warranties is not permitted by some states. Therefore, the above exclusion may not apply to you. This warranty provides you with specific legal rights; there may be other rights that you may have that vary from state to state. The pricing of the book with the Software by Heaton Research, Inc. reflects the allocation of risk and limitations on liability contained in this agreement of Terms and Conditions.

SHAREWARE DISTRIBUTION

This Software may contain various programs that are distributed as shareware. Copyright laws apply to both shareware and ordinary commercial software, and the copyright Owner(s) retains all rights. If you try a shareware program and continue using it, you are expected to register it. Individual programs differ on details of trial periods, registration, and payment. Please observe the requirements stated in appropriate files.

This book is dedicated to my neurons,
without whose constant support
this book would not have been possible.

Acknowledgments

There are several people who I would like to acknowledge. First, I would like to thank the many people who have given me suggestions and comments on the e-book form of this book over the years.

I would like to thank Mary McKinnis for editing the book. I would also like to thank Mary McKinnis for trying out the book examples and offering many helpful suggestions.

I would like to thank my sister Carrie Spear for layout and formatting suggestions. I would like to thank Jeffrey Noedel for suggestions on the book's cover and design.

Contents at a Glance

Contents

Table of Equations

Table of Figures

Table of Tables

Table of Listings

CHAPTER 1: OVERVIEW OF ARTIFICIAL INTELLIGENCE

Chapter Highlights
- **Understanding Biological Neural Networks**
- **How is an Artificial Neural Network Constructed**
- **Finding Good and Bad Uses for Neural Networks**
- **The History of the Neural Network**
- **The Future of Neural Networks**

Computers can perform many operations considerably faster than a human being. Yet there are many tasks where the computer falls considerably short of its human counterpart. There are numerous examples of this. Given two pictures a preschool child could easily tell the difference between a cat and a dog. Yet this same simple task would confound today's computers.

This book shows the reader how to construct neural networks with the Java programming language. As with any technology, it is just as important to learn when to use neural networks as it is to learn when not to use neural networks. This chapter begins to answer that question. What programming requirements are conducive to a neural network?

The structure of neural networks will be briefly introduced in this chapter. This discussion begins with an overview of neural network architecture, and how a typical neural network is constructed. Next you will be shown how a neural network is trained. Ultimately the trained neural network's training must be validated.

This chapter also discusses the history of neural networks. It is important to know where neural networks came from, as well as where they are ultimately headed. Next you will be shown what problems these early networks faced and how current neural networks address these issues.

This chapter gives a broad overview of both the biological and historic context of neural networks. We begin by exploring how real biological neurons store and process information. You will be shown the difference between biological and artificial neurons.

Understanding Neural Networks

Artificial Intelligence (AI) is the field of Computer Science that attempts to give computers humanlike abilities. One of the primary means by which computers are endowed with humanlike abilities, is through the use of a neural network. The human brain is the ultimate example of a neural network. The human brain consists of a network of over a hundred billion interconnected neurons. Neurons are individual cells that can process small amounts of information and then activate other neurons to continue the process.

The term neural network, as it is normally used, is actually a misnomer. Computers attempt to simulate an artificial neural network. However, most publications use the term "neural network" rather than "artificial neural network." This book follows this pattern. Unless the term "neural network" is explicitly prefixed with the terms "biological" or "artificial" you can assume that the term "artificial neural network" is intended. To explore this distinction, you will first be shown the structure of a biological neural network.

How is a Biological Neural Network Constructed

To construct a computer capable of "human like thought," researchers used the only working model they had available—the human brain. To construct an artificial neural network, the brain is not considered as a whole. Taking the human brain as a whole would be far too complex. Rather, the individual cells that make up the human brain are studied. At the most basic level, the human brain is composed primarily of neuron cells.

A neuron cell, as seen in Figure 1.1, is the basic building block of the human brain. It accepts signals from the dendrites. When a neuron accepts a signal, that neuron may fire. When a neuron fires, a signal is transmitted over the neuron's axon. Ultimately the signal will leave the neuron as it travels to the axon terminals. The signal is then transmitted to other neurons or nerves.

Figure 1.1: A Neuron Cell

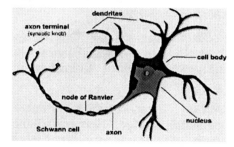

This signal, transmitted by the neuron is an analog signal. Most modern computers are digital machines, and thus require a digital signal. A digital computer processes information as either on or off. This is the basis of the binary digits zero and one. The presence of an electric signal represents a value of one, whereas the absence of an electrical signal represents a value of zero. Figure 1.2 shows a digital signal.

Figure 1.2: A Digital Signal

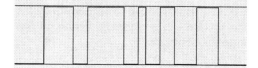

Some of the early computers were analog rather than digital. An analog computer uses a much greater range of values than zero or one. This greater range is achieved as by increasing or decreasing the voltage of the signal. Figure 1.3 shows an analog signal. Though analog computers are useful for certain simulation activates, they are not suited to processing the large volumes of data that digital computers typically process. Because of this, nearly every computer in use today is digital.

Figure 1.3: Sound Recorder Shows an Analog File

Biological Neural Networks are analog. As you will see in the next section, simulating analog neural networks on a digital computer can present some challenges. Neurons accept an analog signal through their dendrites, as seen in Figure 1.1. Because this signal is analog the voltage of this signal will vary. If the voltage is within a certain range, the neuron will fire. When a neuron fires, a new analog signal is transmitted from the firing neuron to other neurons. This signal is conducted over the firing neuron's axon. The regions of input and output are called synapses. Later, in Chapter 3, "Using Multilayer Neural Networks", you will be shown that the synapses are the interface between your program and the neural network.

By firing or not firing, a neuron is making a decision. These are extremely low level decisions. It takes the decisions of a large number of such neurons to read this sentence. Higher level decisions are the result of the collective input and output of many neurons.

These decisions can be represented graphically by charting the input and output of neurons. Figure 1.4 shows the input and output of a particular neuron. As you will be shown in Chapter 3 there are different types of neurons that have different shaped output graphs. As you can see from the graph shown in Figure 1.4, this neuron will fire at any input greater than 0.5 volts.

Figure 1.4: Activation Levels of a Neuron

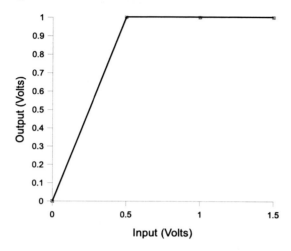

As you can see, a biological neuron is capable of making basic decisions. This model is what artificial neural networks are based on. You will now be shown how this model is simulated using a digital computer.

Simulating a Biological Neural Network with a Computer

This book will show you how to create neural networks using the Java programming language. You will be introduced to the Java Object Oriented Neural Engine (JOONE). JOONE is an open source neural network engine written completely in Java. JOONE is distributed under Lesser GNU Public License, or LGPL. The lesser GNU public license means that JOONE may be freely used in both commercial and non-commercial projects without royalties, so long as you mention that you used JOONE. For more information on the lesser GNU public license, visit the website http://www.gnu.org/copyleft/lesser.html. JOONE will be used in conjunction with many of the examples in this book. JOONE will be introduced in Chapter 3. More information about JOONE can be found at http://jooneworld/.

To simulate a biological neural network JOONE gives you several objects that approximate the portions of a biological neural network. JOONE gives you several types of neurons to construct your networks. These neurons are then connected together with synapse objects. The synapses connect the layers of an artificial neural network just as real synapses connect a biological neural network. Using these objects, you can construct complex neural networks to solve problems.

Solving Problems with Neural Networks

As a programmer of neural networks you must know what problems are adaptable to neural networks. You must also be aware of what problems are not particularly well suited to neural networks. Like most computer technologies and techniques often the most important thing learned is when to use the technology and when not to. Neural networks are no different.

A significant goal of this book is not only to show you how to construct neural networks, but also when to use neural networks. An effective neural network programmer knows what neural network structure, if any, is most applicable to a given problem. First, the problems that are not conducive to a neural network solution will be examined.

Problems Not Suited to a Neural Network

Programs that are easily written out as a flowchart are an example of programs that are not well suited to neural networks. If your program consists of well defined steps, normal programming techniques will suffice.

Another criterion to consider is whether the logic of your program is likely to change. The ability for a neural network to learn is one of the primary features of the neural network. If the algorithm used to solve your problem is an unchanging business rule there is no reason to use a neural network. It might be detrimental to your program if the neural network attempts to find a better solution, and begins to diverge from the expected output of the program.

Finally, neural networks are often not suitable for problems where you must know exactly how the solution was derived. A neural network can become very useful for solving the problem for which the neural network was trained. But the neural network can not explain its reasoning. The neural network knows because it was trained to know. The neural network cannot explain how it followed a series of steps to derive the answer.

Problems Suited to a Neural Network

Although there are many problems that neural networks are not suited for there are also many problems that a neural network is quite useful for solving. In addition, neural networks can often solve problems with fewer lines of code than a traditional programming algorithm. It is important to understand what these problems are.

Neural networks are particularly useful for solving problems that cannot be expressed as a series of steps, such as recognizing patterns, classifying into groups, series prediction and data mining.

Pattern recognition is perhaps the most common use for neural networks. The neural network is presented a pattern. This could be an image, a sound, or any other sort of data. The neural network then attempts to determine if the input data matches a pattern that the neural network has memorized. Chapter 3 will show a simple neural network that recognizes input patterns.

Classification is a process that is closely related to pattern recognition. A neural network trained for classification is designed to take input samples and classify them into groups. These groups may be fuzzy, without clearly defined boundaries. These groups may also have quite rigid boundaries. Chapter 7, "Applying to Pattern Recognition," introduces an example program capable of Optical Character Recognition (OCR). This program takes handwriting samples and classifies them into the correct letter (e.g. the letter "A" or "B").

Training Neural Networks

The individual neurons that make up a neural network are interconnected through the synapses. These connections allow the neurons to signal each other as information is processed. Not all connections are equal. Each connection is assigned a connection weight. If there is no connection between two neurons, then their connection weight is zero. These weights are what determine the output of the neural network. Therefore, it can be said that the connection weights form the memory of the neural network.

Training is the process by which these connection weights are assigned. Most training algorithms begin by assigning random numbers to the weight matrix. Then the validity of the neural network is examined. Next, the weights are adjusted based on how valid the neural network performed. This process is repeated until the validation error is within an acceptable limit. There are many ways to train neural networks. Neural network training methods generally fall into the categories of supervised, unsupervised and various hybrid approaches.

Supervised training is accomplished by giving the neural network a set of sample data along with the anticipated outputs from each of these samples. Supervised training is the most common form of neural network training. As supervised training proceeds, the neural network is taken through several iterations, or epochs, until the actual output of the neural network matches the anticipated output, with a reasonably small error. Each epoch is one pass through the training samples.

Unsupervised training is similar to supervised training except that no anticipated outputs are provided. Unsupervised training usually occurs when the neural network is to classify the inputs into several groups. The training progresses through many epochs, just as in supervised training. As training progresses the classification groups are "discovered" by the neural network. Unsupervised training is covered in Chapter 7, "Applying Pattern Recognition".

There are several hybrid methods that combine several aspects of supervised and unsupervised training. One such method is called reinforcement training. In this method the neural network is provided with sample data that does not contain anticipated outputs, as is done with unsupervised training. However, for each output, the neural network is told whether the output was right or wrong given the input.

It is very important to understand how to properly train a neural network. This book explores several methods of neural network training, including backpropagation, simulated annealing, and genetic algorithms. Chapters 4 through 7 are dedicated to the training of neural networks. Once the neural network is trained, it must be validated to see if it is ready for use.

Validating Neural Networks

Once a neural network has been trained it must be evaluated to see if it is ready for actual use. This final step is important so that it can be determined if additional training is required. To correctly validate a neural network, validation data must be set aside that is completely separate from the training data.

As an example, consider a classification network that must group elements into three different classification groups. You are provided with 10,000 sample elements. For this sample data the group that each element should be classified into is known. For such a system you would divide the sample data into two groups of 5,000 elements. The first group would form the training set. Once the network was properly trained the second group of 5,000 elements would be used to validate the neural network.

It is very important that a separate group always be maintained for validation. First training a neural network with a given sample set and also using this same set to predict the anticipated error of the neural network a new arbitrary set, will surely lead to bad results. The error achieved using the training set will almost always be substantially lower than the error on a new set of sample data. The integrity of the validation data must always be maintained.

This brings up an important question. What exactly does happen if the neural network that you have just finished training performs poorly on the validation set? If this is the case, then you must examine what, exactly, this means. It could mean that the initial random weights were not good. Rerunning the training with new initial weights could correct this. While an improper set of initial random weights could be the cause, a more likely possibility is that the training data was not properly chosen.

If the validation is performing badly this most likely means that there was data present in the validation set that was not available in the training data. The way that this situation should be solved is by trying a different, more random, way of separating the data into training and validation sets. If this fails, you must combine the training and validation sets into one large training set. Then new data must be acquired to serve as the validation data.

For some situations it may be impossible to gather additional data to use as either training or validation data. If this is the case then you are left with no other choice but to combine all or part of the validation set with the training set. While this approach will forgo the security of a good validation, if additional data cannot be acquired this may be your only alterative.

A Historical Perspective on Neural Networks

Neural networks have been used with computers as early as the 1950's. Through the years many different neural network architectures have been presented. In this section you will be shown some of the history behind neural networks and how this history led to the neural networks of today. We will begin this exploration with the Perceptron.

Perceptron

The perceptron is one of the earliest neural networks. Invented at the Cornell Aeronautical Laboratory in 1957 by Frank Rosenblatt, the Perceptron was an attempt to understand human memory, learning, and cognitive processes. In 1960, Rosenblatt demonstrated the Mark I Perceptron. The Mark I was the first machine that could "learn" to identify optical patterns.

The Perceptron progressed from the biological neural studies of neural researchers such as D.O. Hebb, Warren McCulloch and Walter Pitts. McCulloch and Pitts were the first to describe biological neural networks, and are credited with coining the phrase "neural network." They developed a simplified model of the neuron, called the MP neuron that centered on the idea that a nerve will fire an impulse only if its threshold value is exceeded. The MP neuron functioned as a sort of scanning device that read predefined input and output associations to determine the final output. MP neurons were incapable of learning as they had fixed thresholds. As a result MP neurons were able to be hard-wired logic devices that were setup manually.

Because the MP neuron did not have the ability to learn, it was very limited when compared to the infinitely more flexible and adaptive human nervous system upon which it was modeled. Rosenblatt determined that a learning network model could improve its responses by adjusting the weight on its connections between neurons. This was taken into consideration when Rosenblatt designed the perceptron.

The perceptron showed early promise for neural networks and machine learning. The Perceptron had one very large shortcoming. The perceptron was unable to learn to recognize input that was not "linearly separable." This would prove to be huge obstacle that would take some time to overcome.

Perceptrons and Linear Separability

To see why the perceptron failed you must see what exactly is meant by a linearly separable problem. Consider a neural network that accepts two binary digits (0 or 1) and outputs one binary digit. The inputs and output of such a neural network could be represented by Table 1.1.

Table 1.1: A Linearly Separable Function

Input 1	Input 2	Output
0	0	1
0	1	0
1	0	1
1	1	1

This table would be considered to be linearly separable. To see why, examine Figure 1.5. Table 1.1 is shown, in the form of a logic diagram, on Figure 1.5a. Notice how a line can be drawn to separate the output values of 1 from the output values of 0? This is a linearly separable table. Table 1.2 shows a non-linearly separable table.

Figure 1.5: Linearly/Non-Linearly Separable Function

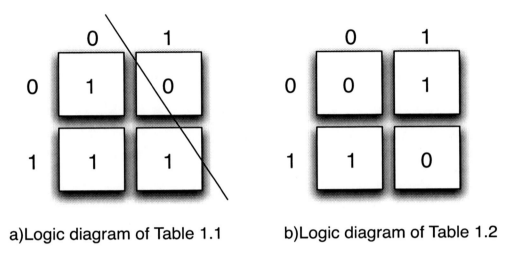

a)Logic diagram of Table 1.1   b)Logic diagram of Table 1.2

Table 1.2: A Non Linearly Separable Function

Input 1	Input 2	Output
0	0	0
0	1	1
1	0	1
1	1	0

The above table, which happens to be the XOR function, is not linearly separable. This can be seen in Figure 1.5b. Table 1.2 is shown on the right side of Figure 1.5. There is no way you could draw a line that would separate the 0 outputs from the 1 outputs. As a result, Table 1.2 is said to be non-linearly separately. A perceptron could not be trained to recognize Table 1.2.

The Perception's inability to solve non-linearly separable problems would prove to be a major obstacle to not only the Perceptron, but the entire field of artificial intelligence. A former classmate of Rosenblatt, Marvin Minsky, along with Seymour Papert, published the book Perceptrons in 1969. This book mathematically discredited the Perceptron model. Fate was to further rule against the Perceptron in 1971 when Rosenblatt died in a boating accident. Without Rosenblatt to defend the Perceptron and neural networks, interest diminished for over a decade.

While the XOR problem was the nemesis of the Perceptron, current neural networks have little problem learning the XOR function or other non-linearly separable problems. In fact, The XOR problem has become a sort of "Hello World" problem for new neural network software. While the XOR problem was eventually surmounted, another test, the Turing Test, remains unsolved to this day.

The Turing Test

The Turing test was proposed in a 1950 paper by Dr. Alan Turing. In this article Dr. Turing introduces the now famous "Turing Test". This is a test that is designed to measure the advance of AI research. The Turing test is far more complex than the XOR problem, and has yet to be solved.

To understand the Turing Test, think of an Internet Instant Message window. Using the Instant Message program you can chat with someone using another computer. Suppose a stranger sends you an Instant Message and you begin chatting. Are you sure that this stranger is a human being? Perhaps you are talking to an AI enabled computer program. Could you tell the difference? This is the "Turing Test." If you are unable to distinguish the AI program from another human being, then that program has passed the "Turing Test".

No computer program has ever passed the Turing Test. No computer program has ever even come close to passing the Turing Test. In the 1950's it was assumed that a computer program capable of passing the Turing Test was no more than a decade away. But like many of the other lofty goals of AI, passing the Turing Test has yet to be realized.

Passing the Turing Test is quite complex. To pass this test requires the computer to be able to read English, or some other human language, and understand the meaning of the sentence. Then the computer must be able to access a database that comprises the knowledge that a typical human has amassed from several decades of human existence. Finally, the computer program must be capable of forming a response, and perhaps questioning the human that it is interacting with. This is no small feat. This goes well beyond the capabilities of current neural networks.

One of the most complex parts of solving the Turing Test is working with the database of human knowledge. This has given way to a new test called the "Limited Turing Test". The "Limited Turing Test" works similarly to the actual Turing Test. A human is allowed to conduct a conversation with a computer program. The difference is that the human must restrict the conversation to one narrow subject area. This limits the size of the human experience database.

Neural Network Today and in the Future

Neural networks have existed since the 1950's. They have come a long way since the early Percptrons that were easily defeated by problems as simple as the XOR operator. Yet neural networks have a long way to go.

Neural Networks Today

Neural networks are in use today for a wide variety of tasks. Most people think of neural networks as attempting to emulate the human mind or passing the Turing Test. Most neural networks used today take on far less glamorous roles than the neural networks frequently seen in science fiction.

Speech and handwriting recognition are two common uses for today's neural networks. Chapter 7 contains an example that illustrates a neural network handwriting recognition program. Neural networks tend to work well for both speech and handwriting recognition because these types of programs can be trained to the individual user.

Data mining is a process where large volumes of data are "mined" for trends and other statistics that might otherwise be overlooked. Very often in data mining the programmer is not particularly sure what final outcome is being sought. Neural networks are often employed in data mining because of their trainability.

Perhaps the most common form of neural network used by modern applications is the feedforward backpropagation neural network. This network feeds inputs forward from one layer to the next as it processes. Backpropagation refers to the way in which the neurons are trained in this sort of neural network. Chapter 3 begins your introduction into this sort of network.

A Fixed Wing Neural Network

Some researchers suggest that perhaps the neural network itself is a fallacy. Perhaps other methods of modeling human intelligence must be explored. The ultimate goal of AI is to produce a thinking machine. Does this not mean that such a machine would have to be constructed exactly like a human brain? That to solve the AI puzzle, we should seek to imitate nature? Imitating nature has not always led mankind to the most optimal solution. Consider the airplane.

Man has been fascinated with the idea of flight since the beginnings of civilization. Many inventors through history worked towards the development of the "Flying Machine". To create a flying machine, most of these inventors looked to nature. In nature we found our only working model of a flying machine, which was the bird. Most inventors who aspired to create a flying machine created various forms of ornithopters.

Ornithopters are flying machines that work by flapping their wings. This is how a bird works, so it seemed only logical that this would be the way to create such a device. However none of the ornithopters were successful. They simply could not generate sufficient lift to overcome their weight. Many designs were tried. Figure 1.6 shows one such design that was patented in the late 1800's.

Figure 1.6: An Ornithopter

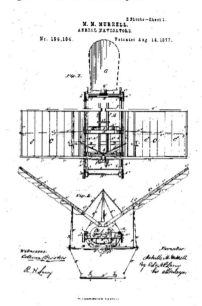

It was not until Wilbur and Orville Wright decided to use a fixed wing design that air plane technology began to truly advance. For years, the paradigm of modeling the bird was pursued. Once the two brothers broke with this tradition, this area of science began to move forward. Perhaps AI is no different. Perhaps it will take a new paradigm, outside of the neural network, to usher in the next era of AI.

Quantum Computing

One of the most promising areas of future computer research is quantum computing. Quantum computing could change the every aspect of how computers are designed. To understand Quantum computers, we must first examine how they are different from the computer systems that are in use today.

Von Neumann and Turing Machines

Practically every computer in use today is built upon the Von Neumann principle. A Von Neumann computer works by following simple discrete instructions, which are the chip-level machine language codes. This type of computer computer's output is completely predictable and serial. This type of machine is implemented by finite state units of data known as "bits", and logic gates that perform operations on the bits. This classic model of computation is essentially the same as Babbage's Analytical Engine in 1834. The computers of today have not strayed from this classic architecture; they have simply become faster and have gained more "bits". The Church-Turing thesis, sums up this idea.

The Church-Turing thesis is not a mathematical theorem in the sense that it can be proven. It simply seems correct and applicable. Alonzo Church and Alan Turing created this idea independently. According to the Church-Turing thesis all mechanisms for computing algorithms are inherently the same. Any method used can be expressed as a computer program. This seems to be a valid thesis. Consider the case where you are asked to add two numbers. You would likely follow a simple algorithm that could be easily implemented as a computer program. If you were asked to multiply two numbers, you would follow another approach implemented as a computer program. The basis of the Church-Turing thesis is that there seems to be no algorithmic problem that a computer cannot solve, so long as a solution does exist.

The embodiment of the Church-Turing thesis is the Turing machine. The Turing machine is an abstract computing device that illustrates the Church-Turing thesis. The Turing machine is the ancestor from which all existing computers descend. The Turing computer consists of a read/write head, and a long piece of tape. This head can read and write symbols to and from the tape. At each step, the Turing machine must decide its next action by following a very simple program consisting of conditional statements, read/write commands or tape shifts. The tape can be of any length necessary to solve a particular problem, but the tape cannot be of an infinite length. If a problem has a solution, that problem can be solved using a Turing machine and some finite length tape.

Quantum Computing

Practically every neural network thus far has been implemented using a Von Neumann computer. But, might the successor to the Von Neumann computer take neural networks to the near human level? Advances in an area called Quantum computing may do just that. A Quantum computer would be constructed very differently than a Von Neumann computer.

But what exactly is a quantum computer? Quantum computers use small particles to represent data. For example, a pebble is a quantum computer for calculating the constant-position function. A quantum computer would use small particles to represent the neurons of a neural network. Before seeing how to construct a Quantum neural network, you must first see how a Quantum computer is constructed.

The most basic level of a Von Neumann computer is the bit. Similarly, the most basic level of the Quantum computer is the "qubit". A qubit, or quantum bit, differs from a normal bit in one very important way. Where a normal bit can only have the value 0 or 1, a qubit can have the value 0, 1 or both simultaneously. To see how this is possible, first you will be shown how a qubit is constructed.

A qubit is constructed with an atom of some element. Hydrogen makes a good example. The hydrogen atom consists of a nucleus and one orbiting electron. For the purposes of Quantum computing, only the orbiting electron is important. This electron can exist in different energy levels, or orbits about the nucleus. The different energy levels would be used to represent the binary 0 and 1. The ground state, when the atom is in its lowest orbit, could represent the value 0. The next highest orbit would represent the value 1. The electron can be moved to different orbits by subjecting the electron to a pulse of polarized laser light. This has he effect of adding photons into the system. So, to flip a bit from 0 to 1, enough light is added to move the electron up one orbit. To flip from 1 to 0, we do the same thing, since overloading the electron will cause the electron to return to its ground state. This is logically equivalent to a NOT gate. Using similar ideas, other gates can be constructed such as AND and OR.

Thus far, there is no qualitative difference between qubits and regular bits. Both are capable of storing the values 0 and 1. What is different is the concept of super position. If only half of the light necessary to move an electron is added, the elector will occupy both orbits simultaneously. Superposition allows two possibilities to be computed at once. Further, if you have one "qubyte", that is 8 qubits, then 256 numbers can be represented simultaneously.

Calculation with super position can have certain advantages. For example, to calculate with the superpositional property, a number of qubits are raised to their superpositions. Then the algorithm is performed on these qubits. When the algorithm is complete, the superposition is collapsed. This results in the true answer being revealed. You can think of the algorithm as being run on all possible combinations of the definite qubit states (i.e. 0 and 1) in parallel. This is called quantum parallelism.

Quantum computers clearly process information differently than their Von Neumann counterpart. But does quantum computing offer anything not already achievable by ordinary classical computers. The answer is yes. Quantum computing provides tremendous speed advantages over the Von Neumann architecture.

To see this difference in speed, consider a problem which takes an extremely long time to compute on a classical computer. Factoring a 250 digit number is a good example. It is estimated that this would take approximately 800,000 years to factor with 1400 present day Von Neumann computers working in parallel. Unfortunately, even as Von Neumann computers improve in speed and methods of large scale parallelism improve, the problem is still exponentially expensive to compute. This same problem, posed to a quantum computer would not take nearly so long. With a Quantum computer it becomes possible to factor 250 digit number in just a few million steps. The key element is that using the parallel properties of superposition all possibilities can be computed simultaneously.

The idea that the Church-Turing thesis is indeed true for all quantum computers is in some doubt. The quantum computer previously mentioned process similar to Von Neumann computers, using bits and logic gates. This is not to say that we cannot use other types of quantum computer models that are more powerful. One such model may be a Quantum Neural Network, or QNN. A QNN could certainly be constructed using qubits. This would be analogous to constructing an ordinary neural network on a Von Neumann computer. The result, would only offer speed, not computability, advantages over Von Neumann based neural networks. To construct a QNN that is not restrained by Church-Turing, a radically different approach to qubits and logic gates must be sought. As of yet, of there does not seem to be any clear way of doing this.

Quantum Neural Networks

How might a QNN be constructed? Currently there are several research institutes around the world working on a QNN. Two such examples are Georgia Tech and Oxford University. Most are reluctant to publish details of their work. This is likely because building a QNN is potentially much easier than an actual quantum computer, which has created a sort of quantum race.

A QNN would likely gain exponentially over classic neural networks through superposition of values entering and exiting a neuron. Another advantage would be a reduction in the number of neuron layers required. This is because neurons can be used to calculate over many possibilities, by using superposition. The model would therefore requires less neurons to learn. This would result in networks with fewer neurons and greater efficiency.

Chapter Summary

Computers can process information considerably faster than human beings. Yet a computer is incapable of performing many of the same tasks that a human can easily perform. For processes that cannot easily be broken into a finite number of steps, a neural network can be an ideal solution.

The term neural network is usually meant to refer to artificial neural network. An artificial neural network attempts to simulate the real neural networks that are contained in the brains of all animals. Neural networks were introduced in the 1950's and have experienced numerous setbacks, and have yet to deliver on the promise of simulating human thought.

Neural networks are constructed of neurons that form layers. Input is presented to the layers of neurons. If the input to a neuron is within the range that the neuron has been trained for, then the neuron will fire. When a neuron fires, a signal is sent to whatever layer of neurons, or their outputs, the firing neuron was connected to. These connections between neurons are called synapses. Java can be used to construct such a network.

One such neural network, which was written in Java, is Java Object Oriented Neural Engine (JOONE). JOONE is an open source library that can be used free of charge. Several of the chapters in this book will explain how to use the JOONE engine.

Neural networks must be trained and validated. A training set is usually split in half to give both a training and validation set. Training the neural network consists of running the neural network over the training data until the neural network learns to recognize the training set with a sufficiently low error rate. Validation begins when the neural network's results are checked.

Just because a neural network can process the training data with a low error, does not mean that the neural network is trained and ready for use. Before the neural network should be placed into production use, the results from the neural network must be validated. Validation involves presenting the validation set to the neural network and comparing the actual results of the neural network with the anticipated results.

At the end of validation, the neural network is ready to be placed into production if the results from the validation set result in an error level that is satisfactory. If the results are not satisfactory, then the neural network will have to be retrained before the neural network is placed into production.

The future of artificial intelligence programming may reside with the quantum computer or perhaps something other than the neural network. The quantum computer promises to speed computing to levels that are unimaginable on today's computer platforms.

Early attempts at flying machines attempted to model the bird. This was done because the bird was our only working model of flight. It was not until Wilbur and Orville Write broke from the model of nature, and created the first fixed wing aircraft that success in flight was finally achieved. Perhaps modeling AI programs after nature is analogous to modeling airplanes after birds, and a much better model than the neural network exists. Only the future will tell.

CHAPTER 2: UNDERSTANDING NEURAL NETWORKS

Chapter Highlights
- **Understanding the Hopfield Neural Network**
- **Recognizing Patterns**
- **Using Autoassociation**
- **Constructing a Neural Network Application**

The neural network has long been the main stay of Artificial Intelligence (AI) programming. As programmers, we can create programs that do fairly amazing things. Programs can automate repetitive tasks such as balancing checkbooks or calculating the value of an investment portfolio. While a program could easily maintain a large collection of images, it could not tell us what any of those images are of. Programs are inherently unintelligent and uncreative. Ordinary computer programs are only able to perform repetitive tasks.

A neural network attempts to give computer programs human like intelligence. Neural networks are usually designed to recognize patterns in data. A neural network can be trained to recognize specific patterns in data. This chapter will teach you the basic layout of a neural network and end by demonstrating the Hopfield neural network, which is one of the simplest forms of neural network.

Neural Network Structure

To study neural networks you must first become aware of their structure. A neural network is composed of several different elements. Neurons are the most basic unit. Neurons are interconnected. These connections are not equal, as each connection has a connection weight. Groups of networks come together to form layers. In this section we will explore each of these topics.

The Neuron

The neuron is the basic building block of the neural network. A neuron is a communication conduit that both accepts input and produces output. The neuron receives its input either from other neurons or the user program. Similarly, the neuron sends its output to other neurons or the user program.

When a neuron produces output, that neuron is said to activate, or fire. A neuron will activate when the sum of its inputs satisfies the neuron's activation function. Consider a neuron that is connected to a number of other neurons. The variable "w" represents the weights between this neuron and the other "k" neurons. We will say that this neuron is connected to "k" other neurons. The variable "x" represents the input to this neuron from each of the other neurons. Therefore we must calculate the sum of every input x multiplied by the corresponding weight "w". This is shown in the following equation. This book will use some mathematical notation to explain how the neural networks are constructed. Often this is theoretical and not absolutely necessary to use neural networks. A review of the mathematical concepts used in this book is covered in Appendix B, "Mathematical Background".

Equation 2.1: Summing the Weight Matrix

$$u = \sum_k w_k x_k$$

This sum must be given to the neurons activation function. An activation function is just a simple Java method that tells the neuron if it should fire or not. For example, if you chose to have your neuron only activate when the input to that neuron is between 5 and 10, the following activation method might be used.

```java
boolean thresholdFunction(double input)
{
  if( (input>=5) && (input<=10) )
    return true;
  else
    return false;
}
```

The above method will return true if the neuron would have activated, false otherwise. The method simply checks to see if the input is between 5 and 10 and returns true upon success. Methods such as this are commonly called threshold methods (or sometimes threshold functions). The threshold for this neuron is any input between 5 and 10. A neuron will always activate when the input causes the threshold to be reached.

There are several threshold methods that are commonly used by neural networks. Chapter 3 will explore several of these threshold methods. The example given later in this chapter uses an activation method called the Hyperbolic Tangent, or TANH. It is not critical to understand exactly what a Hyperbolic Tangent is in order to use such a method. The TANH activation method is just one, of several, activation methods that you may use. Chapter 3 will introduce other activation methods and explain when each is used.

The TANH activation method will be fed the sum of the input patterns and connection weights, as previously discussed. This sum will be referred to as "u". The TANH activation method simply returns the hyperbolic tangent of "u". Unfortunately Java does not contain a hyperbolic tangent method. The formula to calculate the hyperbolic tangent of the variable "u" is shown below.

Equation 2.2: The TANH Function

$$\tanh(u) = \frac{e^u - e^{-u}}{e^u + e^{-u}}$$

A hyperbolic tangent activation can easily be written in Java, even with out a hyperbolic tangent method. The following Java code implements the above formula.

```java
public double tanh (double u)
{
   double a = Math.exp( u );
   double b = Math.exp( -u );
   return ((a-b)/(a+b));
}
```

The hyperbolic tangent threshold method will return values according to Figure 2.1. As you can see this gives it a range of numbers both greater than and less than zero. You will find that you will use the TANH threshold method when you must have output greater than and less than zero. If only positive numbers are needed, then the Sigmoid threshold method will be used. Choosing an activation method is covered in much greater detail in Chapter 3.

Figure 2.1: Hyperbolic Tangent (TANH)

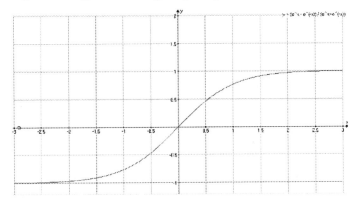

Neuron Connection Weights

The previous section already mentioned that neurons are usually connected together. These connections are not equal, and can be assigned individual weights. These weights are what give the neural network the ability to recognize certain patterns. Adjust the weights, and the neural network will recognize a different pattern.

Adjustment of these weights is a very important operation. Later chapters will show you how neural networks can be trained. The process of training is adjusting the individual weights between each of the individual neurons until we achieve close to the desired output.

Neuron Layers

Neurons are usually grouped into layers. Layers are groups of neurons that perform similar functions. There are three types of layers. The input layer is the layer of neurons that receive input from the user program. The layer of neurons that send data to the user program is the output layer. Between the input layer and output layer can be zero or more hidden layers. Hidden layer neurons are connected only to other neurons and never directly interact with the user program.

Figure 2.2 shows a neural network with one hidden layer. Here you can see the user program sends a pattern to the input layer. The input layer presents this pattern to the hidden layer. The hidden layer then presents information on to the output layer. Finally the user program collects the pattern generated by the output layer. You can also see the connections, which are formed between the neurons. Neuron 1 (N1) is connected to both neuron 5 (N5) and Neuron 6 (N6).

Figure 2.2: Neural Network Layers

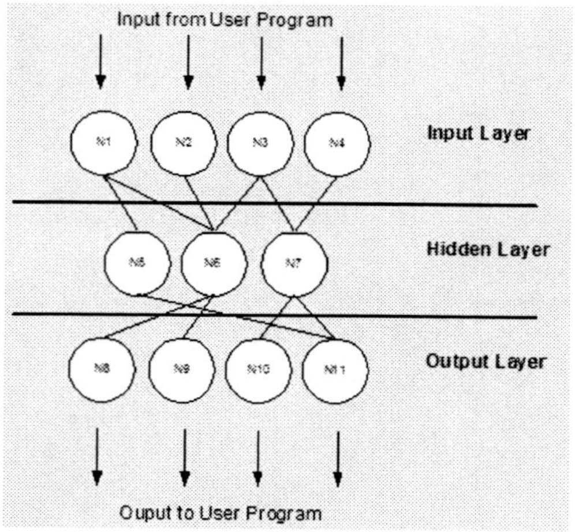

The input and output layers are not just there as interface points. Every neuron in a neural network has the opportunity to affect processing. Processing can occur at any layer in the neural network.

Not every neural network has this many layers. The hidden layer is optional. The input and output layers are required, but it is possible to have one layer act as both an input and output layer. Later, in this chapter you will be shown a Hopfield neural network. This is a single layer (combined input and output) neural network.

Now that you have seen how a neural network is constructed you will be shown how neural networks are used in pattern recognition. Finally, this chapter will conclude with an implementation of a single layer Hopfield neural network that can recognize a few basic patterns.

Pattern Recognition

Pattern recognition is one of the most common uses for neural networks. Pattern recognition is simply the ability to recognize a pattern. The pattern must be recognized even when that pattern is distorted. Consider an every day use of pattern recognition.

Every person who holds a driver's license should be able to accurately identify a traffic light. This is an extremely critical pattern recognition procedure carried out by countless drivers every day. But not every traffic light looks the same. Even the same traffic light can be altered depending on the time of day or the season. In addition, many variations of the traffic light exist. This is not a hard task for a human driver.

How hard would it be to write a computer program that accepts an image and tells you if it is a traffic light? This would be a very complex task. Figure 2.3 shows several such lights. Most common programming algorithms are quickly exhausted when presented with a complex pattern recognition problem.

Figure 2.3: Different Traffic Lights

Recognizing patterns is what neural networks do best. This chapter teaches you how to create a very simple neural network that is capable of only the most basic pattern recognition. The neural network built in this chapter will not recognize traffic lights. In our study of neural networks we will begin simple. This chapter will focus on recognizing very simple 4-digit binary sequences, such as 0101 and 1010. Not every example in the book will be so simple. Later chapters will focus on more complex image recognition. Before you can construct a neural network, you must first be shown how a neural network actually recognizes an image. We've already seen the basic structure of a neural network.

Autoassociation

Autoassociation is a means by which a neural network communicates that it does recognize the pattern that was presented to the network. A neural network that supports autoassociation will pass a pattern directly from its input neurons to the output neurons. No change occurs; to the causal observer it appears as if no work has taken place.

Consider an example. You have an image that you think might be of a traffic light. You would like the neural network to attempt to recognize it. To do this you present the image of the traffic light to the input neurons of the neural network. If the neural network recognizes the traffic light, the output neurons present the traffic light exactly as the input neurons showed it. It does not matter which traffic light is presented. If the neural network, which was trained to recognize traffic lights, identifies it as a traffic light the outputs are the same as the inputs. Figure 2.4 illustrates this process. It does not matter what input pattern is presented. If the presented input pattern is recognized as a traffic light, the outputs will be the same as the inputs. Figure 2.4 shows two different traffic lights, the neural network allows both to pass through, since both are recognized.

Figure 2.4: A Successful Recognition

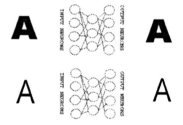

If successful pattern recognition causes an autoassociative neural network to simply pass the input neurons to the output neurons, you may be wondering how it communicates failure. Failed pattern recognition results in anything but the input neurons passing directly to the output neurons. If the pattern recognition fails, some other pattern will be presented to the output neurons. The makeup of that pattern is insignificant. It only matters that the output pattern does not match the input pattern, therefore the recognition failed. Often the output pattern will be some distortion of the input pattern. Figure 2.5 shows what happens when the letter "B" is presented to a autoassociative neural network which is designed to recognize the letter A.

Figure 2.5: A Failed Recognition

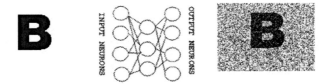

The Hopfield Network

The Hopfield neural network is perhaps the simplest of neural networks. The Hopfield neural network is a fully connected single layer autoassociative network. This means it has one single layer, with each neuron connected to every other neuron. In this chapter we will examine a Hopfield neural network with just four neurons. This is a network that is small enough that it can be easily understood, yet can recognize a few patterns. A Hopfield network, with connections, is shown in figure 2.6.

We will build an example program that creates the Hopfield network shown in Figure 2.6. A Hopfield neural network has every Neuron connected to every other neuron. This means that in a four Neuron network there are a total of four squared or 16 connections. However, 16 connections assume that every neuron is connected to itself as well. This is not the case in a Hopfield neural network, so the actual number of connections is 12.

Figure 2.6: A Hopfield Neural Network with 12 Connections

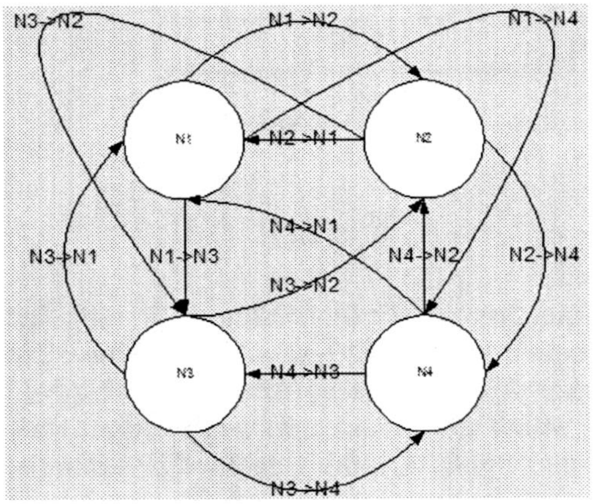

![Hopfield network diagram showing four neurons N1, N2, N3, N4 with connections labeled N3->N2, N1->N2, N1->N4, N2->N1, N3->N1, N1->N3, N4->N1, N4->N2, N2->N4, N3->N2, N4->N3, N3->N4]

As we write an example neural network program, we will store the connections in an array. Because each neuron can potentially be connected to every other neuron a two dimensional array will be used. Table 2.1 shows the layout of such an array.

Table 2.1: Connections on a Hopfield Neural Network

	Neuron 1 (N1)	Neuron 2 (N2)	Neuron 3 (N3)	Neuron 4 (N4)
Neuron 1 (N1)	(n/a)	N2->N1	N3->N1	N4->N1
Neuron 2 (N2)	N1->N2	(n/a)	N3->N2	N3->N2
Neuron 3 (N3)	N1->N3	N2->N3	(n/a)	N4->N3
Neuron 4 (N4)	N1->N4	N2->N4	N3->N4	(n/a)

The connection weights put into this array, also called a weight matrix, allow the neural network to recall certain patterns when presented. For example, the values shown in Table 2.2 show the correct values to use to recall the patterns 0101 and 1010. The method to create the values contained in Table 2.2 will be covered shortly. First you will be shown how the values in Table 2.2 are used to recall 0101 and 1010.

Table 2.2: Weights Used to Recall 0101 and 1010

	Neuron 1 (N1)	Neuron 2 (N2)	Neuron 3 (N3)	Neuron 4 (N4)
Neuron 1 (N1)	0	-1	1	-1
Neuron 2 (N2)	-1	0	-1	1
Neuron 3 (N3)	1	-1	0	-1
Neuron 4 (N4)	-1	1	-1	0

Recalling Patterns

You have been told several times that the connection weight matrix shown in table 2.2 will correctly recall 0101 and 1010. You will now be shown exactly how a neural network is used to recall patterns. First we will take the example of presenting 0101 to the Hopfield network. To do this we present each input neuron, which in this case are also the output neurons, with the pattern. Each neuron will activate based upon the input pattern. For example, when neuron 1 is presented with 0101 its activation will be the sum of all weights that have a 1 in input pattern. For example, we can see from Table 2.2 that Neuron 1 has the following weights with all of the other neurons:

0	-1	1	-1

We must now compare those weights with the input pattern of 0101:

0	1	0	1
0	-1	1	-1

We will sum only the values that contain a 1 in the input pattern. Therefore the activation of the first neuron is –1 + -1, or –2. The activation of each neuron is shown below.

```
N1 = -1 + -1 = -2
N2 = 0 + 1 = 1
N3=  -1 + -1 = -2
N4 = 1 + 0 = 1
```

Therefore, the output neurons, which are also the input neurons, will report the above activations. The final output vector would then be –2, 1, -2, 1. These values are meaningless without a threshold method. We said earlier that a threshold method determines what range of values will cause the neuron, in this case the output neuron, to fire. The threshold usually used for a Hopfield network, is any value greater than zero. So the following neurons would fire.

```
N1 activation is -2, would not fire (0)
N2 activation is 1, would fire (1)
N3 activation is -2, would not fire(0)
N4 activation is 1m would fire (1)
```

As you can see, we assign a binary 1 to all neurons that fired, and a binary 0 to all neurons that did not fire. The final binary output from the Hopfield network would be 0101. This is the same as the input pattern. An autoassociative neural network, such as a Hopfield network, will echo a pattern back if the pattern is recognized. The pattern was successfully recognized. Now that you have seen how a connection weight matrix can cause a neural network to recall certain patterns, you will be shown how the connection weight matrix was derived.

Deriving the Weight Matrix

You are probably wondering how the weight matrix, shown by Table 2.2, was derived. This section will show you how to create a weight matrix that can recall any number of patterns. First you should start with a blank connection weight matrix, as follows.

$$\begin{bmatrix} 0 & 0 & 0 & 0 \\ 0 & 0 & 0 & 0 \\ 0 & 0 & 0 & 0 \\ 0 & 0 & 0 & 0 \end{bmatrix}$$

We will first train this neural network to accept the value 0101. To do this we must first calculate a matrix just for 0101, which is called 0101's contribution matrix. The contribution matrix will then be added to the actual connection weight matrix. As additional contribution matrixes are added to the connection weight matrix, the connection weight is said to learn each of the new patterns.

First we must calculate the contribution matrix of 0101. There are three steps involved in this process. First we must calculate the bipolar values of 0101. Bipolar simply means that you are representing a binary string with –1's and 1's rather than 0's and 1's. Next we transpose and multiply the bipolar equivalent of 0101 by itself. Finally, we set all the values from the north-west diagonal to zero, because neurons do not connect to themselves in a Hopfield network. Lets take each step one at a time and see how this is done, starting with the bipolar conversion.

Step 1: Convert 0101 to Bipolar

Bipolar is nothing more than a way to represent binary values as –1's and 1's rather than zero and 1's. This is done because binary has one minor flaw. Which is that 0 is NOT the inverse of 1. Rather –1 is the mathematical inverse of 1.

To convert 0101 to bipolar we convert all of the zeros to –1's. This results in:

```
0 = -1
1 = 1
0 = -1
1 = 1
```

The final result is the array –1, 1, -1, 1. This array will be used by step 2 to begin to build the contribution matrix for 0101.

Step 2: Multiply –1, 1, -1, 1 by its Inverse

For this step we will consider –1, 1, -1, 1 to be a matrix.

$$\begin{bmatrix} -1 \\ 1 \\ -1 \\ 1 \end{bmatrix}$$

Taking the inverse of this matrix we have.

$$\begin{bmatrix} -1 & 1 & -1 & 1 \end{bmatrix}$$

We must now multiply these two matrixes. Appendix B, "Mathematical Background", tells you where to get additional information about matrix mathematics. It is a relatively easy procedure, where the rows and columns are multiplied against each other, to result in:

-1 X -1 = 1	1 X -1 = -1	-1 X -1 = 1	1 X -1 = -1
-1 X 1 = -1	1 X 1 = 1	-1 X 1 = -1	1 X 1 = 1
-1 X -1 = 1	1 X -1 = -1	-1 X -1 = 1	1 X -1 = -1
-1 X 1 = -1	1 X 1 = 1	-1 X 1 = -1	1 X 1 = 1

Condensed, this the above results in the following matrix.

$$\begin{bmatrix} 1 & -1 & 1 & -1 \\ -1 & 1 & -1 & 1 \\ 1 & -1 & 1 & -1 \\ -1 & 1 & -1 & 1 \end{bmatrix}$$

Now that we have successfully multiplied the matrix by its inverse we are ready for step 3.

Step 3: Set the Northwest Diagonal to Zero

Mathematically speaking we are now going to subtract the identity matrix from the matrix we derived in step two. The net result is that the northwest diagonal gets set to zero. The real reason we do this is Hopfield networks do not have their neurons connected to themselves. So positions [0][0], [1][1], [2][2] and [3][3] in our two dimensional array, or matrix, get set to zero. This results in the final contribution matrix for the bit pattern 0101.

$$\begin{bmatrix} 0 & -1 & 1 & -1 \\ -1 & 0 & -1 & 1 \\ 1 & -1 & 0 & -1 \\ -1 & 1 & -1 & 0 \end{bmatrix}$$

This contribution matrix can now be added to whatever connection weight matrix you already had. If you only want this network to recognize 0101, then this contribution matrix becomes your connection weight matrix. If you also wanted to recognize 1001, then you would calculate both contribution matrixes and add each value in their contribution matrixes to result in a combined matrix, which would be the connection weight matrix.

If this process seems a bit confusing, you might try looking at the next section where we actually build a program that builds connection weight matrixes. There the process is explained in a more Java-centric way.

Before we end the discussion of determination of the weight matrix, one small side effect should be mentioned. We went through several steps to determine the correct weight matrix for 0101. Any time you create a Hopfield network that recognizes a binary pattern; the network also recognizes the inverse of that bit pattern. You can get the inverse of a bit pattern by flipping all 0's to 1's and 1's to zeros. The inverse of 0101 is 1010. As a result, the connection weight matrix we just calculated would also recognize 1010.

Hopfield Neural Network Example

Now that you have been shown some of the basic concepts of neural network we will example an actual Java example of a neural network. The example program for this chapter implements a simple Hopfield neural network that you can used to experiment with Hopfield neural networks.

The example given in this chapter implements the entire neural network. More complex neural network examples will often use JOONE. JOONE will be introduced in Chapter 3. The complete source code to this, and all examples, can be found on the companion download from Heaton Research. To learn how to run the examples, refer to Appendix C, "Compiling Examples under Windows" and Appendix D, "Compiling Examples under Linux/ UNIX". These appendixes give thorough discussion of how to properly compile and execute examples. The classes used to create the Hopfield example are shown in Figure 2.7.

Figure 2.7: Hopfield Example Classes

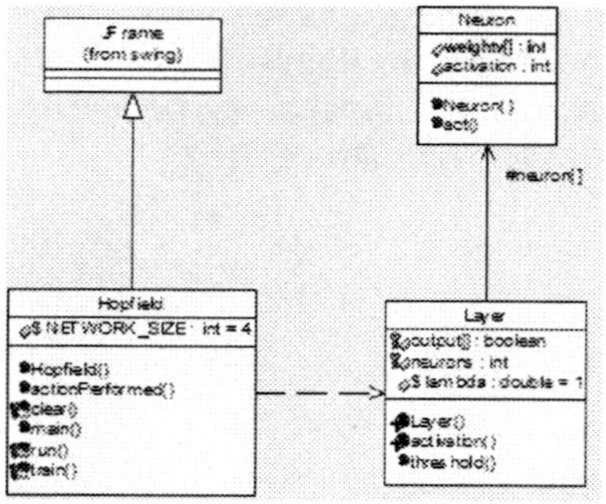

Using the Hopfield Network

You will now be shown a Java program that implements a 4-neuron Hopfield neural network. This simple program is implemented as a Swing Java Application. Figure 2.8 shows the application as it appears when it initially starts up. Initially, the network activation weights are all zero. The network has learned no patterns at this point.

Figure 2.8: A Hopfield Example

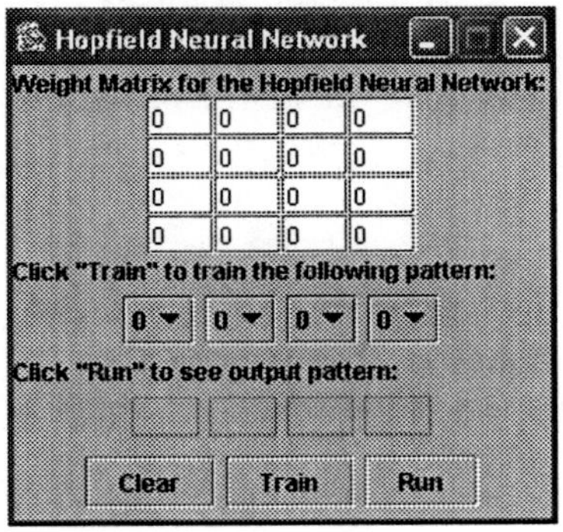

We will begin by teaching it to recognize the pattern 0101. Enter 0101 under the "Input pattern to run or train". Click the "Train" button. Notice the weight matrix adjust to absorb the new knowledge. You should now see the same connection weight matrix as Figure 2.9.

Figure 2.9: Training the Hopfield Network

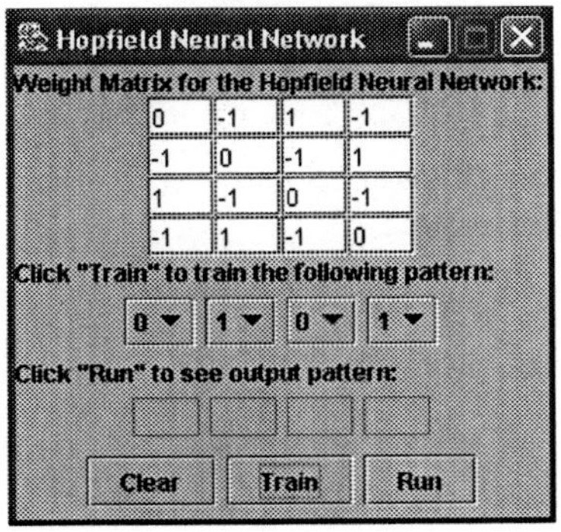

Now you will test it. Enter the pattern 0101 into the "Input pattern to run or train" (it should still be there from your training). The output will be "0101". This is an autoassociative network, therefore it echoes the input if it recognizes it.

Now you should try something that does not match the training pattern exactly. Enter the pattern "0100" and click "Run". The output will now be "0101". The neural network did not recognize "0100", but the closest thing it knew was "0101". It figured you made an error typing and attempted a correction.

Now lets test the side effect mentioned previously. Enter "1010", which is the binary inverse of what the network was trained with ("0101"). Hopfield networks always get trained for the binary inverse too. So if you enter "0101", the network will recognize it.

We will try one final test. Enter "1111", which is totally off base and not close to anything the neural network knows. The neural network responds with "0000", it did not try to correct, it has no idea what you mean. You can play with the network more. It can be taught more than one pattern. As you train new patterns it builds upon the matrix already in memory. Pressing "Clear" clears out the memory.

Constructing the Hopfield Example

Before we examine the portions of the Hopfield example application that are responsible for the actual neural network, we will first examine the user interface. The main application source code is shown in listing 2.1. This listing implements the Hopfield class, which is where the user interface code resides.

Listing 2.1: The Hopfield Application (Hopfield.java)

```java
import java.awt.*;
import javax.swing.*;
import java.awt.event.*;

/**
 * Example: The Hopfield Neural Network
 *
 * This is an example that implements a Hopfield neural
 * network.  This example network contains four fully
 * connected neurons.  This file, Hopfield, implements a
 * Swing interface into the other two neural network
 * classes: Layer and Neuron.
 *
 * @author Jeff Heaton
 * @version 1.0
 */
public class Hopfield extends JFrame implements ActionListener {

  /**
   * The number of neurons in this neural network.
   */
  public static final int NETWORK_SIZE = 4;

  /**
   * The weight matrix for the four fully connected
   * neurons.
   */
  JTextField matrix[][] =
    new JTextField[NETWORK_SIZE][NETWORK_SIZE];
```

```
/**
 * The input pattern, used to either train
 * or run the neural network.  When the network
 * is being trained, this is the training
 * data.  When the neural network is to be ran
 * this is the input pattern.
 */
JComboBox input[] = new JComboBox[NETWORK_SIZE];


/**
 * The output from each of the four neurons.
 */
JTextField output[] = new JTextField[NETWORK_SIZE];


/**
 * The clear button.  Used to clear the weight
 * matrix.
 */
JButton btnClear = new JButton("Clear");


/**
 * The train button.  Used to train the
 * neural network.
 */
JButton btnTrain = new JButton("Train");


/**
 * The run button.  Used to run the neural
 * network.
 */
JButton btnRun = new JButton("Run");


/**
 * Constructor, create all of the components and position
 * the JFrame to the center of the screen.
 */
public Hopfield()
{
  setTitle("Hopfield Neural Network");

  // create connections panel
  JPanel connections = new JPanel();
  connections.setLayout(
    new GridLayout(NETWORK_SIZE,NETWORK_SIZE) );
  for ( int row=0;row<NETWORK_SIZE;row++ ) {
    for ( int col=0;col<NETWORK_SIZE;col++ ) {
```

```
      matrix[row][col] = new JTextField(3);
      matrix[row][col].setText("0");
      connections.add(matrix[row][col]);
    }
  }

Container content = getContentPane();

GridBagLayout gridbag = new GridBagLayout();
GridBagConstraints c = new GridBagConstraints();
content.setLayout(gridbag);

c.fill = GridBagConstraints.NONE;
c.weightx = 1.0;

// Weight matrix label
c.gridwidth = GridBagConstraints.REMAINDER; //end row
c.anchor = GridBagConstraints.NORTHWEST;
content.add(
  new JLabel(
    "Weight Matrix for the Hopfield Neural Network:"),c);

// Weight matrix
c.anchor = GridBagConstraints.CENTER;
c.gridwidth = GridBagConstraints.REMAINDER; //end row
content.add(connections,c);
c.gridwidth = 1;

// Input pattern label
c.anchor = GridBagConstraints.NORTHWEST;
c.gridwidth = GridBagConstraints.REMAINDER; //end row
content.add(
  new JLabel(
    "Click \"Train\" to train the following pattern:"),c);

// Input pattern

String options[] = { "0","1"};

JPanel inputPanel = new JPanel();
inputPanel.setLayout(new FlowLayout());
for ( int i=0;i<NETWORK_SIZE;i++ ) {
  input[i] = new JComboBox(options);
  inputPanel.add(input[i]);
}
```

```
c.gridwidth = GridBagConstraints.REMAINDER; //end row
c.anchor = GridBagConstraints.CENTER;
content.add(inputPanel,c);

// Output pattern label
c.anchor = GridBagConstraints.NORTHWEST;
c.gridwidth = GridBagConstraints.REMAINDER; //end row
content.add(
  new JLabel("Click \"Run\" to see output pattern:"),c);


// Output pattern

JPanel outputPanel = new JPanel();
outputPanel.setLayout(new FlowLayout());
for ( int i=0;i<NETWORK_SIZE;i++ ) {
  output[i] = new JTextField(3);
  output[i].setEditable(false);
  outputPanel.add(output[i]);
}
c.gridwidth = GridBagConstraints.REMAINDER; //end row
c.anchor = GridBagConstraints.CENTER;
content.add(outputPanel,c);

// Buttons

JPanel buttonPanel = new JPanel();
btnClear = new JButton("Clear");
btnTrain = new JButton("Train");
btnRun = new JButton("Run");
btnClear.addActionListener(this);
btnTrain.addActionListener(this);
btnRun.addActionListener(this);
buttonPanel.setLayout(new FlowLayout());
buttonPanel.add(btnClear);
buttonPanel.add(btnTrain);
buttonPanel.add(btnRun);
content.add(buttonPanel,c);

// adjust size and position
pack();
Toolkit toolkit = Toolkit.getDefaultToolkit();
Dimension d = toolkit.getScreenSize();
setLocation(
            (int)(d.width-this.getSize().getWidth())/2,
```

```
                    (int) (d.height-this.getSize().getHeight())/2 );
      setDefaultCloseOperation(WindowConstants.DISPOSE_ON_CLOSE);
      setResizable(false);


  }

  /**
   * Used to dispatch events from the buttons
   * to the handler methods.
   *
   * @param e The event
   */
  public void actionPerformed(ActionEvent e)
  {
    if ( e.getSource()==btnRun )
      run();
    else if ( e.getSource()==btnClear )
      clear();
    else if ( e.getSource()==btnTrain )
      train();
  }

  /**
   * Called when the neural network is to be ran against
   * the input.
   */
  protected void run()
  {
    boolean pattern[] = new boolean[NETWORK_SIZE];
    int wt[][] = new int[NETWORK_SIZE][NETWORK_SIZE];

    for ( int row=0;row<NETWORK_SIZE;row++ )
      for ( int col=0;col<NETWORK_SIZE;col++ )
        wt[row][col]=Integer.parseInt(matrix[row][col].getText());
    for ( int row=0;row<NETWORK_SIZE;row++ ) {
      int i = input[row].getSelectedIndex();
      if ( i==0 )
        pattern[row] = false;
      else
        pattern[row] = true;
    }

    Layer net = new Layer(wt);
    net.activation(pattern);
```

```
    for ( int row=0;row<NETWORK_SIZE;row++ ) {
      if ( net.output[row] )
        output[row].setText("1");
      else
        output[row].setText("0");
      if ( net.output[row]==pattern[row] )
        output[row].setBackground(java.awt.Color.green);
      else
        output[row].setBackground(java.awt.Color.red);
    }

}


/**
 * Called to clear the weight matrix.
 */
protected void clear()
{
  for ( int row=0;row<NETWORK_SIZE;row++ )
    for ( int col=0;col<NETWORK_SIZE;col++ )
      matrix[row][col].setText("0");
}


/**
 * Called to train the weight matrix based on the
 * current input pattern.
 */
protected void train()
{
  int work[][] = new int[NETWORK_SIZE][NETWORK_SIZE];
  int bi[] = new int[NETWORK_SIZE];

  for ( int x=0;x<NETWORK_SIZE;x++ ) {
    if ( input[x].getSelectedIndex()==0 )
      bi[x] = -1;
    else
      bi[x] = 1;
  }

  for ( int row=0;row<NETWORK_SIZE;row++ )
    for ( int col=0;col<NETWORK_SIZE;col++ ) {
      work[row][col] = bi[row]*bi[col];
    }

  for ( int x=0;x<NETWORK_SIZE;x++ )
    work[x][x] =-1;
```

```
    for ( int row=0;row<NETWORK_SIZE;row++ )
      for ( int col=0;col<NETWORK_SIZE;col++ ) {
        int i = Integer.parseInt(matrix[row][col].getText());
        matrix[row][col].setText( "" + (i+work[row][col]));
      }

  }

  /**
   * Main program entry point, display the
   * frame.
   *
   * @param args Command line arguments are not used
   */
  static public void main(String args[])
  {
    JFrame f = new Hopfield();
    f.show();
  }
}
```

The Hopfield Application Components

The most significant components are the matrix array, the input array and the output array. The weight matrix is stored in a two dimensional array of JTextField elements. It is here that you enter the weights for each neuron. Because there are four neurons in our sample applications, and each neuron is fully connected to the other four (including itself), a four by four two dimensional array is used.

In addition to the weight array, you must have an area where you can input new patterns for the application to either recognize or learn from. This is the purpose of the input array. The input array is a one-dimensional array that contains four elements. These four elements correspond to each of the four input neurons to the Hopfield neural network (the four input neurons are also the output neurons in this example). When you click the Train button, the weight matrix is adjusted so the pattern you stored in the input array will be recalled in the future. If you click the Run button, then the values stored in the input array will be presented to the Neural Network for possible recognition.

The output of this recognition is stored in the output array. If the pattern was successfully recognized, then the output array should exactly mimic the input array. If the input pattern was slightly different than the pattern the network was trained with, then the Neural Network attempts to find the closest match. Therefore, after an input pattern is presented to the Neural Network, the output array will reflect the Neural Network's best guess at the pattern that was input to it.

How exactly the Neural Network derives this output will be discussed later. Next you will be shown how the matrix was determined. Determining the matrix that will produce the desired output is called training the network.

Training the Network

When the Train button is clicked, the application calls the method train. The train method is responsible for adjusting the weight matrix so that the new pattern can be correctly recalled. This process takes several steps. You will now be shown how the network trains.

The mathematical basis for training a Hopfield Neural Network was already explained earlier in the "Deriving the Weight Matrix" section. Now we will examine the process from a more programmatic basis. The first thing that the train method must do is retrieve the input pattern from the TextField controls. As the input is retrieved, the values are converted to bipolar values. As was discussed previously, conversion to bipolar simply involves converting every 0 to a –1 of a binary number; the output is stored in the "bi" array. This is done as follows.

```
// first convert to bipolar(0=-1, 1=1)
    for ( int x=0;x<4;x++ ) {
      if ( input[x].getSelectedIndex()==0 )
        bi[x] = -1;
      else
        bi[x] = 1;
    }
```

The next step is to multiply the input sequence by its transposition. To see exactly what this means refer back to the "Deriving the Weight Matrix" section. To perform this operation, a new matrix is constructed, called work, that is perfectly square. Its width is determined by the width of the input sequence. In this case the work matrix is exactly 4X4, which is the same size as the weight matrix array shown on the application. Here, each element of the work matrix is filled with a value that is derived by multiplying the value of the input sequence that contains the same row and column. This is done with the following code.

```
// now multiply the matrix by its transposition
    for ( int row=0;row<4;row++ )
      for ( int col=0;col<4;col++ ) {
        work[row][col] = bi[row]*bi[col];
      }
```

A Hopfield Neural network does not generally assign weights between the same neurons. For example, there would be no weight between neuron 0 and itself. The weight of each of the four neurons back to itself must be set to –1 (0 in bipolar). This is done with the following code.

```
// next set the northwest diagonal to -1
   for ( int x=0;x<4;x++ )
     work[x][x] =-1;
```

Finally, the work matrix must be added to the existing weight matrix. This is done by taking each element of the work matrix and adding it to the corresponding element of the actual weight matrix. The result of this is displayed on the application.

```
// finally add to the existing weight matrix
   for ( int row=0;row<4;row++ )
     for ( int col=0;col<4;col++ ) {
       int i = Integer.parseInt(matrix[row][col].getText());
       matrix[row][col].setText( "" + (i+work[row][col]));
     }
```

Determining the Neuron Output

You will now be shown how the application is able to recall a pattern. This is done by presenting the input sequence to the Neural Network and determining the output for each Neuron. The mathematical basis for this process was already described in the section "Recalling Patterns." The application determines the output of the Neural Network by using the Layer class, shown in Listing 2.2.

Listing 2.2: The Layer Class (Layer.java)

```
public class Layer {

  /**
   * An array of neurons.
   */
  protected Neuron neuron[] = new Neuron[4];

  /**
   * The output of the neurons.
   */
  protected boolean output[] = new boolean[4];

  /**
   * The number of neurons in this layer.  And because this is a
   * single layer neural network, this is also the number of
   * neurons in the network.
   */
  protected int neurons;
```

```java
/**
 * A constant to multiply against the threshold function.
 * This is not used, and is set to 1.
 */
public static final double lambda = 1.0;


/**
 * The constructor.  The weight matrix for the
 * neurons must be passed in.  Because this is
 * a single layer network the weight array should
 * always be perfectly square(i.e.  4x4).  These
 * weights are used to initialize the neurons.
 *
 * @param weights A 2d array that contains the weights
 * between each
 * neuron and the other neurons.
 */
Layer(int weights[][])
{
  neurons = weights[0].length;

  neuron = new Neuron[neurons];
  output = new boolean[neurons];

  for ( int i=0;i<neurons;i++ )
    neuron[i]=new Neuron(weights[i]);
}


/**
 * The threshold method is used to determine if the neural
 * network will fire for a given pattern.  This threshold
 * uses the hyperbolic tangent (tanh).
 *
 * @param k The product of the neuron weights and the input
 * pattern.
 * @return Whether to fire or not to fire.
 */
public boolean threshold(int k)
{
  double kk = k * lambda;
  double a = Math.exp( kk );
  double b = Math.exp( -kk );
  double tanh = (a-b)/(a+b);
  return(tanh>=0);
}
```

```
/**
 * This method is called to actually run the neural network.
 *
 * @param pattern The input pattern to present to the
 * neural network.
 */
void activation(boolean pattern[])
{
  int i,j;
  for ( i=0;i<4;i++ ) {
    neuron[i].activation = neuron[i].act(pattern);
    output[i] = threshold(neuron[i].activation);
  }
 }
}
```

When the constructor is called for the Layer class, the weight matrix is passed in. This will allow the Layer class to determine what the output should be for a given input pattern. To determine the output sequence, an input sequence should be passed to the activation method of the Layer class. The activation method calls each of the neurons to determine their output. The following code does this.

```
for ( i=0;i<4;i++ ) {
  neuron[i].activation = neuron[i].act(pattern);
  output[i] = threshold(neuron[i].activation);
}
```

The above loop stores each neuron's activation value in the same neuron. Each activation is determined by calling the act method of the Neuron. To see how each neuron calculates its activation, we must first examine the Neuron class, which is shown in Listing 2.3.

Listing 2.3: The Neuron Class (Neuron.java)

```
public class Neuron {

  /**
   * The weights between this neuron and the other neurons on
   * the layer.
   */
  public int weightv[];

  /**
   * Activation results for this neuron.
   */
  public int activation;
```

```
/**
 * The constructor.  The weights between this neuron and
 * every other neuron(including itself) is passed in as
 * an array.  Usually the weight between this neuron and
 * itself is zero.
 *
 * @param in The weight vector.
 */
public Neuron(int in[])
{
  weightv = in;
}

/**
 * This method is called to determine if the neuron would
 * activate, or fire.
 *
 * @param x Neuron input
 * @return If the neuron would activate, or fire
 */
public int act(boolean x[] )
{
  int i;
  int a=0;

  for ( i=0;i<x.length;i++ )
    if ( x[i] )
      a+=weightv[i];
  return a;
}

}
```

To calculate a neuron's activation, that neuron simply sums all of its weight values. Only those weight values that have a 1 in the input pattern are calculated. This is accomplished by using the following code.

```
      for ( i=0;i<x.length;i++ )
        if ( x[i] )
          a+=weightv[i];
      return a;
```

Summary

Neural Networks are one of the most commonly used systems in Artificial Intelligence. Neural Networks are particularly adept at recognizing patterns. This allows them to recognize something, even when distorted.

A Neural Network may have input, output and hidden layers. The input and output layers are the only required layers. The input and output layer may be the same neurons. Neural networks are typically presented input patterns that will produce some output pattern.

If a Neural network mimics the input pattern it was presented with, then that network is said to be autoassociative. For example, if a neural network were presented with the pattern "0110", and the output were also "0110", then that network would be said to be autoassociative.

A neural network calculates its output based on the input pattern and the neural network's internal connection weight matrix. The values for these connection weights will determine the output from the neural network, based upon input pattern.

A Hopfield neural network is a fully connected autoassociative neural network. What this means, is that each neuron is connected to every other neuron in a Hopfield Neural Network. A Hopfield Neural Network can be trained to recognize certain patterns. Training a Hopfield Neural Network involves performing some basic matrix manipulations on the input pattern that is to be recognized.

This chapter showed how to construct a simple Hopfield Neural Network. The next chapter will show how to create a multilayered neural network. To do this, you will be introduced to the JOONE package that is freely available for Java.

CHAPTER 3: USING MULTILAYER NEURAL NETWORKS

Chapter Highlights
- **Using the JOONE Editor**
- **Using the JOONE Engine**
- **Neural Network Input from Files**
- **Neural Network Input from Memory**

In this chapter you will see how to use the feedforward multilayer neural network. This neural network architecture has become the mainstay of modern neural network programming. In this chapter you will be shown two ways that you can implement such a neural network.

We will begin by examining an open source neural network engine called JOONE. JOONE can be downloaded from http://www.jooneworld.com. JOONE contains a neural network editor that allows you to quickly model and test neural networks. We will use this editor to introduce the concept of how a multilayer network fits together.

Using the JOONE Editor

JOONE is an open source, 100% Java implementation. JOONE is released under a Lesser GNU Public License (LPGL). What this means is that you are free to use JOONE in any project, be it commercial or private, without paying any sort of royalty or licensing free.

JOONE is maintained at the website JooneWorld (http://www.jooneworld.com). Because JOONE is always being updated to include new features, it is a good idea to check the site to see if a new version of JOONE exists. This book uses the latest version of JOONE that was available at the time of printing, which is version 0.9.0 of the engine and version 0.6.0 of the editor. JOONE contains several components. To begin learning how to use JOONE, you will first be introduced to the JOONE editor.

JOONE includes a neural network editor, which provides a way to graphically layout neural networks. This allows you to quickly see the components of a neural network and how they fit together. With this tool you can create neural network solutions that do not require any customized coding. If your solution can be accomplished with only a neural network and no other supporting code, then you might use only the JOONE editor.

Of course few programming tasks can be accomplished with only a neural network. You will often have to write support code that encapsulates the neural network, such as the user interface.

Because of this, most applications that use JOONE make use of the JOONE engine. The JOONE engine is the set of core neural network classes that you can use directly from within your own Java programs. What the JOONE editor is primarily used for is to quickly try out several neural network architectures before deciding which is best for your program. The JOONE editor allows you to see your neural networks in a very graphical format.

Setting Up Your Environment

Before you can begin using the JOONE editor or engine, you must make sure that the Java environment is correctly setup on your computer, and that JOONE is installed. The instructions for setting up your environment differ greatly depending on what sort of operating system you are running. If you are running a Windows based operating system, refer to Appendix C, "Compiling Examples Using Windows". If you are running on a UNIX or Linux based system refer to Appendix D, "Compiling Examples Using UNIX/Linux". Once you have your environment properly setup and JOONE installed, you can begin using JOONE.

JOONE consists of several components. At the heart of everything is the JOONE engine. The JOONE engine has no user interface, however it implements all of the low level functions of the network. If you write programs that make use of the JOONE system, these programs will most likely make use of the engine. JOONE also contains a GUI editor that can be used to quickly design and test neural networks. As most new programs are introduced in this book, I will provide a Uniform Modeling Language (UML) diagram. UML is a standard way of drawing object diagrams. Figure 3.1 shows a UML diagram of some of the main JOONE Engine components.

Figure 3.1: JOONE Components

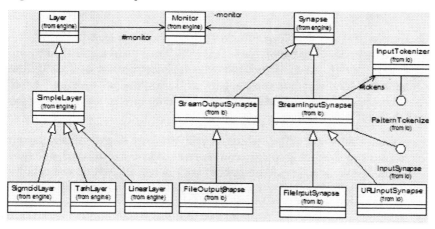

Regardless of if you are using the JOONE Editor or the JOONE Engine you will be using these components. These components are pictured above. As you build the neural networks in this chapter you will see how many of these objects are actually used. Table 3.1 summarizes these components.

Table 3.1: JOONE Components

Class	Purpose
FileInputSynapse	A synapse that is designed to input from a disk file.
FileOutputSynapse	A synapse that is designed to output to a disk file.
InputSynapse	An interface that defines a input synapse, or data source.
InputTokenizer	A tokenizer is used to transform underlying input formats into arrays of floating point numbers that will be fed to the neural network.
Layer	The layer object is the basic element in JOONE. A layer transfers the input pattern to the output pattern while executing a transfer function. The output pattern is then sent to all output synapses that are attached to the layer.
LinerLayer	A neuron layer that uses a linear function to activate.
Monitor	The monitor is used to control the behavior of the neural net. It controls the start/stop actions. Each layer and synapse is connected to a monitor.
PatternTokenizer	An interface that is used to define a tokenizer.
SigmoidLayer	A neuron layer that uses a sigmoid function to activate.
SimpleLayer	This abstract class represents layers that are made up of neurons that implement some transfer function.
StreamInputSynapse	This abstract class forms the base for any of the stream based input synapses.
StreamOutputSynapse	This abstract class forms the base for any of the stream based output synapses.
Synapse	The Synapse is the connection element between two Layer objects. Each connection between neurons in these layers is represented by a weight. The values of these weights are the memory of the neural network.
TanhLayer	A neuron layer that uses the hyperbolic tangent to activate its neurons.
URLInputSynapse	A synapse that is designed to receive input from a HTTP connection.

To see how to use JOONE objects an example is in order. You will now be shown how to use the JOONE Editor and the JOONE Engine. Our discussion of JOONE will begin with the JOONE editor.

Solving the XOR Problem with the JOONE Editor

The examples given in this chapter will revisit the XOR problem. First you will see how to use the JOONE editor to create a neural network that is capable of solving the XOR problem. In addition to modeling the neural network, the JOONE editor also allows you to run training data against the neural network. This allows the neural network to learn, by adjusting neuron weights, to solve the XOR problem. This XOR solution neural network will first be created in the JOONE editor so that you can visually see what the neural network looks like.

Once you have seen how to use the JOONE editor to solve the XOR problem, you will be shown how to use the JOONE engine to create a standalone Java application that solves the XOR problem.

The JOONE editor is used to quickly model neural networks and observe the output. The JOONE editor will not generate code, nor is it ever used in conjunction with any program you might create. The JOONE editor is simply a rapid prototype tool that can be used to visually see neural networks in action. In this chapter you will be stepped through the process of creating a simple multilayer feedforward neural network.

This section shows you how to layout a neural network using the editor. The next section of this chapter will show you how to take that model and turn it into a working program. You will begin with a relatively simple problem; creating a neural network that can learn the XOR problem.

You will recall from Chapter 1, "Introduction to AI," that the XOR problem confounded the perceptron. In this chapter we will use the JOONE Editor to create a neural network that is capable of solving the XOR problem. The XOR function is summarized in Table 3.2.

Table 3.2: The XOR Function

Input 1	Input 2	Ouput
0	0	0
0	1	1
1	0	1
1	1	0

To have JOONE solve the XOR problem, as presented in Table 3.1, the XOR problem must be presented to JOONE in a manor that JOONE can process. JOONE requires that all such input be in a standard data file format.

Understanding JOONE Data Files

JOONE is programmed to only perform input and output from files. This is true for both the JOONE Editor, as well as the JOONE Engine. There are three types of data files that you will likely process with JOONE. They are summarized as follows.

Training Files are used to provide JOONE with sample inputs to train with. If you are using supervised learning, this file will also contain the anticipated output from the neural network.

Input Files are used to provide input that the neural network should process. Once the neural network has been trained, the network can be fed input files. This will produce result files.

Result Files contain the results from the output neurons. A result file is generated when the neural network is fed input files.

To have JOONE solve the XOR problem you must create the appropriate data files. The format for all three files is exactly the same. Just by looking at the file contents of a JOONE data file it is impossible to discern one file from another.

A JOONE data file consists of individual lines of floating point numbers which are delineated by semicolons. Decimal points are not required, if the numbers are integer. The individual numbers can be either input values or the expected result. This will be communicated to JOONE when these files are specified. When a training file is provided as input, you tell the JOONE Editor or Engine which columns are input and which columns are expected output. The training file that would be created to train the XOR network is shown in Listing 3.1.

Listing 3.1: The XOR Function Training File (training.txt)

```
0.0;0.0;0.0
0.0;1.0;1.0
1.0;0.0;1.0
1.0;1.0;0.0
```

The training file shown in Listing 3.1 provides the neural network with all anticipated neural network inputs. It is not necessary, and usually impossible, to provide JOONE with every possible combination of inputs. However, for a simple function like XOR it is easy enough to provide every combination. This is the purpose of the first two columns of Listing 3.1. The remaining column specifies the output for each of the input pairs. For example, the input zero followed by one should produce an output of one.

Understanding JOONE Layer File

Neural networks are composed of layers of a neurons. A layer consists of one or more neurons that have similar properties. JOONE provides you with several different layer types. To allow the editor to easily be expanded, a special configuration file is used to identify what layer types are supported by JOONE.

When you launch the JOONE editor you must specify the location of the "layers.xml" file. A copy of "layers.xml" is included on the companion download along with this JOONE editor. For more information on the proper installation of the JOONE Editor and Engine, refer to Appendix C and D.

This chapter will make user of only one layer type, the Sigmoid layer. Chapter 4, "How a Machine Learns," will introduce the other layer types supported by JOONE. Chapter 4 will also show how JOONE can easily be extended to support additional neuron layer types. With the JOONE Editor and your layers file properly installed, you are now ready to construct a neural network.

Constructing the Neural Network

To begin creating your neural network you must first launch the JOONE editor. This requires that your environment be properly setup. The section "Setting up Your Environment" presented earlier in this chapter shows how to do this. To launch the JOONE editor you should issue the following command from a command or terminal window.

```
java org.joone.edit.JoonEdit c:\jar\layers.xml
```

This command can be executed from any location on your computer. The first parameter, which specifies the location of your layers file, may be different depending on where you have your layers file stored. Refer to the previous section for more information about the layers file.

When the editor first comes up, a blank neural network will be presented. You can add components to this network and then later save. The companion download already has a copy of this neural network saved under the name "xor.ser".

To create the XOR solution neural network, you must add three sigmoid layers. Individual neurons are not shown on JOONE diagrams, only neuron layers. These three layers will be the input, hidden and output layers.

First create the input layer. This is done by clicking on the sigmoid layer button on the toolbar. As you hover your mouse over each of the buttons the meaning of the button is shown in the status bar that is at the very bottom of the JOONE editor. On some operating systems popup will also be shown to tell you what component your mouse is currently hovering over. If this is done correctly your screen should look like Figure 3.2.

Figure 3.2: A Sigmoid Layer

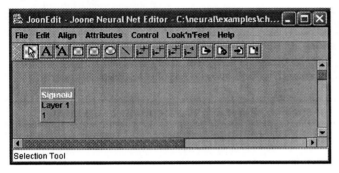

You must now set the properties for the input layer. Clicking on the input layer will display the properties dialog box. You should rename this layer to "Input Layer" and set the rows parameter to two. This dialog box is shown in Figure 3.3. The current version of JOONE contains no "Save" or "Apply" button in JOONE property dialog boxes, your changes are saved when you click the close button for a window. There is no way to discard changes.

The JOONE editor will open the properties window for any object that you click. This can be an annoying side effect, as you will get the properties window opened even when you simply select a object to move it. A more elegant solution is on the current request list for the JOONE project. The best way to counter this is to simply leave the properties window open all the time, and allow it to change to whatever the currently selected object is. Of course, you should move the properties window away from your current work area so it does not interfere with your work.

Figure 3.3: Sigmoid Layer Properties

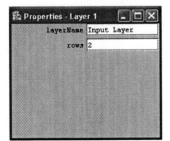

As you can see there are several properties that a sigmoid layer allows you to set. These properties remain the same regardless of if you are creating a neural network in the JOONE Editor, or if you are directly programming the JOONE Engine from Java. The meanings of each of these fields are summarized below.

Table 3.3: Sigmoid Layer Options

Property	Purpose
Layer Name	This is the layer name, its value is not directly used by JOONE. When it becomes necessary to debug a program, a layer name can be invaluable for determining exactly which layer a particular Java reference is pointing to.
Rows	The rows parameter specifies the number of neurons in this level.

Next, the hidden layer must be created. The steps to create a hidden layer are nearly the same as the steps to create the input layer. Create another sigmoid layer and set its name to "Hidden Layer" and the rows parameter to three.

Finally, you must create the output layer. The steps to create the output layer are nearly the same as the steps to create the previous layers. Create a third sigmoid layer and set its name to "Output Layer" and the rows parameter to one.

You now have three disjointed neural layers. For these layers to function they must be linked together. Begin by connecting the input layer to the hidden layer. This is done by dragging a line from the small circle on the right hand side of the input layer. You must have the input layer selected to see this circle. This should draw an arrow. (JOONE will likely open up the properties window when you complete this operation. Simply close the properties window as you do not need to make any changes.) You should also draw a line from the hidden to the output layer in exactly the same way. At this point your network is complete. This is the point at which the "startXor.ser" sample was saved, which is included on the companion download. Your neural network should now look like Figure 3.4.

Figure 3.4: The Completed Neural Network

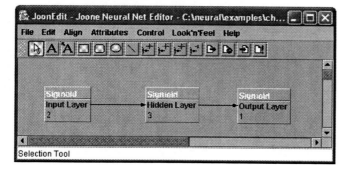

Now the neural network must be trained. However, before the network can be trained, some additional objects must be added to the neural network. First a "File Input Layer" must be added to the left of the input layer. This layer can be obtained from the toolbar, just like the sigmoid layer. The small circle from the file input layer should be dragged to the input layer. This is done in the same way as when the other layers are connected. This will cause the training file to feed its data to the input layer.

You must also set the properties for the file input layer. To bring up the properties, click the input layer. Set the firstCol and lastCol parameters to one and two respectively. This specifies which columns specify the input data in the data file. The filename should contain the complete path to your train.xml file. This file can be found on the companion download. All other parameters should remain the same. Figure 3.5 shows a completed file input layer dialog box.

Figure 3.5: A Completed file Input Layer Dialog Box

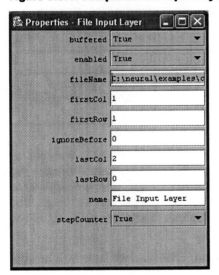

As you can see, there are several properties that a file input layer allows you to set. The meanings of each of these fields are summarized below. Table 3.4 summarizes these properties.

Table 3.4: Input Layer Options

Property	Purpose
Buffered	Sets whether JOONE buffer the values or read them from disk each time.
Enabled	Is this layer enabled.
FirstCol	One input file can serve multiple purposes. This parameter specifies the starting column to use. Column indexes begin with one.
FirstRow	This parameter specifies the starting row. Set to one to specify the first row.
IgnoreBefore	Specifies the number of input patterns to ignore for each training cycle. I have not found much practical use for this property.
LastCol	This is the last column index that this layer should read.
LastRow	This is the last row that the layer should read from the file. To instruct the layer to read the entire contents of the file a value of zero should be passed.
Name	The name of this layer.
StepCounter	If this property is set to true, then the file will automatically rewind when the end is reached. Because most neural networks are rapidly trained with the same data, this is often desired.

Next, a teacher layer must be added to the output layer. This will allow the weights for the input, hidden and output layers to be modified to cause the neural network to learn the XOR pattern. Add a teacher layer to the right of the output layer. Connect the output layer to the teacher layer by dragging the small circle from the output layer to the teacher layer. The only property of the teacher layer that should be set is the name. The name property of the teacher layer should be set to "Teacher Layer".

The teacher layer requires access to the input data too. The teacher layer will be concerned with the last column of Listing 3.1, which is the anticipated output. A second file input layer should be added to the neural network. This file input layer should be named "Teacher File Input", as it will be connected to the teacher layer. The properties of the teacher file input layer are set as follows. The input file to the teacher file input layer is the same input file as was specified for the main "File Input Layer". The teacher layer uses the desired output column of Listing 3.1; as a result both the firstCol and lastCol properties must be set to three.

The "Teacher File Input Layer" should be connected to the "Teacher Layer". This is done by dragging the small box on the edge of the "Teacher File Input Layer" to the "Teacher Layer". With these steps complete your neural network is now ready to begin learning. The completed neural network should look like Figure 3.6.

Figure 3.6: A Neural Network Ready for Training

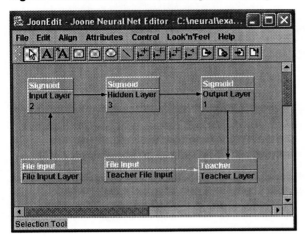

Training the Neural Network

Now that the neural network has been constructed, the training process can begin. Select the "Control Panel" menu. From here select the "Control Panel" menu item. They are both named "Control Panel". This will display a window that allows you to specify the training parameters. These parameters should be filled in as seen in Figure 3.7. The totCycles parameter should be set to 10,000. The patterns parameter should be set to 4. The learning rate parameter should be set to 0.8 and the momentum parameter to 0.3. Finally, to specify that you are training you should set the learning property to true.

Figure 3.7: Setting Training Parameters

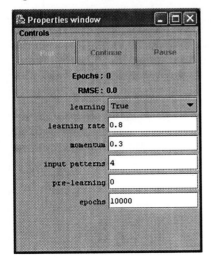

As you can see there are several properties that a sigmoid layer allows you to set. These properties remain the same regardless of if you are creating a neural network in the JOONE Editor, or if you are directly programming the JOONE Engine from Java. The meanings of each of these fields are summarized below in table 3.5.

Table 3.5: Training Properties

Property	Purpose
Learning Set	This value to true if you are training the neural network. If you are presenting patters to the neural network for recognition this property should be set to false.
Learning Rate	The learning rate for the neural network controls the rate at which changes are made to the weights store in the synapses. This will be covered in greater detail in Chapter 4.
Momentum	A parameter used for backpropagation learning. The use of momentum will be covered in Chapter 9, "Understanding Backpropagation".
Input Patterns	The number of input patterns that will be presented to the neural network.
Pre-learning	Prelearning allows several cycles to be designation as learning cycles, even though the learning property is set to false.
Total Cycles	How many times the input pattern should be run. This is usually used with training to determine how long to train for.

To begin the training process, click the start button. JOONE is completely multi-threaded and other tasks can be performed while the network is training. The neural network will be taken through 10,000 training cycles. For very large or complex neural networks this can take considerable time. For such tasks, JOONE can operate in a distributed mode, using many computers to train the neural network.

At the end of the training, the error, specified as RMSE (root mean square error), should be very small. An error below 0.1 is acceptable. If this fails to happen you must retrain the neural network. To do this, select the "Randomize" menu item under the "Control Panel" menu. Now train the neural network again. You may wish to save your neural network now that it is trained.

Now that the neural network has been trained we can present data and observe the results. The neural network should now be properly trained to respond with the correct XOR result for any given input. The neural networks objects must be rearranged slightly to allow the neural network to be executed. This will be discussed in the next section.

Preparing to Execute the Neural Network

Before the neural network can be tested, a few changes must be made to the neural network diagram. The teacher must be disconnected from the neural network and a file output layer must be added. Add a file output layer to the right of the output layer. Click on the new file output layer and enter a file name in which to store the results. The companion download contains a sample results file that is named "results.txt". You should also name this layer "Results".

The "Results" layer must be attached to the output layer in place of the teacher layer. To do this, click the line that connects the output layer to the teacher layer. Now press the delete button to sever this link. Next drag a new link from the "Output Layer" to the newly created "Results" layer. Your model should now look like Figure 3.8.

Figure 3.8: A Neural Network Ready to Run

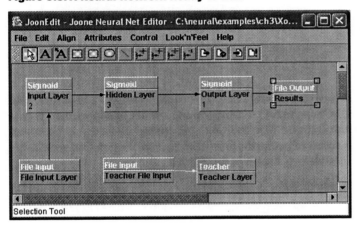

Now that the neural network has been properly configured for running or executing; you can see if the neural network properly learned the XOR function. Select the "Control Panel" menu. From here, select the "Control Panel" menu item. They are both named "Control Panel". This will display a window that allows you to specify the neural network parameters. This is the same window as was used to train the neural network. These parameters should be filled in as seen in Figure 3.9. The totCycles parameter should be set to 1. The patterns parameter should be set to 4. Finally, to specify that you are no longer training you should set the learning property to false.

Figure 3.9: Ready to Run the Neural Network

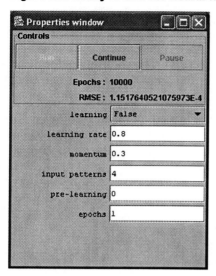

Once these fields are properly set you should click the "Begin" button. The neural network will run very quickly. The file "results.txt" will be created. What has happened is that every input pattern specified in the training file "train.txt", discussed earlier, has been run through the neural network. The result of each row is written to a corresponding row in the "result.txt" file. The contents of this file are shown in Listing 3.2.

Listing 3.2: Neural Network Results (result.txt)

```
0.012022188543571214
0.9850650966922243
0.9848523804373928
0.018901538819852792
```

Your results may vary from Listing 3.2. However, you should always see two numbers which are close to one, and two numbers which are close to zero. This shows that the neural network has recalled one for the second and fourth rows and zero for the first and third.

Using the JOONE Engine

As you saw in the previous section, it is possible to construct a neural network using the JOONE Editor. With the neural network complete, you can both train and execute neural networks using input files. While the JOONE Editor is user friendly and makes it easy to edit neural network layouts, it does not lend itself well to more complex programming tasks.

Generally neural networks do not stand alone as independent programs. A neural network is almost always integrated into a much larger program. The neural network is responsible for performing pattern recognition, and the larger program handles the user interface. To use JOONE with a larger Java program, you must use the JOONE Engine, rather than the JOONE Editor. The JOONE Engine gives you a library of classes that you can use to implement neural networks.

The JOONE engine is written to be very multi-threaded. On computer systems with many processors, or in a distributed environment, JOONE can achieve great performance. Unfortunately these additional layers mean a great deal of overhead, and programming complexity for otherwise simple projects. In this book we will not use the JOONE Engine. In the next section we will examine a reusable class named "Network.java" that we will use in later chapters as well to implement the feedforward backpropagation neural network. In this chapter we will focus mainly on how to use it. Later chapters will explain how it process information, as well as how it learns.

Using a Java Neural Network

In this section you will see how to use a feedforward backpropagation neural network from a Java program. In this chapter we will see mainly how the program is structured. In Chapter 5 we will examine the internal workings of how the feedforward backpropagation neural network was implemented using JOONE. The next section will be introduce the neural network class that will be used in this book, when we are not using JOONE. While it is usually a good idea to use JOONE, this class will demonstrate to you exactly how to create a neural network completely on your own. Then in the following section you will be shown how a simple example can be created that demonstrates the neural network class solving the XOR problem. We begin by examining the neural network class.

Using the Network Class

All programs in this book that make use of the feedforward neural network will make use of the Neural class. This class implements a feedforward neural network with an input, hidden and output layer. Most examples in this book will use only a single layer of hidden neurons.

There are several methods that make up the Network class. In the next sections, we will examine each of these and see how they are called.

The Network Constructor

Like most classes in Java, the network class makes available a specialized constructor that will accept some basic configuration information about how the neural network is to be constructed. The signature for the neural network constructor is shown below.

```
public Network(int inputCount,
               int hiddenCount,
               int outputCount,
               double learnRate,
               double momentum)
```

As you can see from the above constructor, several configuration parameters must be passed to the neural network class as it is instantiated. These parameters are summarized as follows in Table 3.6.

Table 3.6: Network Constructor Parameters

Property	Purpose
inputCount	The number of neurons that are in the input layer.
hiddenCount	The number of neurons that are in the hidden layer.
outputCount	The number of neurons that are in the output layer.
learnRate	The learning rate for the backpropagation training algorithm. This parameter will be discussed in much greater detail in Chapter 5.
momentum	The momentum for the backpropagation training algorithm. This parameter will be discussed in much greater detail in Chapter 5.

The input and output layers are determined by how you represent your problem as a neural network. There are many ways to determine this. Through this book you will be presented with problems that will be adapted to neural networks.

The learning rate and momentum are both backpropagation algorithms that will affect the learning process of the neural network. These two parameters will be covered in much greater detail in Chapter 5. In general, both of these values should be set to values that are greater than zero, but also less than 1.

Once the neural network has been instantiated using the constructor, it is ready for use. At this point the neural network has a random weight matrix and should be trained before any patterns are to be recalled from the neural network. In the next section you will see how the neural network is used to recall a pattern.

The Output Computation Method

The output computation method allows you to present a pattern to the input layer and receive a pattern back from the output layer. Both the input and output patterns are passed using an array of doubles. The signature for the output computation method is shown here.

```
public double [] computeOutputs(double input[])
```

The size of this array must correspond to the number of input neurons for the neural network. An array will be returned from this method. The array that is returned will have one element that represents the output of each of the output neurons. The following code shows how you would present a simple two number pattern to the output computation method and display the result.

```
double input[] = { 0.0, 1.0 };
double output[];
```

```
output = neural.computeOutputs(input);

for(int i=0;i<output.length;i++)
{
  System.out.println( output[i] );
}
```

As you can see the above code passes the input array to the output computation method and receives the output from the neural network. The output from this method may not match the desired output. To calculate the amount of error in the output of the neural network you will use the error calculation methods. The error calculation methods will be discussed in the next section.

The Error Calculation Method

The error calculation methods allow you to determine the amount of variance between the expected and actual output of a neural network. In the next section, you will be shown how to train the neural network. Calling the error calculation methods is the first step in training the neural network. Once the error has been determined, the network can be trained so that the next time the error will likely be lower.

There are two methods that are used for error calculation. The first is shown here.

```
public void calcError(double ideal[])
```

This method is to be called after each output set is presented during a training process. This method does not make any modifications to the weight matrix. Yet, this method does store the "deltas" needed to modify the weight matrix so that the neural network will produce the ideal output better next time. To actually implement these changes, you must call the learn method of the neural network. The learn method will be covered in the next section.

The second way to calculate error is called the root mean-square (RMS) error for a complete set of training data. Once you have submitted a number of a complete training sets through the learning process, you can call the "getError" method to calculate the average error for the entire set. The signature for the "getError" method is shown below.

```
public double getError(int len)
```

Now that you have seen how to calculate errors, you are ready to see the methods that are used to train the neural network. These methods are covered in the next section.

The Training and Resetting Methods

Once you have obtained the neural network output and calculated the error for an input pattern, you can train the neural network to better recognize this pattern next time. This is done very simply calling the learn method. Before you call the learn method you must insure that you have calculated the output and errors. The signature for the learn method is shown below.

```
public void learn()
```

The neural network begins with a completely random weight matrix. You may wish to completely reset the neural network back to this state. This can be done at any time by calling the reset method. The signature for the reset method is shown here.

```
public void reset()
```

As you can see, you must use the output calculation, error calculation and training methods in a specific order. The following code segment shows how this would be done.

```
double input[] = {
  { 0,0 },
  { 0,1 },
  { 1,0 },
  { 1,1 } };

double ideal[] = { {0}, {1}, {1}, {0 }};

for( int i=0;i<input.length; i++)
{
  neural.calcOutputs( input[i] );
  neural.calcError(ideal[i]);
  neural.learn();
}

System.out.println("Total error: " +
  neural.getError(input.length) );
```

As you can see from the above code, the training set used is for the XOR operator. This training set is then presented to the "calcOutputs" method. Though the "calcOutputs" calculates the output for the neural network, these outputs are discarded as they are not needed. At this point we are only calling the "calcOutputs" method to prepare to call the "calcError" method. This is because we are simply training and we do not care about the actual outputs of the neural network. Once the "calcOutputs" method has been called the "calcError" method is called. The ideal outputs, which are the outputs we expected from the neural network, are passed into the "calcError" method. The "calcError" method will then determine how close the actual outputs from the neural network match these ideal outputs. With this all complete, we can finally call the "learn" method of the neural network. The "learn" method will make any adjustments to the weight matrix to allow an in network to better recognize this training set and produce the ideal outputs.

The above code loops through all four of the possibilities for the XOR problem. Just as the human often does not learn a new skill the first time, so too the neural network learns through repetition. The example program that you will see in the next section runs through a similar process up to 10,000 times, to properly train the neural network. Generally, you'll write neural network programs to evaluate the overall error and continue looping through the training set, so long as the error is above a desired amount, such as 10 percent.

Activation Functions

You may recall from earlier in the chapter that JOONE allowed you to choose different neuron layer types. These layer types differed in the sort of threshold method that they used. By default, the neural network class uses a sigmoid activation method. This activation method is shown below.

```
public double threshold(double sum) {
    return 1.0 / (1 + Math.exp(-1.0 * sum));
}
```

You may wish to use other types of activation methods. To do this, you must override the neural network class and provide a new threshold method.

XOR Problem Example

Now that you have see how to use the neural network class, we will examine a more complex example function. We will create a simple program that allows you to solve the XOR problem. You will also be able to enter other logic gates as well. The program that we will examine is shown in Figure 3.10.

Figure 3.10: The XOR Problem

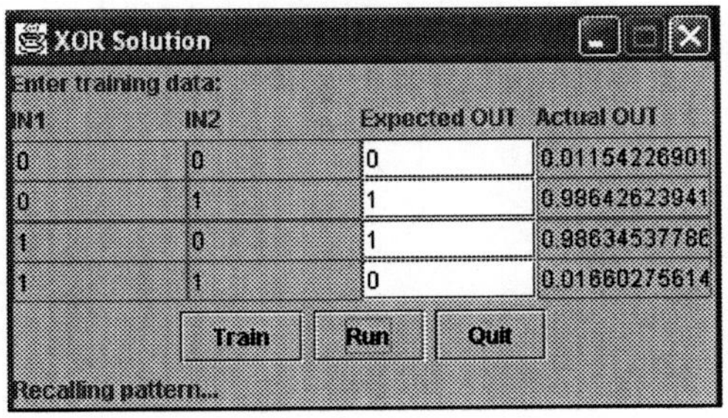

This program is implemented as a single class. The complete listing for this example is shown in Listing 3.3.

Listing 3.3: User Interface to an XOR Problem Solution

```java
import javax.swing.*;
import java.awt.*;
import java.awt.event.*;
import java.text.*;

public class XorExample extends JFrame implements
ActionListener,Runnable {

  protected JButton btnTrain;
  protected JButton btnRun;
  protected JButton btnQuit;
  protected JLabel status;
  protected Thread worker = null;
  protected final static int NUM_INPUT = 2;
  protected final static int NUM_OUTPUT = 1;
  protected final static int NUM_HIDDEN = 3;
  protected final static double RATE = 0.5;
  protected final static double MOMENTUM = 0.7;
  protected JTextField data[][] = new JTextField[4][4];
  protected Network network;

  /**
   * Constructor.  Setup the components.
   */
  public XorExample()
  {
    setTitle("XOR Solution");
    network = new Network(
                        NUM_INPUT,
                        NUM_HIDDEN,
                        NUM_OUTPUT,
                        RATE,
                        MOMENTUM);

    Container content = getContentPane();

    GridBagLayout gridbag = new GridBagLayout();
    GridBagConstraints c = new GridBagConstraints();
    content.setLayout(gridbag);

    c.fill = GridBagConstraints.NONE;
    c.weightx = 1.0;
```

```
// Training input label
c.gridwidth = GridBagConstraints.REMAINDER; //end row
c.anchor = GridBagConstraints.NORTHWEST;
content.add(
          new JLabel(
                    "Enter training data:"),c);

JPanel grid = new JPanel();
grid.setLayout(new GridLayout(5,4));
grid.add(new JLabel("IN1"));
grid.add(new JLabel("IN2"));
grid.add(new JLabel("Expected OUT    "));
grid.add(new JLabel("Actual OUT"));

for ( int i=0;i<4;i++ ) {
  int x = (i&1);
  int y = (i&2)>>1;
  grid.add(data[i][0] = new JTextField(""+y));
  grid.add(data[i][1] = new JTextField(""+x));
  grid.add(data[i][2] = new JTextField(""+(x^y)));
  grid.add(data[i][3] = new JTextField("??"));
  data[i][0].setEditable(false);
  data[i][1].setEditable(false);
  data[i][3].setEditable(false);
}

content.add(grid,c);

// the button panel
JPanel buttonPanel = new JPanel(new FlowLayout());
buttonPanel.add(btnTrain = new JButton("Train"));
buttonPanel.add(btnRun = new JButton("Run"));
buttonPanel.add(btnQuit = new JButton("Quit"));
btnTrain.addActionListener(this);
btnRun.addActionListener(this);
btnQuit.addActionListener(this);

// Add the button panel
c.gridwidth = GridBagConstraints.REMAINDER; //end row
c.anchor = GridBagConstraints.CENTER;
content.add(buttonPanel,c);

// Training input label
c.gridwidth = GridBagConstraints.REMAINDER; //end row
c.anchor = GridBagConstraints.NORTHWEST;
```

```
    content.add(
              status = new JLabel(
      "Click train to begin training..."),c);

    // adjust size and position
    pack();
    Toolkit toolkit = Toolkit.getDefaultToolkit();
    Dimension d = toolkit.getScreenSize();
    setLocation(
              (int)(d.width-this.getSize().getWidth())/2,
              (int)(d.height-this.getSize().getHeight())/2 );
    setDefaultCloseOperation(WindowConstants.DISPOSE_ON_CLOSE);
    setResizable(false);

    btnRun.setEnabled(false);
  }

  /**
   * The main function, just display the JFrame.
   *
   * @param args No arguments are used.
   */
  public static void main(String args[])
  {
    (new XorExample()).show(true);
  }

  /**
   * Called when the user clicks one of the three
   * buttons.
   *
   * @param e The event.
   */
  public void actionPerformed(ActionEvent e)
  {
    if ( e.getSource()==btnQuit )
      System.exit(0);
    else if ( e.getSource()==btnTrain )
      train();
    else if ( e.getSource()==btnRun )
      evaluate();
  }

  /**
   * Called when the user clicks the run button.
   */
```

```
protected void evaluate()
{
  double xorData[][] = getGrid();
  int update=0;

  for (int i=0;i<4;i++) {
    NumberFormat nf = NumberFormat.getInstance();
    double d[] = network.computeOutputs(xorData[i]);
    data[i][3].setText(nf.format(d[0]));
  }

}


/**
 * Called when the user clicks the train button.
 */
protected void train()
{
  if ( worker != null )
    worker = null;
  worker = new Thread(this);
  worker.setPriority(Thread.MIN_PRIORITY);
  worker.start();
}

/**
 * The thread worker, used for training
 */
public void run()
{
  double xorData[][] = getGrid();
  double xorIdeal[][] = getIdeal();
  int update=0;

  int max = 10000;
  for (int i=0;i<max;i++) {
    for (int j=0;j<xorData.length;j++) {
      network.computeOutputs(xorData[j]);
      network.calcError(xorIdeal[j]);
      network.learn();
    }

    update++;
    if (update==100) {
      status.setText( "Cycles Left:" + (max-i) + ",Error:"
```

```
                + network.getError(xorData.length) );
                update=0;
            }
        }
      btnRun.setEnabled(true);
    }


  /**
   * Called to generate an array of doubles based on
   * the training data that the user has entered.
   *
   * @return An array of doubles
   */
  double [][]getGrid()
  {
    double array[][] = new double[4][2];

    for ( int i=0;i<4;i++ ) {
      array[i][0] =
      Float.parseFloat(data[i][0].getText());
      array[i][1] =
      Float.parseFloat(data[i][1].getText());
    }

    return array;
  }

  /**
   * Called to set the ideal values that that the neural network
   * should return for each of the grid training values.
   *
   * @return The ideal results.
   */
  double [][]getIdeal()
  {
    double array[][] = new double[4][1];

    for ( int i=0;i<4;i++ ) {
      array[i][0] =
      Float.parseFloat(data[i][2].getText());
    }
    return array;
  }
}
```

As you can see, there are several properties that are defined for this class. These properties are shown in Table 3.7.

Table 3.7: Variables Used by the XOR Example

Variable	Purpose
btnTrain	The button that allows the user to begin the training process.
btnRun	The button that allows the user to actually run the neural network and see the output.
btnQuit	The button that allows the user to quit the program.
status	A status display that shows the user the progress of training.
worker	The background thread that handles the training process.
NUM_INPUT	The number of neurons in the input layer of the neural network.
NUM_OUTPUT	The number of output neurons in the output layer of the neural network.
NUM_HIDDEN	The number of neurons in the hidden layer.
RATE	The learning rate for the neural network.
MOMENTUM	The momentum for training the neural network.
data	An array that holds the grid of input and ideal results for the neural network.
network	Holds the actual neural network.

We will now examine three of the major activities that this program carries out. First, we will see how the program sets up the neural network. Second, we will see how the neural network is trained. Finally, we will see how data is presented to the neural network and the output of the neural network is displayed. We will begin by examining how the neural network is initialized.

Setting Up the Neural Network

Setting up the neural network is fairly straight forward. To setup the neural network, the constructor for the neural network class is called with the input layer size, the hidden layer size, the output layer size, the rate and momentum. The following lines of code do this:

```
network = new Network(
                NUM_INPUT,
                NUM_HIDDEN,
                NUM_OUTPUT,
                RATE,
                MOMENTUM);
```

A method is needed that will pull the training sets from the grid. A method named "get-Grid" is provided to do this. The "getGrid" method is shown here.

```java
double [] []getGrid()
{
  double array[] [] = new double[4] [2];

  for ( int i=0;i<4;i++ ) {
    array[i] [0] =
    Float.parseFloat(data[i] [0] .getText());
    array[i] [1] =
    Float.parseFloat(data[i] [1] .getText());
  }

  return array;
}
```

As you can see, the get grid method simply passes over the 4X2 grid that allows the user to input the training data. This method will be used both for the training and execution methods. When the neural network is training, this method, along with the "getIdeal" method allows the neural network to construct training sets of input signals, along with the anticipated output. When the neural network is run to produce output, the "getGrid" method is used to obtain the input signals for the neural network.

Along with the "getGrid" method the "getIdeal" method is used to obtain an array of the ideal outputs for each of the training sets. The "getIdeal" method is shown below.

```java
double [] []getIdeal()
{
  double array[] [] = new double[4] [1];

  for ( int i=0;i<4;i++ ) {
    array[i] [0] =
    Float.parseFloat(data[i] [2] .getText());
  }
  return array;
}
```

As you can see, the "getIdeal" method moves across the same grid used by the "getGrid" method. The "getIdeal" method only returns the output column. Now that you have seen how the neural network is setup and the training data is accessed, you will be shown how the neural network is trained.

Training the Neural Network

The neural network must be trained if it is to output the correct data. The code from the training method will now be discussed. First, the training data must be acquired. This is done by calling the "getGrid" and "getIdeal" methods to access the training data.

```
double xorData[][] = getGrid();
double xorIdeal[][] = getIdeal();
int update=0;
```

An update variable is also kept to keep track of the last time that the status line is updated. This is done because we do not want to update the user interface every time through the training algorithm. There could be thousands of loops of the training algorithm. It would be too slow to update the status line for each iteration. Rather, we will update the status line for each 1,000 iterations.

Here you can see that we will be looping through 10,000 iterations. For the XOR problem, 10,000 iterations is usually quite sufficient to get a low error rate. If the error rate is still high you can click the "Train" button again and retrain the neural network further.

```
int max = 10000;
for (int i=0;i<max;i++) {
```

Each iteration we will present the neural network with teach training set. For this example program, the number of training sets is the four possible combinations for the XOR problem.

```
for (int j=0;j<xorData.length;j++) {
  network.computeOutputs(xorData[j]);
  network.calcError(xorIdeal[j]);
  network.learn();
}
```

As you can see from the above code, each training set is first run through the compute-Ouputs method. Then the error rate is calculated by calling the "calcError" method. Finally, the "learn" method is called to update the weight matrix for this training set. Finally the user interface is updated with the progress of the training.

```
update++;
if (update==100) {
  status.setText( "Cycles Left:" + (max-i) + ",Error:"
    + network.getError(xorData.length) );
  update=0;
}
```

Now that you have seen how to present data to the neural network for training we will discuss how to present data to the neural network for recognition.

Presenting Data to the Neural Network

The ultimate goal of a neural network is to be able to present data and have the neural network recognize or classify the data in some way. The following lines of code show how data is presented to the neural network for recognition. First, the grid of input values is read.

```
double xorData[][] = getGrid();
```

In this case, we do not care what the ideal values are. The neural network will have hopefully learned this for itself by this point. The example program then proceeds to loop through each of the four sample inputs and displays the output that the neural network produced for each.

```
for (int i=0;i<4;i++) {
  NumberFormat nf = NumberFormat.getInstance();
  double d[] = network.computeOutputs(xorData[i]);
  data[i][3].setText(nf.format(d[0]));
}
```

It is important to understand that the above code is actually presenting four individual patterns to the neural network. Each of the possible inputs to the XOR problem are presented.

Summary

Multilayer neural networks are necessary to allow more advanced patterns to be recognized. Multilayer networks are particularly necessary for non-linearly separable problems such as XOR. This chapter showed you how to use a neural network class to process the XOR problem.

We began by looking at an open source editor for neural networks. JOONE includes a graphical editor that allows you visually create a neural network. This editor works fine for prototyping networks, but neural networks created by the editor cannot easily be incorporated into an actual Java program. To incorporate JOONE neural networks into an actual Java program, the JOONE Engine must be used. In this book we will develop our own class to evaluate neural networks. The internal workings of this class will be explained further in Chapter 5.

In this chapter, we saw the process by which the neural network is trained, and ultimately used. An array of input signals is presented to the neural network, and a corresponding array of output signals is processed. Error can be calculated based on how different the actual output was from the anticipated output. In the next chapter you will be introduced to some of the methods by which neural networks can be trained. Then Chapter 5 will introduce you to the backpropagation method that the neural network class presented in this chapter uses to train.

CHAPTER 4: HOW A MACHINE LEARNS

Chapter Highlights
- **Understanding Layers**
- **Supervised Training**
- **Unsupervised Training**
- **Error Calculation**
- **Understanding Hebb's Rule and Delta Rule**

In the preceding chapters, we have seen that a neural network can be taught to recognize patterns by adjusting the weights of the neuron connections. Using the provided neural network class, we were able to teach a neural network to learn the XOR problem. We only touched briefly on how the neural network was able to learn the XOR problem. In this chapter we will begin to see how a neural network learns.

There are many different ways that a neural network can learn. Every learning algorithm somehow involves modifying the weight matrixes between the neurons. In this chapter, we will examine some of the more popular ways of adjusting these weights. In chapter 5 we will follow this up by learning the backpropagation method of training, which is the most common neural network training method used today.

Learning Methods

Training is a very important process for a neural network. As we saw in Chapter 1, there are two forms of training that can be employed with a neural network. Supervised training provides the neural network with training sets and the anticipated output. Unsupervised training supplies the neural network with training sets, but there is no anticipated output provided. In this book, we will examine both supervised and unsupervised training. We will now briefly cover each type of training. Supervised and unsupervised training will be covered in much greater detail in later chapters of this book.

Unsupervised Training

What is meant by training without supervision? As previously mentioned, the neural network is provided with training sets, which are collections of defined input values. But the unsupervised neural network is not provided with anticipated outputs.

Unsupervised training is usually used in a classification neural network. A classification neural network takes input patterns, which are presented to the input neurons. These input patterns are then processed, causing one single neuron on the output layer to fire. This firing neuron can be thought of as the classification of which group the neural input pattern belonged to.

A common application for unsupervised training is data mining. In this case, you have a large amount of data, but you do not often know exactly what you are looking for. You want the neural network to classify this data into several groups. You do not want to dictate, ahead of time, to the neural network, which input pattern should be classified into to which group. As the neural network trains, the input patterns will fall into similar groups. This will allow you to see which input patterns were in common groups.

Unsupervised training is a very common training technique for Kohonen neural networks. In Chapter 6, we will discuss how to construct a Kohonen neural network and the general process for training without supervision.

In Chapter 7, you will be shown a practical application of the Kohonen neural network. The example program presented in Chapter 7, learns by using the unsupervised training method. This example program is designed to be able to read handwriting. Handwriting recognition is a good application of a classification neural network.

The input patterns presented to the Kohonen neural network are the dot image of the character that was hand written. We may then have 26 output neurons, which correspond to the 26 letters of the English alphabet. The Kohonen neural network should classify the input pattern into one of the 26 input patterns.

During the training process, the Kohonen neural network in Chapter 7 is presented with 26 input patterns. The network is configured to also have 26 output patterns. As the Kohonen neural network is trained, the weights should be adjusted so that the input patterns are classified into the 26 output neurons. As you will see in Chapter 7, this technique results in a relatively effective method for character recognition.

As you can see unsupervised training can be applied to a number of uses, and will be covered in much greater detail in Chapters 6 and 7.

Supervised Training

The supervised training method is similar to the unsupervised training method in that training sets are provided. Just as with unsupervised training, these training sets specify input signals to the neural network. The neural network that was introduced in Chapter 3 used the supervised training method.

The primary difference between supervised and unsupervised training, is that in supervised training, the expected outputs are provided. This allows the supervised training algorithm to adjust the weight matrix based on the difference between the anticipated output of the neural network, and the actual output.

There are several popular training algorithms that make use of supervised training. One of the most common is the backpropagation algorithm. Backpropagation will be discussed in Chapter 5. It is also possible to use an algorithm such as simulated annealing or a genetic algorithm to implement supervised training. Simulated annealing and genetic algorithms will be discussed in Chapters 8 through 10. We will now discuss how errors are calculated as a part of both the supervised and unsupervised training algorithms.

Error Calculation

Error calculation is an important aspect of any neural network. Whether the neural network is supervised or unsupervised, an error rate must be calculated. The goal of virtually all training algorithms is to minimize the error. In this section we will examine how the error is calculated for a supervised neural network. We will also discuss how the error is determined for an unsupervised training algorithm. We will begin this section by discussing two error calculation steps used for supervised training.

Error Calculation and Supervised Training

Error calculation is an important part of the supervised training algorithm. In this section, we will examine an error calculation method that can be employed by supervised training. Further, we will see how this training algorithm is applied to the neural network class that was introduced in Chapter 3.

For supervised training there are two components to the error that must be considered. First, we must calculate the error for each of the training sets as they are processed. Secondly, we must take the average error across each sample for the training set. For example, consider the XOR problem that has only four items in its training set. An output error would be calculated on each element of the training set. Finally, after all training sets have been processed, the root mean square (RMS) error is determined.

Output Error

The output error is simply an error calculation that is done to determine how far off a neural network's output was from the ideal network. This value is rarely used for any purpose other than a stepping stone on the way to the calculation of root mean square (RMS) error. Once all training sets have been used the RMS error can be calculated. This error acts as the global error for the entire neural network.

You will recall from Chapter 3 that there is a method provided by the neural network class named "calcError". This method has two primary responsibilities. First, it calculates the output error for each member of the training set. This error is allowed to grow until all of the training sets have been presented. Then the RMS error is calculated. The calculation of the RMS error is covered in the next section.

The second task that is accomplished by the "calcError" method, is the calculation of backpropagation deltas. This aspect of the "calcError" method will be covered in much greater detail in Chapter 5. We will now examine how the output error for a training set member is calculated. The source code for the "calcError" method is shown below.

```
public void calcError(double ideal[]) {
   int i, j;
   final int hiddenIndex = inputCount;
   final int outputIndex = inputCount + hiddenCount;

   // clear hidden layer errors
```

```
    for (i = inputCount; i < neuronCount; i++) {
      error[i] = 0;
    }

    // layer errors and deltas for output layer
    for (i = outputIndex; i < neuronCount; i++) {
      error[i] = ideal[i - outputIndex] - fire[i];
      globalError += error[i] * error[i];
      errorDelta[i] = error[i] * fire[i] * (1 - fire[i]);
    }

    // hidden layer errors
    int winx = inputCount * hiddenCount;

    for (i = outputIndex; i < neuronCount; i++) {
      for (j = hiddenIndex; j < outputIndex; j++) {
        accMatrixDelta[winx] += errorDelta[i] * fire[j];
        error[j] += matrix[winx] * errorDelta[i];
        winx++;
      }
      accThresholdDelta[i] += errorDelta[i];
    }

    // hidden layer deltas
    for (i = hiddenIndex; i < outputIndex; i++) {
      errorDelta[i] = error[i] * fire[i] * (1 - fire[i]);
    }

    // input layer errors
    winx = 0;  // offset into weight array
    for (i = hiddenIndex; i < outputIndex; i++) {
      for (j = 0; j < hiddenIndex; j++) {
        accMatrixDelta[winx] += errorDelta[i] * fire[j];
        error[j] += matrix[winx] * errorDelta[i];
        winx++;
      }
      accThresholdDelta[i] += errorDelta[i];
    }
  }
```

As you can see from the above source code, the error is calculated by the first block of code in the method. The error calculation begins with the following lines.

```
    // layer errors and deltas for output layer
    for (i = outputIndex; i < neuronCount; i++) {
```

First, we are going to loop through every neuron in the output layer. Each element in the neural network's output is compared against the ideal output. The difference between these two values is calculated. This value is then squared and stored. Until it is later added to the output error, and finally stored in the global error property, as well.

```
    error[i] = ideal[i - outputIndex] - fire[i];
    globalError += error[i] * error[i];
    errorDelta[i] = error[i] * fire[i] * (1 - fire[i]);
}
```

At the end of processing, we now have added the error of this training set element to the global error accumulator. This process continues for each of the training set elements. Once the error of each element in the set has been calculated, you are ready to calculate the RMS error. Calculation of the RMS error will be discussed in the next section.

You will also notice that the above method calculates the "responsibility" of each of the neurons in the other layers for the error, which is stored in the "error" array. This will be used when the train method is called to adjust the weights of the neural network. This method uses the backpropagation method, which will be discussed in greater detail in Chapter 5. For now, we will continue by examining how the RMS is calculated.

Root Mean Square (RMS) Error

The RMS error is the error that was displayed by Chapter 3's example, as the neural networked trained. It is the RMS error that allows the neural network to know if enough training has taken place. The RMS error can be calculated at any time after the "calcErrors" method has been called. This calculation is done by the "getError" method. The "getError" method is shown here.

```
public double getError(int len) {
    double err = Math.sqrt(globalError / (len * outputCount));
    globalError = 0;  // clear the accumulator
    return err;
}
```

As you can see, you must pass in the length of the training set. This is necessary because the RMS is an average. To take the average error across all training set elements, you must know the size of the training set. The RMS error is then calculated by dividing the global error by the product of the training set length and the number of output neurons. The square root of this ratio produces the RMS. Finally, after the RMS error has been calculated the globalError is set back to zero. This is done so that it can begin accumulating for a new error.

Error Calculation and Unsupervised Training

We have discussed how errors are calculated for supervised training. Errors must also be calculated for unsupervised training as well. How this is done may not be initially obvious. How can an error be calculated when no correct output is provided? The exact procedure by which this is done will be covered in Chapter 6 when the Kohonen neural network is discussed. For now we will simply highlight the major details of the process, as well as compare and contrast unsupervised training error calculation to supervised training error calculation.

Most unsupervised neural networks are designed to classify input data. The input data should be classified into one of the output neurons. The degree to which each output neuron fires for the input data is studied, to produce an error for unsupervised training. Ideally, we would like just one single neuron to fire at a high level for each member of the training set. If this is not the case, we adjust the weights to the neuron with the highest firing, that is the winning neuron, consolidates its win. This training method causes more and more neurons to fire for the different elements in the training set.

Neuron Layers

Neuron layers also play an important part in the neural network's ability to learn. The neural network class, presented in Chapter 3, allows you to define any number of different neuron layer types by overriding one or more of the methods of the neural network class. One such method is the threshold method. This method determines the activation function that will be used for the neural network. We will now examine some of the different neuron layer types you may wish to use.

The Sigmoid Layer

A sigmoid neural network layer uses the sigmoid function to determine its activation. The sigmoid function is as follows.

Equation 4.1: The Sigmoid Function

$$y(u) = \frac{1}{1 + e^{-u}}$$

The term, sigmoid, means curved in two directions, like the letter "S". You can see the sigmoid function in Figure 4.1. One important thing to note about the sigmoid layer, is that it only positive values are returned. If you need negative numbers as a result from the neural network, the sigmoid function will be unsuitable. Most examples in this book will use the sigmoid layer if positive values are required, and the TanH layer if negative values are required.

Figure 4.1: The Sigmoid Function

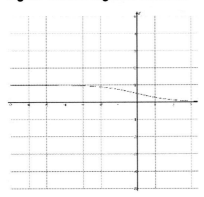

The TanhLayer Layer

As previously mentioned, the sigmoid layer does not return values less than zero. However, it is possible to "move" the sigmoid layer to a region of the graph so that it provides negative numbers. This is done using the TanhLayer. The equation for the TanhLayer activation function is given below.

Equation 4.2: The TANH Function

$$y(u) = \frac{e^u - e^{-u}}{e^u + e^{-u}}$$

Though this looks considerably more complex than the sigmoid function you can safely think of it as a positive and negative compatible version of the sigmoid function. The graph for the TanhLayer is shown in Figure 4.2.

Figure 4.2: The Sigmoid Function

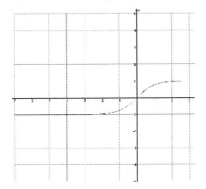

The LinearLayer

The LinearLayer is essentially no layer at all. It is probably the least commonly used of the layers. The linear layer does no modification on the pattern before outputting it. The function for the linear layer is given as follows.

Equation 4.3: A Linear Function

$$y(u)=u$$

The LinearLayer is useful in situations when you need the entire range of numbers to be output. Usually, you will want to think of your neurons as active or non-active. Because the TanhLayer and SigmoidLayer both have established upper and lower bounds, they tend to be used for more Boolean (on or off) type operations. The LinearLayer is useful for presenting a range. The graph of the linear layer is given in Figure 4.3.

Figure 4.3: The Linear Layer

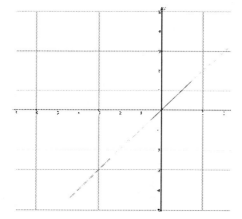

Training Algorithm

Training occurs as the neuron connection weights are modified to produce more desirable results. There are several ways that this training can take place. In this chapter we will observe two simple methods for training the connection weights of the neural network. In Chapter 5, "Understanding Backpropagation" we will see backpropagation, which is a much more complex training algorithm. Backpropagation is the most common form of neural network training.

Neuron connection weights are not just modified in one pass. The process by which neuron weights are modified occurs over iterations. The neural network is presented with training data, and then the results are observed. These results must in some way change the connection weights in order for the neural network to be learn. The exact process by which this happens is determined by the learning algorithm.

These learning algorithms, which are commonly called learning rules, are almost always expressed as functions. What you want to know from this function, is how should the weight between two neurons be changed. Consider a weight matrix between four neurons, such as we saw in Chapter 2. This is expressed as an array of doubles.

```
double weights[][] = new double[4][4];
```

This stores the weights between four neurons. Because Java array indexes begin with zero we shall refer to these neurons as neurons zero through three. Using the above array, the weight between neuron two and neuron three would be contained in the variable weights[2][3]. Therefore, we would like a learning function that would return the new weight between neurons "i" and "j", such as

```
weights[i][j] += learningRule(...)
```

The hypothetical method learningRate calculates the change (delta) that must occur between the two neurons in order for learning to take place. We never discard the previous weight value altogether, rather, we compute a delta value that is used to modify the original weight. It does not take just one modification for the neural network to learn. Once the weight of the neural network has been modified, the network is presented with the training data again, and the process continues. These iterations continue until the neural network's error rate has dropped to an acceptable level.

Another common input to the learning rule, is the error. The error is the degree to which the actual output of the neural network differed from the anticipated output. If such an error is provided to the training function, then the method is called supervised training. In supervised training, the neural network is constantly adjusting the weights to attempt to better line up with the anticipated outputs that were provided.

Conversely, if no error was provided to the training function, then we are using an unsupervised training algorithm. In unsupervised training the neural network is not told what the "correct output" is. Unsupervised training leaves the neural network to determine this for itself. Often, unsupervised training is used to allow the neural network to group the input data. The programmer does not know ahead of time exactly what these groups are. Figure 4.4 shows the flow chart of supervised training. Figure 4.5 shows the flow chart of unsupervised training.

Figure 4.4: Supervised Training

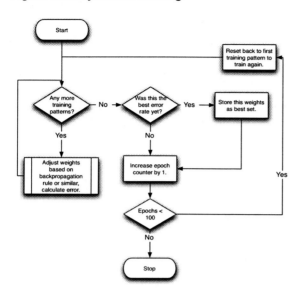

Figure 4.5: Unsupervised Training

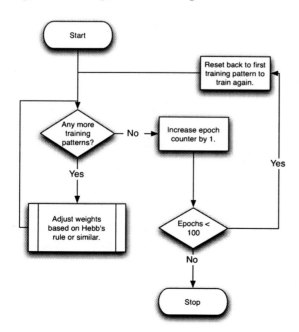

We will now examine two common training algorithms. The first, Hebb's rule, is used for unsupervised training, and does not take into account network error. The second, the delta rule, is used with supervised training and adjusts the weights so that the input to the neural network will more accurately produce the anticipated output. We will begin with Hebb's Rule.

Hebb's Rule

One of the most common learning algorithms is called Hebb's Rule. This rule was developed by Donald Hebb to assist with unsupervised training. We previously examined a hypothetical learning rule given by the following expression.

```
weights[i][j] += learningRule(...)
```

Rules for training neural networks are almost always represented as algebraic formulas. Hebbs rule is expressed as:

Equation 4.4: Hebb's Rule

$$\Delta W_{ij} = \mu \, a_i a_j$$

The above equation calculates the needed change (delta) in weights from the connection from neuron "i" to neuron "j". The Greek letter mu (μ) represents the learning rate. The activation of each neuron, when provided with the training pattern, is given as a_i and a_j. This equation can easily be translated into the following Java method.

```java
double learningRule(double rate,double act_i,double act_j)
{
  return(rate*act_i*act_j);
}
```

We will now examine how this training algorithm actually works. To see this, we will consider a simple neural network with only two neurons. In this neural network, these two neurons make up both the input and output layer. There is no hidden layer. Table 4.1 summarizes some of the possible scenarios using Hebbian training. Assume that the learning rate is one.

Table 4.1: Using Hebb's Rule

Case	Neuron I Output (activation)	Neuron J Output (activation)	Hebb's Rule (R*I*J)	Weight Modification ΔW
Case 1	+1	-1	1*1*-1	-1
Case 2	-1	+1	1*-1*1	-1
Case 3	+1	+1	1*1*1	+1

As you can see from the above table, if the activations of neuron "I" was +1 and the activation of neuron J were -1, the neuron connection weight between neuron "I" and neuron "J" would be decreased by one.

Delta Rule

The delta rule is also known as the least mean squared error rule (LMS). Using this rule, actual output of a neural network is compared against the anticipated output. Because the anticipated output is specified, using the delta rule is considered supervised training. Algebraically, the delta rule is written as follows.

Equation 4.5: The Delta Rule

$$\Delta W_{ij} = \mu x_i (d-a)_j$$

The above equation calculates the needed change (delta) in weights from the connection from neuron "i" to neuron "j". The Greek letter mu represents the learning rate. The variable d represents the desired output of the neuron. The variable "a" represents the actual output of the "j" neuron. The variable "d" represents the desired output for the j neuron. As a result, "d-a" is the error. This equation can easily be translated into the following Java method.

```
protected double trainingFunction(
  double rate,double input,double error)
{
  return rate*input*error;
}
```

We will now examine how the delta training algorithm actually works. To see this we will look at the example program shown in Listing 4.1.

Listing 4.1: Using the Delta Rule

```java
public class Delta {

  /**
   * Weight for neuron 1
   */
  double w1;

  /**
   * Weight for neuron 2
   */
  double w2;

  /**
   * Weight for neuron 3
   */
  double w3;

  /**
   * Learning rate
   */
  double rate = 0.5;

  /**
   * Current epoch #
   */
  int epoch = 1;

  /**
   * @param i1 Input to neuron 1
   * @param i2 Input to neuron 2
   * @param i3 Input to neuron 3
   * @return the output from the neural network
   */
  protected double recognize(double i1,double i2,double i3)
  {
    double a = (w1*i1)+(w2*i2)+(w3*i3);
    return(a*.5);
  }

  /**
   * This method will calculate the error between the
   * anticipated output and the actual output.
```

```java
 *
 * @param actual The actual output from the neural network.
 * @param anticipated The anticipated neuron output.
 * @return The error.
 */
protected double getError(double actual,double anticipated)
{
  return(anticipated-actual);
}


/**
 * The learningFunction implements the delta rule.
 * This method will return the weight adjustment for
 * the specified input neuron.
 *
 * @param rate The learning rate
 * @param input The input neuron we're processing
 * @param error The error between the actual output
 * and anticipated output.
 * @return The amount to adjust the weight by.
 */
protected double trainingFunction(
  double rate,double input,double error)
{
  return rate*input*error;
}


/**
 * Present a pattern and learn from it.
 *
 * @param i1 Input to neuron 1
 * @param i2 Input to neuron 2
 * @param i3 Input to neuron 3
 * @param anticipated The anticipated output
 */
protected void presentPattern(
  double i1,double i2,double i3,double anticipated)
{
  double error;
  double actual;
  double delta;

  // run the net as is on training data
  // and get the error
  System.out.print("Presented [" + i1 + "," + i2
                  + "," + i3 + "]");
```

```java
    actual = recognize(i1,i2,i3);
    error = getError(actual,anticipated);
    System.out.print(" anticipated=" + anticipated);
    System.out.print(" actual=" + actual);
    System.out.println(" error=" + error);

    // adjust weight 1
    delta = trainingFunction(rate,i1,error);
    w1+=delta;

    // adjust weight 2
    delta = trainingFunction(rate,i2,error);
    w2+=delta;

    // adjust weight 3
    delta = trainingFunction(rate,i3,error);
    w3+=delta;
}
/**
 * Process one epoch.  Here we learn from all three training
 * samples and then update the weights based on error.
 */

protected void epoch()
{
    System.out.println("***Beginning Epoch #" + epoch+"***");
    presentPattern(0,0,1,0);
    presentPattern(0,1,1,0);
    presentPattern(1,0,1,0);
    presentPattern(1,1,1,1);
    epoch++;
}

/**
 * This method loops through 100 epochs.
 */
public void run()
{
    for ( int i=0;i<100;i++ ) {
        epoch();
    }
}

/**
 * Main method just instanciates a delta object and calls
 * run.
```

```
     *
     * @param args Not used
     */
    public static void main(String args[])
    {
      Delta delta = new Delta();
      delta.run();
    }
}
```

This program will train for 100 iterations. It is designed to teach the neural network to recognize three patterns. These patterns are summarized as follows.

```
For 001 output 0
For 011 output 0
For 101 output 0
For 111 output 1
```

For each epoch you will be shown what the actual and anticipated results were. By epoch 100 the network is trained. The output from epoch 100 is shown here.

```
***Beginning Epoch #100***
Presented [0.0,0.0,1.0] anticipated=0.0 actual=-0.33333333131711973 error=0.33333333131711973
Presented [0.0,1.0,1.0] anticipated=0.0 actual=0.333333333558949 error=-0.333333333558949
Presented [1.0,0.0,1.0] anticipated=0.0 actual=0.3333333370649876 error=-0.3333333370649876
Presented [1.0,1.0,1.0] anticipated=1.0 actual=0.6666666655103011 error=0.33333333448969893
```

As you can see from the above display there are only two possible outputs 0.333 and 0.666. The output of 0.333 corresponds to 0 and the output of 0.666 corresponds to 1. A neural network will never produce exactly the required output, but through rounding it gets pretty close. While the delta rule is efficient at adjusting the weights it is not the most commonly used. In the next chapter we will examine the feedforward backpropagation network, which is one of the most commonly used neural networks.

Summary

The error of a neural network is a very important statistic to be used as a part of the training process. This chapter showed you how to calculate the output error for an individual training set element, as well as how to calculate the RMS error for the entire training set.

Layers are collections of related neurons. JOONE supports several layer types. In this chapter we examined the sigmoid layer, which can handle only positive output. We also examined the hyperbolic tangent layer which can handle both positive and negative outputs. Lastly, we examined the linear layer, which performs no modification of the input at all.

Synapses form the connection between layers. Synapses maintain individual weights between connected neurons. When you connect two layers with a synapses, each neuron is automatically connected to the neuron in the other layer. These connection weights make up the memory of the neural network. These weights determine the degree to which the neuron will pass information on to the connected neuron.

Training occurs when the weights of the synapse are modified to produce a more suitable output. Unsupervised training occurs when the neural network is left to determine the correct responses. Supervised training occurs when the neural network is provided with training data and anticipated outputs. Hebb's rule can be used for unsupervised training. The delta rule is used for supervised training.

In this chapter we learned how a machine learns by modifying the connection weights between the neurons. This chapter only introduced the basic concepts of how a machine learns. In the next chapter we will explore backpropagation and see how the neural network class implements it. We will also create an example of an artificial mouse that is trained to run a maze.

CHAPTER 5: UNDERSTANDING BACKPROPAGATION

Chapter Highlights
- **Introducing the Feeforward Backpropagation Neural Network**
- **Understanding the Feedforward Algorithm**
- **Implementing the Feedforward Algorithm**
- **Understanding the Backpropagation Algorithm**
- **Implementing the Backpropagation Algorithm**

In this chapter we shall examine one of the most common neural network architectures—the feedforword backpropagation neural network. This neural network architecture is very popular because it can be applied to many different tasks. To understand this neural network architecture, we must examine how it is trained and how it processes the pattern. The name "feedforward backpropagation neural network" gives some clue as to both how this network is trained, and how it processes the pattern.

The first term, "feedforward" describes how this neural network processes the pattern and recalls patterns. When using a "feedforward neural network," neurons are only connected foreword. Each layer of the neural network contains connections to the next layer (for example, from the input to the hidden layer), but there are no connections back. This differs from the Hopfield neural network that was examined in Chapter 2. The Hopfield neural network was fully connected, that is, each neuron was connected to every other neuron in the network—even to itself. Exactly how a "feedforward neural network" recalls the pattern will be explored in this chapter.

The term backpropagation describes how this type of neural network is trained. Backpropagation is a form of supervised training. When using a supervised training method, the network must be provided with sample inputs and anticipated outputs. These anticipated outputs will be compared against the actual output from the neural network. Using these anticipated outputs, the "backpropagation" training algorithm then takes a calculated error and adjusts the weights of the various layers backwards from the output layer all the way back to the input layer. The exact process by which backpropagation occurs will be discussed later in this chapter.

The algorithms "backpropagation" and "feedforward" are often used together. This, by no means, needs to be the case. It would be quite permissible to create a neural network that uses the feedforward algorithms to determine its output, and yet does not use the "backpropagation training algorithm". Similarly if you choose to create a neural network that uses "backpropagation training methods," you are not necessarily limited to a "feedforward" algorithm to determine the output of the neural network. Though such cases are less common than the "feedforward backpropagation neural network", examples can be found. In this book we will examine only the case of using the "feedforward" and "backpropagation" algorithms together. We will begin this discussion by examining how a feedforward neural network functions.

A Feedforward Neural Network

A "feedforward" neural network is similar to the types of neural networks that we have already examined. Just like many other neural network types, the feedforward neural network begins with an input layer. This input layer must be connected to a hidden layer. This hidden layer can then be connected to another hidden layer or directly to the output layer. There can be any number of hidden layers, so long as at least one hidden layer is provided. In common use, most neural networks will have only one hidden layer. It is very rare for a neural network to have more than two hidden layers. We will now examine, in detail, the structure of a "feedforward neural network".

The Structure of a Feedforward Neural Network

A "feedforward" neural network differs from the neural networks previously examined. Figure 5.1 shows a typical feedforward neural network with a single hidden layer.

Figure 5.1: A Typical Feedforward Neural Network (single hidden layer)

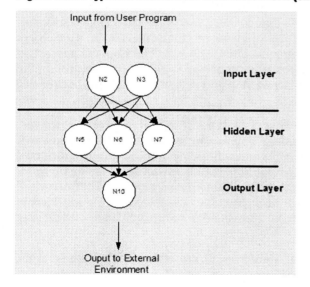

As previously mentioned, neural networks with more than two hidden layers are less common.

Choosing your Network Structure

As we saw the previous section, there are many ways that feedforward neural networks can be constructed. You must decide how many neurons will be inside the input and output layers. You must also decide how many hidden layers you're going to have, as well as how many neurons will be in each of these hidden layers.

There are many techniques for choosing these parameters. In this section we will cover some of the general "rules of thumb" that you can use to assist you in these decisions. Rules of thumb will only take you so far. In nearly all cases, some experimentation will be required to determine the optimal structure for your "feedforward neural network". There are many books dedicated entirely to this topic. For a thorough discussion on structuring feedforward neural networks, you should refer to the book "Neural Smithing: Supervised Learning in Feedforward Artificial Neural Networks" (MIT Press, 1999).

The Input Layer

The input layer to the neural network is the conduit through which the external environment presents a pattern to the neural network. Once a pattern is presented to the input layer of the neural network, the output layer will produce another pattern. In essence, this is all the neural network does. The input layer should represent the condition for which we are training the neural network for. Every input neuron should represent some independent variable that has an influence over the output of the neural network.

It is important to remember, that the inputs to the neural network are floating point numbers. These values are expressed as the primitive Java data type "double". This is not to say that you can only process numeric data with the neural network. If you wish to process a form of data that is non-numeric, you must develop a process that normalizes this data to a numeric representation. In chapter 7, "Applying Pattern Recognition," I will show you how to communicate graphic information to a neural network.

The Output Layer

The output layer of the neural network is what actually presents a pattern to the external environment. Whatever pattern is presented by the output layer can be directly traced back to the input layer. The number of a output neurons should be directly related to the type of work that the neural network is to perform.

To determine the number of neurons to use in your output layer, you must first consider the intended use of the neural network. If the neural network is to be used to classify items into groups, then it is often preferable to have one output neuron for each group that the item is to be assigned into. If the neural network is to perform noise reduction on a signal, then it is likely that the number of input neurons will match the number of output neurons. In this sort of neural network, you would want the patterns to leave the neural network in the same format as they entered.

For a specific example of how to choose the numbers of input and output neurons consider a program that is used for optical character recognition, or OCR. This is the example program that will be presented in Chapter 7. To determine the number of neurons used for the OCR example, we will first consider the input layer. The number of input neurons that we will use is the number of pixels that might represent any given character. Characters processed by this program are normalized to a universal size that is represented by a 5x7 grid. A 5x7 grid contains a total of 35 pixels. The optical character recognition program therefore has 35 input neurons.

The number of output neurons used by the OCR program will vary depending on how many characters the program has been trained for. The default training file that is provided with the optical character recognition program, is trained to recognize 26 characters. As a result, using this file, the neural network would have 26 output neurons. Presenting a pattern to the input neurons will fire the appropriate output neuron that corresponds to the letter that the input pattern corresponds to.

The Number of Hidden Layers

There are really two decisions that must be made regarding the hidden layers: how many hidden layers to actually have in the neural network and how many neurons will be in each of these layers. We will first examine how to determine the number of hidden layers to use with the neural network.

Problems that require two hidden layers are rarely encountered. Differences between the numbers of hidden layers are summarized in Table 5.1. However, neural networks with two hidden layers can represent functions with any kind of shape. In addition, there is currently no theoretical reason to use neural networks with any more than two hidden layers. In fact, further for many practical problems, there's no reason to use any more than one hidden layer.

Table 5.1: Determining the Number of Hidden Layers

Number of Hidden Layers	Result
none	Only capable of representing linear separable functions or decisions.
1	Can approximate arbitrarily with any functions which contains a continuous mapping from one finite space to another.
2	Represent an arbitrary decision boundary to arbitrary accuracy with rational activation functions and can approximate any smooth mapping to any accuracy.

Just deciding the number of hidden neuron layers is only a small part of the problem. You must also determine how many neurons will be in each of these hidden layers. This process is covered in the next section

The Number of Neurons in the Hidden Layers

Deciding the number of hidden neurons in layers is a very important part of deciding your overall neural network architecture. Though these layers do not directly interact with the external environment, these layers have a tremendous influence on the final output. Both the number of hidden layers and number of neurons in each of these hidden layers must be carefully considered.

Using too few neurons in the hidden layers will result in something called underfitting. Underfitting occurs when there are too few neurons in the hidden layers to adequately detect the signals in a complicated data set.

Using too many neurons in the hidden layers can result in several problems. First, too many neurons in the hidden layers may result in overfitting. Overfitting occurs when the neural network has so much information processing capacity that the limited amount of information contained in the training set is not enough to train all of the neurons in the hidden layers. A second problem can occur even when there is sufficient training data. An inordinately large number of neurons in the hidden layers can increase the time it takes to train the network. The amount of training time can increase enough so that it is impossible to adequately train the neural network. Obviously, some compromise must be reached between too many and too few neurons in the hidden layers.

There are many rule-of-thumb methods for determining the correct number of neurons to use in the hidden layers. Some of them are summarized as follows.

- The number of hidden neurons should be between the size of the input layer and the size of the output layer.
- The number of hidden neurons should be 2/3 of the input layer size, plus the size of the output layer.
- The number of hidden neurons should be less than twice the input layer size.

These three rules are only starting points that you may want to consider. Ultimately, the selection of the architecture of your neural network will come down to trial and error. But what exactly is meant by trial and error. You do not want to start throwing random layers and numbers of neurons at your network. To do so would be very time-consuming. There are two methods that can be used to organize your trial and error search for the optimum network architecture.

The "forward" and "backward" selection methods are the two trial and error approaches that you may use in determining the number of hidden neurons. The first method, the "forward selection method", begins by selecting a small number of hidden neurons. This method usually begins with only two hidden neurons. Then the neural network is trained and tested. The number of hidden neurons is then increased, and the process is repeated so long as the overall results of the training and testing improved. The "forward selection method" is summarized in figure 5.2.

Figure 5.2: Forward Selection

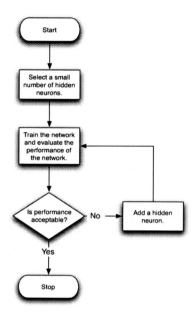

The second method, the "backward selection method", begins by using a large number of hidden neurons. Then the neural network is trained and tested. This process continues until about the performance improvement of the neural network is no longer significant. The backward selection method is summarized in Figure 5.3.

Figure 5.3: Backward Selection

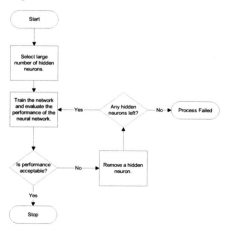

One additional method that can be used to reduce the number of hidden neurons is called pruning. In the simplest sense, pruning involves evaluating the weighted connections between the layers. If the network contains any hidden neurons which contain only zero weighted connections, they can be removed. Pruning is a very important concept for neural networks and will be discussed in Chapter 11, "Pruning Neural Networks".

Java and Threads

Before we explain how to implement the feedforward backpropagation neural network in Java, it is important to understand how threads work in Java. Many programmers have not worked with threads a great deal. The JOONE neural network is designed to make extensive use of threading. This allows JOONE to achieve great speed advantages on a multi-processor computer, as the task is already divided for the CPU's.

Threads can enhance performance and functionality in Java, by allowing a program to perform multiple tasks simultaneously. We will now take a look at the implementation of threads using Java, and offer a step-by-step overview of the fundamentals needed to incorporate threads into a Java program.

First we must examine what exactly a thread is. Basically, a thread is a path of execution through the program. Most programs written today run as a single thread, and thus have just one single path of execution. This can cause problems when multiple events or actions need to occur at the same time. For example, single threaded program is not capable downloading data from the network while responding to mouse or keyboard input from the user. The single threaded program must give its full attention to either the keyboard input or the network download. The ideal solution to this problem is the seamless execution of two or more sections of a program at the same time. This is the problem that threads were designed to solve.

Multithreaded applications are capable of running many threads concurrently within a single program. From a logical point of view, multithreading means multiple lines of a single program can be executed at the same time. This is not the same as starting a program twice and saying that there are multiple lines of a program being executed at the same time. In the case of simply running a program twice, the operating system is treating the programs as two separate and distinct processes. Take for example, the UNIX forking process. UNIX creates a child process with a different address space for both code and data when the fork() function is evoked. However, fork() creates a lot of overhead for the operating system, making it a very CPU-intensive operation. By starting a thread instead, an efficient path of execution is created while still sharing the original data area from the parent. The idea of sharing the data area is very beneficial, but brings up some areas of concern that we'll discuss later in this chapter.

Creating Threads

Java was designed to allow threads to be created in two ways. To create a Java thread you must either implement the Runnable interface or extend the Thread class. When a Java class is extended, the new class inherits methods and variables from a parent class. Java only allows a class to extend from one parent. To overcome this limitation, interfaces are used. This brings us to the second, more common way, that threads are created. By implementing the Runnable interface any class can act as a thread.

Interfaces provide a template which provide a way for programmers to lay the groundwork of a class. They are used to design the requirements for a set of classes to implement. The interface sets everything up, and the class or classes that implement the interface do all the work. The different set of classes that implement the interface all have to follow the same rules.

There are several differences between a class and an interface. An interface can only contain abstract methods and/or static final variables (constants). Classes, on the other hand, can implement methods and contain variables that are not constants. An interface may (unlike classes) extend from multiple interfaces. Finally, an interface cannot be instantiated with the new operator; for example, "Runnable a=new Runnable();" is not allowed.

The first method of creating a thread, is to simply extend from the Thread class. This method should only be used if this new class does not need to extend from another class. Because Java classes can only extend from one class, the thread class is the ONLY class you will be extending from when using this method. The Thread class is defined in the java.lang package, so it does not need to be imported (java.lang is always automatically imported by Java).

```
public class MyThread extends Thread
{
  public void run()
  {
    // perform actual thread work here
  }
}
```

The above example creates a new class named MyThread that extends the Thread class and overrides the Thread.run() method for its own implementation. The run() method is where all the work of the MyThread class thread is done. This same functionality could also be achieved by implementing the Runnable interface.

```
public class MyRunnable implements Runnable
{
  Thread T;
  public void run()
  {
    // perform actual thread work here
  }
```

}

In the above example, the abstract run () method is implemented in the Runnable interface. We have an instance of the Thread class as a variable of the MyRunnable class. The only difference between the two methods, is that by implementing Runnable, there is greater flexibility in the creation of the class Counter. In the above example, the opportunity still exists to extend the Counter class, if needed. The majority of classes created that need to be run as a thread will implement Runnable since they probably are extending some other functionality from another class.

The Runnable interface is not doing any real work when the thread is being executed. It is merely a class to hold the code to be executed by the thread. The Runnable interface is very small and contains only one abstract method. The following is the definition of the Runnable interface directly from the Java source:

```
public interface Runnable
{
  public abstract void run();
}
```

These few lines of code are all that there is to the Runnable interface. An interface provides only a foundation upon which classes should be implemented. In the case of the Runnable interface, it forces the definition of only the run () method.

Controlling the Thread's Execution

Now that we have examined the different ways to create an instance of a thread, we now will discuss the ways available to start and stop a thread. We will also examine a short example program that uses several threads that remain synchronized. To cause a thread to begin execution, the start method must be called. To cause a thread to cease execution, the stop method must be called.

```
public static void main(String args[])
{
  MyRunnable run = new MyRunnable();
  Thread t = new Thread(run);
  t.start();
}
```

Once the above code is called, a new thread is created that will begin by executing the run method of the MyRunnable class. Once this method is running, it is important to sleep somewhere in a thread. If not, the thread may consume all CPU time for the process and may not allow any other threads to be executed. Another way to cease the execution of a thread is to call the stop () method.

It is not generally recommended to stop threads. It is better to let the thread stop itself by allowing the run method to return.

Suspending and Resuming Threads

The execution of threads can be controlled. You can pause the execution of a thread with the sleep() method. The thread will sleep for a certain period of time and then begin executing when the time limit is reached. But, this is not ideal if the thread needs to be started when a certain event occurs. In this case, the suspend() method allows a thread to temporarily cease executing and the resume() method allows the suspended thread to start again.

To keep track of the current state of the application, the boolean variable suspended is used. Distinguishing the different states of an application is important because some methods will throw exceptions if they are called while in the wrong state. For example, if the thread has stopped, executing the start() method will throw an IllegalThreadStateException exception.

Thread Scheduling

The Java Thread Scheduler monitors all running threads in all programs and decides which threads should be running and which are in line to be executed. There are two characteristics of a thread that the scheduler identifies in its decision process. The first, and most important, is the priority of the thread. The other, and less used, is the daemon flag. The scheduler's basic rule is if there are only daemon threads running, the Java Virtual Machine (JVM) will exit. New threads inherit the priority, and daemon flag, from the thread that created it. The scheduler determines which thread should be executed by analyzing the priorities of all threads. Those with the highest priority are allowed execution before any lower priority threads.

There are two types of thread scheduling algorithms commonly used, preemptive or non-preemptive. Preemptive schedulers give a certain time-slice to all threads running on the system. The scheduler decides which thread is next to run and resume that thread for some constant period of time. When the thread has executed for that time period it will be suspended() and the next thread scheduled will be resumed. Non-preemptive schedulers decide which thread should run and run it until the thread is complete. The thread has full control of the system for as long as it likes. The yield() method is a way for a thread to force the scheduler to start executing another waiting thread. Unfortunately Java uses both algorithms, depending on the operating system Java is running on.

Thread priority determines what percent of CPU time one thread should get relative to another thread. This is based on a priority number assigned to each thread. The range of priorities is from 1 to 10. The default priority of a thread is Thread.NORM_PRIORITY, which is assigned the value of 5. Two other static variables are made available; they are Thread.MIN_PRIORITY, which is set to 1, and Thread.MAX_PRIORITY, which is set to 10. The getPriority() method can be used to find the current property of a thread.

Daemon threads run at a low priority in the background. Daemon threads are sometimes called "service" threads, as they provide a basic service to a program or programs when activity on a machine is reduced. An example of a daemon thread that is continuously running is the garbage collector thread. This thread, provided by the JVM, will scan programs for variables that will never be accessed again and release their resources back to the system. A thread can set the daemon flag by passing a true boolean value to the setDaemon() method. If a false boolean value is passed, the thread will become a user thread. However, this must occur before the thread has been started.

Synchronizing Threads

Up to this point we have only talked about independent, asynchronous threads. That is, each thread contains all of the data and methods required for its execution. Threads of this type don't require any outside resources or methods. Threads of this nature may run at their own pace without concern over the state or activities of any other threads that may be running in the background.

This is not usually the case. Threads must usually work with other related threads. In this case, these concurrent threads must share data and must consider the state and activities of other threads. The threads used to create a the neural network are of this type. These threads must communicate with each other to ensure that new work is obtained and no new work duplicates work already completed.

Java provides several mechanisms to facilitate this thread synchronization. Most Java synchronization centers around object locking. Every object in Java that descends from the object named Object has an individual lock. And since every object in Java must descend from "Object", every object in Java has its own lock.

The code segments within a program that access the same object from separate, concurrent threads are called critical sections. In the Java language, a critical section can be a block or a method and is identified using the synchronized keyword. Java associates a lock with every object that contains code that uses the synchronized keyword.

Generally the "put" and "get" methods of an object are ideal candidates for the synchronized keyword. This is because the get method reads the internal state of any object and the set method changes the internal state of an object. You do not want the state changing right in the middle of a get operation. Likewise, you do not want the state to change while another thread is changing the state with the set operation. The following code shows just such an example.

```
public class MySynchronizedObject
{
  int myInt;

  public synchronized int getMyInt()
  {
    return myInt;
  }

  public synchronized void putMyInt(int value)
  {
    myInt = value;
  }
}
```

The method declarations for both putMyInt() and getMyInt() make use of the synchronized keyword. As a result, the system creates a unique lock with every instantiation of MySynchronizedObject. Whenever control enters a synchronized method, the thread that called the method locks the object whose method has been called. Other threads cannot call a synchronized method on the same object until the object is unlocked.

Once a thread calls either putMyInt() or getMyInt(), that thread now owns the lock of that instance of MySynchronizedObject, until the putMyInt() or getMyInt() method exits. This acquisition and release of a lock is done automatically and atomically by the Java. This ensures multiple threads do not access the same data simultaneously, thus ensuring data integrity. Synchronization isn't the whole story. The two threads must also be able to notify one another when they've done their job.

Each object only has one lock that is shared by all synchronized areas of that program. A common misconception is that each synchronized area contains its own lock.

Using the notifyAll and wait Methods

The MySynchronizedObject stores its variable called contents. A boolean, named available, is also declared. The available variable has a value of true when the value has just been "put" but not yet "gotten," and is false when the value has been "gotten" but not yet "put". We will first consider a simple implementation of synchronized get and put methods.

```
public synchronized int get()
{
  if (available == true)
  {
    available = false;
    return contents;
  }
}
public synchronized void put(int value)
{
  if (available == false)
  {
    available = true;
    contents = value;
  }
}
```

These two methods will not work. Consider, first, the get method. What happens if nothing has yet been put in the MySynchronizedObject and available isn't true? In this case get does nothing. Likewise, if the something is put into the object before the get method was called the put does nothing.

What is needed, is for the caller of the get method to wait until the there is something to read. Likewise, the caller of the put method should wait until there is no data and it is safe to store its value. The two threads must coordinate more fully and they can use Object's wait and notifyAll() methods to do so.

Consider this new implementation of both get and put that wait on and notify each other of their activities:

```
public synchronized int get()
{
  while (available == false)
  {
    try
    {
      // wait for a thread to put a value
      wait();
    }
    catch (InterruptedException e)
    {
    }
  }
  available = false;
  // notify that value has been retrieved
  notifyAll();
  return contents;
}

public synchronized void put(int value)
{
  while (available == true)
  {
    try
    {
      // wait for to get value
      wait();
    }
    catch (InterruptedException e)
    {
    }
  }
  contents = value;
  available = true;
  // notify that value has been set
  notifyAll();
}
```

The get method loops until the put method has been called and there is data to read. The wait method is called each time through this loop. Calling the wait method relinquishes the lock held on the MySynchronizedObject (thereby allowing other threads to get the lock and update the MySynchronizedObject) as it waits for a notify method to be called. Once something is put in the MySynchronizedObject, it notifies any waiting threads by calling notify-All(). These waiting threads will then come out of the wait state. The variable "available" will be set to true, causing the loop to exit. This causes the get method to return the value in the MySynchronizedObject. The put method works in a similar fashion, waiting for the a thread to consume the current value before allowing the other threads to add more values.

The notifyAll() method wakes up all threads waiting on the object in question (in this case, the MySynchronizedObject). The awakened threads compete for the lock. One thread gets it, and the others go back to waiting. The Object class also defines the notify method, which arbitrarily wakes up one of the threads waiting on this object. I say arbitrarily, because Java does not allow you to choose the thread that will be awoken.

You should now be familiar with the basics of thread handling in Java. You are now ready to learn how a feedforward backpropagation neural network can be implemented. This will be the topic of the next two sections of this chapter.

Examining the Feedforward Process

In this section I will show you how the output for a feedforward neural network is calculated. First we will examine the algorithm used for a feedforward network. Once the algorithm is understood, we can examine how JOONE implements a feedforward neural network.

Understanding Feedforward Calculations

We will now look in greater detail at how a "feedforward" neural network processes data and recalls a pattern. Once we have examined this process, we can begin to explore "backpropagation" and see how the "feedforward" neural network is actually trained. First, we will examine a very simple feedforward neural network. We will examine a neural network that has only three layers, which include a hidden, input, and output layer. A basic picture of a neural network is shown in figure 5.1.

You may recall that this is the same neural network that was presented in Chapter 3 to solve the XOR problem. To generalize our discussion of feedforward neural networks we will use three variables. The variable "i" represents the number of neurons in the input layer, the variable "j" represents the number of neurons in the single hidden layer, and the variable "k" represents the number of neurons in the output layer. For this example there are two neurons in the input and output layer, and three neurons in the hidden layer. This causes the variables to hold the values i=2,k=2 and j=3.

The output of the input neurons is easy enough to calculate. It is the same as the input. In this neural network, the input neurons are doing no processing, they serve only as an interface to the external environment. The only processing that will occur is between the input and hidden layer, and then the hidden to the output layer. In the next section we will see how JOONE implements these ideas in a Java program.

Implementing a Feedforward Neural Network

We will now examine the process that JOONE uses to implement a feedforward neural network. As we step through the various classes and methods in JOONE, it is important to keep one of JOONE's design principles in mind. JOONE was designed to run as a distributed system.

By structuring JOONE to optimize for running as a distributed system, two clear advantages were achieved. First, JOONE will run considerably faster on a multi-processor machine. Secondly, components of a JOONE neural network can be ran on different machines. This allows JOONE to distribute its workload across a "farm" of computers.

Central to JOONE's distributed design is the fact that each of the neural network layers is designed to operate as autonomously as possible. When running on a single computer each of the neural network layers is run on a different thread. These neuron layers begin running in the background and wait for data to be transmitted to them. Data is transmitted to JOONE objects using the synapse objects. You will now be shown how JOONE recalls a pattern. Listing 5.1 shows the run method of the Layer class.

Listing 5.1: The Layer.run Method

```
public void run() {
  while ( running ) {
    int dimI = getRows();
    int dimO = getDimension();
    // Recall
    inps = new double[dimI];
    this.fireFwdGet();
    if ( m_pattern != null ) {
      forward(inps);
      m_pattern.setArray(outs);
      fireFwdPut(m_pattern);
    }
    if ( step != -1 )
      // Checks if the next step is a learning step
      m_learning = monitor.isLearningCicle(step);
    else
      // Stops the net
      running = false;
    //if ((m_learning) && (m_batch != 1))
    if ( (m_learning) && (running) ) {   // Learning
      gradientInps = new double[dimO];
      fireRevGet();
      backward(gradientInps);
      m_pattern = new Pattern(gradientOuts);
      m_pattern.setCount(step);
      fireRevPut(m_pattern);
    }
  }  // END while (running = false)
  myThread = null;
}
```

As you can see, the run method begins a loop that is constantly waiting for a new input pattern and then transmits an output pattern. As soon as a layer is started, this run method begins its loop. For the case of the XOR neural network that we examined in the previous section, there are actually three such layers that are running as threads. These layers are the input, hidden and output layer. We will now examine how the input pattern is processed by the input layer.

Examining the run method, we see that the process is began by calling the fireFwdGet() method.

```
this.fireFwdGet();
```

This method will wait, or block, if there is no pattern waiting on its input synapse. When a pattern is retrieved, it is stored in the m_pattern variable that is associated with the layer class. Next, the code makes sure that a valid pattern has been retrieved.

```
if ( m_pattern != null ) {
```

If a valid pattern has been retrieved, we will call our forward method. The forward method is resposable for applying the weights of the output synapse to the input pattern. Finally, the fireFwdPut method is called to pass the pattern into the output synapse.

```
forward(inps);
m_pattern.setArray(outs);
fireFwdPut(m_pattern);
}
```

Just by examining the run method of the Layer class, you are able to see the high level process that JOONE goes through as a neural network recalls a pattern. We will now examine in closer detail how these methods work. As the forward and fireFwdPut methods are called, three important actions occur:

- The connection weights are applied
- The bias weight is applied
- The threshold function is applied

The first method that is called by the Layer class' run method is the fireFwdGet method. This method is more specific to JOONE than it is to the "feedforward" neural network algorithm. The primary task of this method is to accept the pattern from the input synapse and wait if no pattern is present. To understand the "fireFwdGet" method, you must understand how Java thread synchronization works. Java thread synchronization will be covered as we discuss this method. The fireFwdGet method of the Layer class is shown in Listing 5.2.

Listing 5.2: The Layer.fireFwdGet Method

```
protected synchronized void fireFwdGet() {
    while (aInputPatternListener == null) {
        try {
            wait();
        } catch (InterruptedException ie) {
            ie.printStackTrace();
            return;
        }
    }
    double[] patt;
    int currentSize = aInputPatternListener.size();
    InputPatternListener tempListener = null;
    for (int index = 0; index < currentSize; index++){
        tempListener = (InputPatternListener)
          aInputPatternListener.elementAt(index);
        if (tempListener != null) {
            m_pattern = tempListener.fwdGet();
            if (m_pattern != null) {
                patt = m_pattern.getArray();
                if (patt.length != inps.length)
                    inps = new double[patt.length];
                sumInput(patt);
                step = m_pattern.getCount();
            }
        };
    };
}
```

The "fireFwdGet" method is used to consolidate the input from several layers. It could be that the current layer that is being processed receives input from several layers. It is the "fireFwdGet" method that consolidates these inputs. You will notice from the above code that the variable "aInputPatternListener" holds multiple pattern sources. The code loops through each of these input sources and sums the input. This summation is accomplished by calling the sumInput method inside of the loop.

Usually this is not the case, and you will have only layer to input from. If there is only one layer to input from, then the "fireFwdGet" method does little more than return the pattern that is being presented to the current level. When the "fireFwdGet" method is done receiving the input it returns back to the Layer.run() method.

For the case of the XOR example, the input layer is simply receiving a pattern to recall, such as {0,1}. The input layer will take this value, and then apply the threshold function, and pass it onto the next layer. For the XOR example, we used a sigmoid type input layer. JOONE implements the sigmoid through the class SigmoidLayer. When the "Layer.run()" method calls the forward method, it is actually the "SigmoidLayer.forward()" method that is being called, since we are using a SigmoidLayer class. Listing 5.3 shows the SigmoidLayer. forward() method.

Listing 5.3: The SigmoidLayer.forward Method

```java
public void forward(double[] pattern) {
  int x;
  double in;
  int n = getRows();
  try {
    for ( x = 0; x < n; ++x ) {
      in = pattern[x] + bias.value[x][0];
      outs[x] = 1 / (1 + Math.exp(-in));
    }
  } catch ( Exception aioobe ) {
    aioobe.printStackTrace();
  }
}
```

As you can see from Listing 5.3, the "SigmoidLayer.forward()" method applies the sigmoid function to each of the neurons in this layer. The sigmoid function was discussed in Chapter 2.

Now that the Layer.run method has processed its input using the sigmoid threshold function, the layer is ready to pass the pattern to the next layer. As the pattern is passed to the next layer, the appropriate weights must be applied.

In the case of the XOR problem, examined in the previous section, the pattern presented to the input layer consists of simply our two binary numbers that we are inputting into the XOR problem, such as {0,1}. The three hidden layer neurons of the neural network will next receive the pattern. Each of these three neurons will each receive two numbers, one from each input neuron in the previous layer. The hidden layer, therefore will receive a total of six numbers from the previous layer, two input neurons for each of the three hidden neurons. The input pattern will not be simply passed unmodified to the hidden layer, though. First the connection weights, threshold method and bias must all be applied. We will first examine how the connection weight between layers is applied. In the case of a single hidden layer neural network there will be two groups of connection weights. The first is from the input layer to the hidden layer. The second is from the hidden layer to the output layer.

To process the connection weights, JOONE uses synapses. Now that the Layer.run method has applied the threshold function to each of the neuron values, the layer must pass the pattern onto the synapse. It will be the synapse that applies the connection weights and actually sends the pattern to the next layer. Do not forget that in JOONE each layer is running as a separate thread. So passing the pattern from one layer to the next does not involve a simple function call. As I show you how the pattern is passed from the layer to the next layer, you will see how the thread synchronization works. The Layer method has a method called fireFwdPut() that helps with this process. You will notice from Listing 5.1 that the Layer. fireFwdPut() method is called once the input has been obtained, and processed by the Layer. forward methods. The Layer.fireFwdPut method is shown in Listing 5.4.

Listing 5.4: The Layer.fireFwdPut Method

```
protected void fireFwdPut(Pattern pattern) {
  if ( aOutputPatternListener == null ) {
    return;
  };
  int currentSize = aOutputPatternListener.size();
  OutputPatternListener tempListener = null;
  for ( int index = 0; index < currentSize; index++ ){
    tempListener = (OutputPatternListener)
      aOutputPatternListener.elementAt(index);
    if ( tempListener != null ) {
      tempListener.fwdPut((Pattern)pattern.clone());
    };
  };
}
```

The Layer.fireFwdPut method has two responsibilities. First, it must apply the connection weights between each of the neurons of the current level, and those of the next level. Second, it must transmit this pattern to the synapse.

There may be zero or more synapses that will receive input from the current layer. Most likely, there will be only one. The for loop seen in Listing 5.4, loops through the collection of synapses and calls the fireFwdPut() method for each. This method will carry the pattern to the synapse by calling the Synapse.fireFwdPut method. The Synapse.fireFwdPut method is shown in Listing 5.5.

Listing 5.5: The Synapse.fireFwdPut Method

```
public synchronized void fwdPut(Pattern pattern) {
  if ( isEnabled() ) {
    count = pattern.getCount();
    while ( items > 0 ) {
      try {
        wait();
```

```
      } catch ( InterruptedException e ) {
        //e.printStackTrace();
        return;
      }
    }
    m_pattern = pattern;
    inps = (double[])pattern.getArray();
    forward(inps);
    ++items;
    notifyAll();
  }
}
```

One of the first things that you should notice about the fireFwdPut method is that it is designed to support thread synchronization. You can see this by the fact that the keyword, synchronized, is in the method signature. The fireFwdPut method will call the wait method if there is a pattern already being processed at the destination layer. This will cause the fireFwdPut method to wait, and therefore not consume processor resources, if the receiving layer is not ready to handle the input yet.

Once the wait loop completes, the synapse will process the input, and then pass the pattern to the next layer. The only processing that the synapse will perform on the pattern is to apply the bias. As the Synapse.fwdPut method processes, it first copies the pattern that was passed to the m_pattern class variable.

```
m_pattern = pattern;
```

The pattern array is then copied to an array of double values for processing.

```
inps = (double[])pattern.getArray();
```

The pattern, as an array of doubles, is then passed to the forward method. In all of the JOONE classes, the forward method is always used to perform whatever processing the current object is to perform. In the case of the synapse, the processing that is to be applied is the application of the bias.

```
forward(inps);
```

Once the bias has been applied, the pattern is ready to be processed by the next layer. The next layer is in a separate thread and is likely already waiting to process this pattern. To cause the next layer to accept the pattern, the next layer's thread must be notified. This is done by calling the Java notifyAll method that will release all threads that are waiting on this method.

```
notifyAll();
```

We will now examine the FullSynapse.forward method that applies the bias. You will notice that this method is inside of the FullSynapse class rather than the Synapse class. This is because the Synapse class is an abstract class that does not actually implement the forward method. This allows multiple synapse types to be created in the JOONE library that can handle the bias in different ways. The FullSynapse.forward method is shown in Listing 5.6.

Listing 5.6: The FullSynapse.forward Method

```
public void forward(double[] pattern) {
  int x;
  double in;
  int n = getRows();
  try {
    for ( x = 0; x < n; ++x ) {
      in = pattern[x] + bias.value[x][0];
      outs[x] = 1 / (1 + Math.exp(-in));
    }
  } catch ( Exception aioobe ) {
    aioobe.printStackTrace();
  }
}
```

As you can see, the bias is applied to each element of the pattern. The bias is not simply multiplied against the pattern like a connection weight. Rather, the pattern is summed with the bias. The sign of this value is inverted and the reciprocal is taken. This value will be returned to the calling method to be passed onto the next level.

You have observed the process that JOONE goes through as an input pattern is passed from one layer to the next layer. This process will be repeated for each layer of the neural network. In the case of the "single hidden layer neural network" being used for the XOR problem, this process will be repeated as the pattern then goes from the hidden layer to the output layer.

Examining the Backpropagation Process

You have now seen how to calculate the output for a feedforward neural network. You have seen both the mathematical equations and the Java implementation. As we examined how to calculate the final values for the network, we used the connection weights and bias values to determine the final result. You may be wondering where these values actually came from.

The values contained in the weight matrix and bias variables were determined using the backpropagation algorithm. This is a very useful algorithm for training neural networks. The backpropagation algorithm works by running the neural network just as we did when doing a recognition, as shown in the previous section. The main difference is, we are presenting the neural network with training data. As each item of training data is presented to the neural network, the error is calculated between the actual output of the neural network, and the output that was expected (and specified in the training set). The weights and bias' are then modified so that there is a greater chance of the network returning the correct result when the network is next presented with the same input.

Backpropagation is a very common method for training multilayered feedforward networks. Backpropagation can be used with any feedforward network that uses a threshold function which is differentiable.

It is this derivative function that we will use during training. It is not necessary that you understand Calculus or how to take the derivative of an equation to work with this chapter. If you are using one of the common threshold functions, you can simply get the threshold function from a chart.

To train the neural network, a method must be determined to calculate the error. As the neural network is trained, the net is presented with samples from the training set. The result obtained from the neural network is then compared with the anticipated result that is part of the training set. The degree to which the output from the neural network matches this anticipated output is the error.

To train the neural network, we must try to minimize this error. To minimize the error, the neuron connection weights and biases must be modified. We must define a function that will calculate the error of the neural network. This error function must be mathematically differentiable. Because the network uses a differential threshold function, the activations of the output neurons can be thought of as differentiable functions of the input, weights and bias. If the error function is also differentiable error, such as the "sum of square" error function, the error function itself is a differentiable function of the these weights. This allows us to evaluate the derivative of the error using the weights. Then using these derivatives, we find weights and bias that will minimize the error function.

There are several ways that weights which minimize the error function can be found. The most popular, is by using the gradient descent method. The algorithm that evaluates the derivative of the error function, is known as backpropagation, because it propagates the errors backward through the network. In the next section, we will walk through how JOONE implements the backpropagation algorithm. As we step through this process you will see how the backpropagation algorithm actually works.

Implementing Backpropagation

I will now show you how the JOONE neural network implements backpropagation training. The training process uses many of the same methods as the recognition process that we just evaluated. In fact the backpropagation method works by first running a recognition against the training data and then adjusting the weights and biases to improve the error.

You can see this process by examining the Layer.run method, which is shown in Listing 5.1. We already examined the first part of the Layer.run method in the previous section. It is the second half of the Layer.run method that is responsible for providing training for the neural network. The second half of the Layer.run method can be thought of as the main loop for the training process. It is this section of code that will be ran against each item in the training set, and the training data will be ran repeatedly until the error of the neural network falls within an acceptable level. The Layer.run method first checks to see if the neural network is in training mode.

```
if ( step != -1 )
  // Checks if the next step is a learning step
  m_learning = monitor.isLearningCicle(step);
else
  // Stops the net
  running = false;
```

To determine if we are learning, we examine the step variable. If there is no current step, then we are not training.

```
if ( (m_learning) && (running) ) {  // Learning
```

If we are in fact learning, then we must calculate the gradient inputs. The concept of gradient was discussed earlier in this chapter. For now, we simply allocate an array large enough to hold the gradient values.

```
gradientInps = new double[dimO];
```

Next we call the fireRevGet method.

```
        fireRevGet();

        backward(gradientInps);
        m_pattern = new Pattern(gradientOuts);
        m_pattern.setCount(step);

        fireRevPut(m_pattern);
    }
  }  // END while (running = false)
```

The code that we just examined implements backpropagation learning from a high level. Next we will examine the individual methods that were called by the Layer.run method to see how the learning actually takes place.

Listing 5.7: The Layer.fireRevGet Method

```
protected void fireRevGet() {
  if ( aOutputPatternListener == null )
    return;
  double[] patt;
  int currentSize = aOutputPatternListener.size();
  OutputPatternListener tempListener = null;
  for ( int index = 0; index < currentSize; index++ ){
    tempListener = (OutputPatternListener)
      aOutputPatternListener.elementAt(index);
    if ( tempListener != null ) {
      m_pattern = tempListener.revGet();
      if ( m_pattern != null ) {
        patt = m_pattern.getArray();
        if ( patt.length != gradientInps.length )
          gradientInps = new double[patt.length];
        sumBackInput(patt);
      }
    };
  };
}
```

The Layer.fireRevGet method is very similar to the fireFwdGetMethod in that they are both used to sum the patterns obtained from multiple levels into one. In most cases there will only be one layer that you are summing. This is the case with the XOR example. This summation process is assisted by the Synapse.sumBackInput method that is shown in Listing 5.8.

Listing 5.8: The Synapse.sumBackInput Method

```
protected void sumBackInput(double[] pattern) {
  int x;
  int n = getRows();
  for ( x=0; x < n; ++x )
    gradientInps[x] += pattern[x];

}
```

As you can see, the Synapse.sumBackInput method essentially just sums every element of each pattern that it is passed. This is a cumulative effect as the sumBackInput method is called repeatedly.

Once the fireRevPut method completes, it returns back to the Layer.run method. The next method that the Layer.run method calls, is the SigmoidLayer.backward method that is shown in Listing 5.9.

Listing 5.9: The SigmoidLayer.backward Method

```
public void backward(double[] pattern) {
  super.backward(pattern);
  double dw, absv;
  int x;
  int n = getRows();
  for ( x = 0; x < n; ++x ) {
    gradientOuts[x] = pattern[x] * outs[x] * (1 - outs[x]);
    // Adjust the bias
    if ( getMomentum() < 0 ) {
      if ( gradientOuts[x] < 0 )
        absv = -gradientOuts[x];
      else
        absv = gradientOuts[x];
      dw = getLearningRate() * gradientOuts[x] + absv *
           bias.delta[x][0];
    } else
      dw = getLearningRate() * gradientOuts[x] + getMomentum() *
           bias.delta[x][0];
    bias.value[x][0] += dw;
    bias.delta[x][0] = dw;
  }
}
```

This method is where much of the training actually takes place. It is here that gradient output and new bias values will be calculated. The weights will be adjusted later. Next, the other layers will be given a chance to update and train. To do this, the layer must now pass control to the synapse. It is here, in the synapse, that the connection weights will be updated. To pass control to the synapse, the Layer.fireRevPut method is called. The fireRevPut method will call all synapses that are connected to this layer. This method can be seen in Listing 5.10.

Listing 5.10: The Layer.fireRevPut Method

```
protected void fireRevPut(Pattern pattern) {
  if ( aInputPatternListener == null ) {
    return;
  };
  int currentSize = aInputPatternListener.size();
  InputPatternListener tempListener = null;
  for ( int index = 0; index < currentSize; index++ ){
    tempListener = (InputPatternListener)
      aInputPatternListener.elementAt(index);
    if ( tempListener != null ) {
      tempListener.revPut((Pattern)pattern.clone());
    };
  };
}
```

As you can see, from the above listing the fireRevPut method will loop through each input synapse that is connected. You may notice that we are passing data to our own input synapse. It may seem backward to pass data to your inputs, but that is exactly the pattern that backpropagation follows. The revPut method that is called in each of the input synapses, is shown in Listing 5.11.

Listing 5.11: The Synapse.revPut Method

```
public synchronized void revPut(Pattern pattern) {
  if ( isEnabled() ) {
    count = pattern.getCount();

    while ( bitems > 0 ) {
      try {
        wait();
      } catch ( InterruptedException e )
      {
        e.printStackTrace();
        return;
      }
    }
```

```
    m_pattern = pattern;
    backward(pattern.getArray());
    ++bitems;
    notifyAll();
  }
}
```

As you can see, the Synapse.revPut method is designed to be synchronized. This allows training to take advantage of a multi-processor computer or a distributed environment, while training, as the program can operate concurrently.

The Synapse.revPut method then makes any adjustments needed to the neuron biases by calling the Synapse.backward method. Finally, once all this is done the revPut method calls notifyAll() to inform any thread that might be waiting on data, that data is available. You will now be shown how the Synapse.backward method works.

Listing 5.12: The Synapse.backward Method

```
protected void backward(double[] pattern) {
  int x;
  int y;
  double s, dw;
  int m_rows = getInputDimension();
  int m_cols = getOutputDimension();

  // Weights adjustement
  for ( x=0; x < m_rows; ++x ) {
    double absv;
    s = 0;
    for ( y=0; y < m_cols; ++y ) {
      s += pattern[y] * array.value[x][y];
      if ( getMomentum() < 0 ) {
        if ( pattern[y] < 0 )
          absv = -pattern[y];
        else
          absv = pattern[y];
        dw = getLearningRate() * pattern[y] * inps[x] + absv *
            array.delta[x][y];
      } else
        dw = getLearningRate() * pattern[y] * inps[x] +
            getMomentum() * array.delta[x][y];
      array.value[x][y] += dw;
      array.delta[x][y] = dw;
    }
    bouts[x] = s;
  }
}
```

The Synapse.backward method very closely parallels the SigmoidLayer.backward layer. Both layers mathematically adjust the weights based on the backpropagation training algorithm. Only this time, we are modifying the connection weights, not the biases of the neurons.

Summary

In this chapter, you learned how a feedforward backpropagation neural network functions. You saw how the JOONE neural network implemented such a neural network. The feedforward backpropagation neural network is actually composed of two neural network algorithms. It is not necessary to always use "feedforward" and "backpropagation" together, but this is usually the case. The term "feedforward" refers to a method by which a neural network recognizes a pattern, where as the term "backpropagation" describes a process by which the neural network will be trained.

A feedforward neural network is a network where, neurons are only connected to the next layer. There are no connections between neurons in previous layers or between neurons and themselves. Additionally neurons will not be connected to neurons beyond the next layer. As the pattern is processed by a feedforward design, the bias and connection weights will be applied.

Neural networks can be trained using backpropagation. Backpropagation is a form of supervised training. The neural network is presented with the training data, and the results from the neural network are compared with the expected results. The difference between the actual results and the expected results produces an error. Backpropagation is a method whereby the weights and input bias of the neural network are altered in a way that causes this error to be reduced.

The feedforward backpropagation neural network is a very common network architecture. This neural network architecture can applied to many cases. There are other neural network architectures that may be used. In the next chapter, we will examine the Kohonen neural network. The most significant difference between the Kohonen neural network and the feedforward backpropagation neural network that we just examined, is the training method. The backpropagation method uses a supervised training method. In the next chapter we will see how an unsupervised training method is used.

CHAPTER 6: UNDERSTANDING THE KOHONEN NEURAL NETWORK

Chapter Highlights
- **What is a Kohonen Neural Network**
- **How a Kohonen Neural Network Classifies Patterns**
- **Training a Kohonen Neural Network**
- **Dealing with Neurons that do not Learn to Classify**

In the previous chapter, you learned about the feedforward backpropagation neural network. While feedforward neural networks are very common, they are not the only architecture for neural networks. In this chapter, we will examine another very common architecture for neural networks.

The Kohonen neural network, sometimes called the self organizing map (SOM), contains no hidden layer. This network architecture is named after its creator, Tuevo Kohonen. The Kohonen neural network differs from the feedforward backpropagation neural network in several important ways. In this chapter we will examine the Kohonen neural network and see how it is implemented. Chapter 7 will continue by showing a practical application of the Kohonen neural network, optical character recognition.

Introducing the Kohonen Neural Network

The Kohonen neural network differs considerably from the feedforward backpropagation neural network, in how it is trained and how it recalls a pattern. The Kohohen neural network does not use any sort of activation function. Further, the Kohonen neural network does not use any sort of a bias weight.

Output from the Kohonen neural network does not consist of the output of several neurons. When a pattern is presented to a Kohonen network one of the output neurons is selected as a "winner". This "winning" neuron is the output from the Kohonen network. Often these "winning" neurons represent groups in the data that is presented to the Kohonen network. For example, in Chapter 7 we will examine an OCR program that uses 26 output neurons. These 26 output neurons map the input patterns into the 26 letters of the Latin alphabet.

The most significant difference between the Kohonen neural network and the feedforward backpropagation neural network, is that the Kohonen network trains in an unsupervised mode. This means that the Kohonen network is presented with data, but the correct output that corresponds to that data is not specified. Using the Kohonen network, data can be classified into groups. We will begin our review of the Kohonen network by examining the training process.

It is also important to understand the limitations of the Kohonen neural network. You will recall from the previous chapter that neural networks with only two layers can only be applied to linearly separable problems. This is the case with the Kohonen neural network. Kohonen neural networks are used because they are a relatively simple network to construct that can be trained very rapidly.

How a Kohonen Network Recognizes

I will now show you how the Kohonen neural network recognizes a pattern. We will begin by examining the structure of the Kohonen neural network. Once you understand the structure of the Kohonen neural network, and how it recognizes patterns, you will be shown how to train the Kohonen neural network to properly recognize the patterns you desire. We will begin by examining the structure of the Kohonen neural network.

The Structure of the Kohonen Neural Network

The Kohonen neural network works differently than the feedforward neural network that we learned about in Chapter 5. The Kohonen neural network contains only an input and output layer of neurons. There is no hidden layer in a Kohonen neural network. First we will examine the input and output to a Kohonen neural network.

The input to a Kohonen neural network is given to the neural network using the input neurons. These input neurons are each given the floating point numbers that make up the input pattern to the network. A Kohonen neural network requires that these inputs be normalized to the range between -1 and 1. Presenting an input pattern to the network will cause a reaction from the output neurons.

The output of a Kohonen neural network is very different from the output of a feedforward neural network. Recall from Chapter 5, that if we had a neural network with five output neurons we would be given an output that consisted of five values. This is not the case with the Kohonen neural network. In a Kohonen neural network, only one of the output neurons actually produces a value. Additionally, this single value is either true or false. When the pattern is presented to the Kohonen neural network, one single output neuron is chosen as the output neuron. Therefore, the output from the Kohonen neural network is usually the index of the neuron (i.e. Neuron #5) that fired. The structure of a typical Kohonen neural network is shown in Figure 6.1.

Figure 6.1: A Kohonen Neural Network

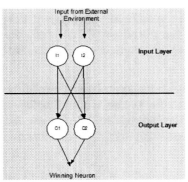

Now that you understand the structure of the Kohonen neural network we will examine how the network processes information. To examine this process we will step through the calculation process. For this example, we will consider a very simple Kohonen neural network. This network will have only two input and two output neurons. The input given to the two input neurons is shown in Table 6.1.

Table 6.1: Sample Inputs to a Kohonen Neural Network

Input Neuron 1 (I1)	0.5
Input Neuron 2 (I2)	0.75

We must also know the connection weights between the neurons. These connection weights are given in Table 6.2.

Table 6.2: Connection Weights in the Sample Kohonen Neural Network

I1->O1	0.1
I2->O1	0.2
I1->O2	0.3
I2->O2	0.4

Using these values, we will now examine which neuron would win and produce output. We will begin by normalizing the input.

Normalizing the Input

The Kohonen neural network requires that its input be normalized. Because of this, some texts refer to the normalization as a third layer. For the purposes of this book, the Kohonen neural network is considered a two layer network, because there are only two actual neuron layers at work in the Kohonen neural network.

The requirement that the Kohonen neural network places on its input data, is one of the most sever limitations of the Kohonen neural network. Input to the Kohonen neural network must be between the values -1 and 1. In addition, each of the inputs should fully use the range. If one, or more, of the input neurons were to use only the numbers between 0 and 1, the performance of the neural network would suffer.

To normalize the input we must first calculate the "vector length" of the input data, or vector. This is done by summing the squares of the input vector. In this case it would be.

```
(0.5 * 0.5) + (0.75 * 0.75)
```

This would result in a "vector length" of 0.8125. If the length becomes too small, then the length will be set some arbitrarily small value. In this case, the "vector length" is a sufficiently large number. Using this length, we can now determine the normalization factor. The normalization factor is the reciprocal of the square root of the length. For our value the normalization factor is calculated as follows.

$$\frac{1}{\sqrt{0.8125}}$$

This results in a normalization factor of 1.1094. This normalization process will be used in the next step where the output layer is calculated.

Calculating Each Neuron's Output

To calculate the output, the input vector and neuron connection weights must both be considered. First the "dot product" of the input neurons and their connection weights must be calculated. To calculate the dot product between two vectors you must multiply each of the elements in the two vectors. We will now examine how this is done.

Equation 6.1: Calculating the Kohonen output

$$|0.5 \quad 0.75| \cdot |0.1 \quad 0.2| = (0.5 * 0.75) + (0.1 * 0.2)$$

As you can see from the above calculation the dot product would be 0.395. This calculation will have to be done for each of the output neurons. Through this example, we will only examine the calculations for the first output neuron. The calculations necessary for the second output neuron are calculated in the same way.

This output must now be normalized by multiplying it by the normalization factor that was determined in the previous step. You must now multiply the dot product of 0.395 by the normalization factor of 1.1094. This results in an output of 0.438213. Now that the output has been calculated and normalized it must be mapped to a bipolar number.

Mapping to Bipolar

As you may recall from Chapter 2, a bipolar number is an alternate way of representing binary numbers. In the bipolar system, the binary zero maps to -1 and the binary remains a 1. Because the input to the neural network normalized to this range, we must perform a similar normalization to the output of the neurons. To make this mapping, we multiply by two and subtract one. For the output of 0.438213 this would result in a final output of -0.123574.

The value -0.123574 is the output of the first neuron. This value will be compared with the outputs of the other neuron. By comparing these values we can determine a "winning" neuron.

Choosing the Winner

We have seen how to calculate the value for the first output neuron. If we are to determine a winning output neuron we must also calculate the value for the second output neuron. We will now quickly review the process to calculate the second neuron. For a more detailed description you should refer to the previous section.

The second output neuron will use exactly the same normalization factor as was used to calculate the first output neuron. As you recall from the previous section the normalization factor is 1.1094. If we apply the dot product for the weights of the second output neuron and the input vector we get a value of 0.45. This value is multiplied by the normalization factor of 1.1094 to give the value of 0.0465948. We can now calculate the final output for neuron 2 by converting the output of 0.0465948 to bipolar which yields -0.9068104.

As you can see, we now have an output value for each of the neurons. The first neuron has an output value of -0.123574 and the second neuron has an output value of -0.9068104. To choose the winning neuron we choose the output that has the largest output value. In this case, the winning neuron is the second output neuron with an output of -0.9068104, which beats neuron two's output of -0.123574.

You have now seen how the output of the Kohonen neural network was derived. As you can see, the weights between the input and output neurons determine this output. In the next section we will see to adjust these weights can be adjusted to produce output that is more suitable for the desired task. The training process is what modified these weights. The training process will be described in the next section.

How a Kohonen Network Learns

In this section, you will learn to train a Kohonen neural network. There several steps involved in this training process. Overall, the process for training a Kohonen neural network involves stepping through several epochs until the error of the Kohonen neural network is below an acceptable level. In this section, we will learn these individual processes. You'll learn how to calculate the error rate for Kohonen neural network and you'll learn how to adjust the weights for each epoch. You will also learn to determine when no more epochs are necessary to further train the neural network.

The training process for the Kohonen neural network is competitive. For each training set one neuron will "win". This winning neuron will have its weight adjusted so that it will react even more strongly to the input the next time. As different neurons win for different patterns, their ability to recognize that particular pattern will be increased.

We will first examine the overall process involving training the Kohonen neural network. These individual steps are summarized in figure 6.2.

Figure 6.2: Training the Kohonen Neural Network

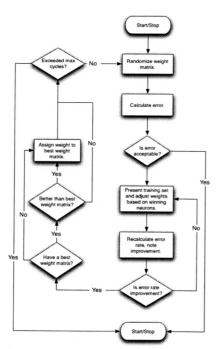

As you can see from the above diagram the Kohonen neural network is trained by repeating epochs until one of two things happens. If the calculated error is below an acceptable level, the training process is complete. On the other hand, if the error rate has changed by only a very marginal amount, this individual cycle will be aborted without any additional epochs taking place. If it is determined that the cycle is to be aborted, the weights will be "initialized random values" and a new training cycle begins.

The most important part in the network's training cycles, are the individual epochs. We will now examine what happens turning each of these epochs. We will began by examining how the weights are adjusted for each epoch.

Learning Rate

The learning rate is a constant that will be used by the learning algorithm. The learning rate must be a positive number less than 1. Typically, the learning rate is a number such as .4 or .5. In the following section, the learning rate will be specified by the symbol alpha.

Generally, setting the learning rate to a larger value will cause the training to progress faster. Though setting the learning rate to too large of a number, could cause the network to never converge. This is because the oscillations of the weight vectors will be too great for the classification patterns to ever emerge. Another technique, is to start with a relatively high learning rate and decrease this rate as training progresses. This allows initial rapid training of the neural network that will be "fine tuned" as training progresses.

The learning rate is just a variable that is used as part of the algorithm used to adjust the weights of the neurons. In the next section we will see how these weights are adjusted using the learning rate.

Adjusting Weights

The entire memory of the Kohonen neural network is stored inside of the weighted connections between the input and output layer. The weights are adjusted in each epoch. An epoch occurs when training data is presented to the Kohonen neural network and the weights are adjusted based on the results of this data. The adjustments to the weights should produce a network that will yield more favorable results the next time the same training data is presented. Epochs continue as more and more data is presented to the network and the weights are adjusted.

Eventually, the return on these weight adjustments will diminish to the point that it is no longer valuable to continue with this particular set of weights. When this happens, the entire weight matrix is reset to new random values. This forms a new cycle. The final weight matrix that will be used, will be the best weight matrix determined from each of the cycles. We will now examine how these weights are transformed.

The original method for calculating the changes to weights, which was proposed by Kohonen, is often called the additive method. This method uses the following equation:

Equation 6.2: Adjusting the Kohonen Weight

$$w^{t+1} = \frac{w^t + \alpha x}{\|w^t + \alpha x\|}$$

The variable "x" is the training vector that was presented to the network. This variable "w" is the weight of the winning neuron, and result of the equation is the new weight. The double vertical bars represent the vector length. This method will be implemented in the Kohonen example shown later in this chapter.

The additive method generally works well for Kohonen neural networks. Though in cases where the additive method shows excessive instability, and fails to converge, an alternate method can be used. This method is called the subtractive method. The subtractive method uses the following equations:

Equation 6.3: Adjusting the Kohonen Weight (subtractive)

$$e = x - w^t$$

Equation 6.4: Adjusting the Kohonen Weight (subtractive, cont.)

$$w^{t+1} = w^t + \alpha e$$

These two equations show you the basic transformation that will occur on the weights of the network. In the next section, you will see how these equations are implemented as a Java program, and their use will be demonstrated.

Calculating the Error

Before we can understand how to calculate the error, for the neural network we must first understand what the error means. This neural network is trained in an unsupervised fashion, so the definition of the error is somewhat different than what we normally think of as an error.

In the previous chapter, supervised training involved calculating the error. The error was the difference between the anticipated output of the neural network and the actual output of the neural network. In this chapter, we are examining unsupervised training. In unsupervised training, there is no anticipated output. Because of this, you may be wondering exactly how we can calculate an error. The answer is that the error we are calculating is not a true error, or at least not an error in the normal sense of the word.

The purpose of the Kohonen neural network is to classify the input into several sets. The error for the Kohonen neural network, therefore, must be able to measure how well the network is classifying these items. We will examine two methods for determining the error in this section. There is no official way to calculate the error for a Kohonen neural network.

The error is just a percent that gives an idea of how well the Kohonen network is classifying the input into the output groups. The error itself is not used to modify the weights, as was done in the backpropagation algorithm. The method to determine this error will be discussed when we see how to implement a Java training method.

Implementing the Kohonen Neural Network

Now that you understand how the Kohonen neural network functions, we will implement one using Java. In this section, we will see how several classes can be used together to create a Kohonen neural network. Following this section you will be shown an example of how to use the Kohonen neural network classes to create a simple Kohonen neural network. Finally, in Chapter 7 you will be shown how to construct a more complex application based on the Kohonen neural network that can recognize handwriting.

First you must understand the structure of the Kohonen neural network classes that we are constructing. Many of the neural network examples in this book use the Java Object Oriented Neural Engine (JOONE). JOONE is constructed to primarily support supervised training. As a result, we will not use JOONE to construct the Kohonen neural network in this chapter. The classes used to implement the Kohonen Neural Network are summarized in Table 6.3.

Table 6.3: Classes Used to Implement the Kohonen Neural Network

Class	Purpose
KohonenNetwork	Implements the methods that are unique to the Kohonen neural network. This is where the Kohonen neural network is trained and recalls patterns.
Network	Contains the methods that are not unique to the Kohonen neural network. This class contains methods to calculate the dot product and vector length, among other common tasks.
NeuralReportable	A simple interface that allows the Kohonen neural network to return progress information as the neural network is trained.
TrainingSet	A training set holder object that can contain arrays of individual training items. The training set can hold both input and output elements. For the Kohonen neural network examples shown in this chapter, only the input elements are used.

Now that you understand the overall structure of the Kohonen neural network classes we will examine each individual class. You will see how these classes work together to provide Kohonen network functionality. We will begin by examining how the training set is constructed using the TrainingSet class.

Training Sets

To train the Kohonen neural network, training sets must be provided. This training data will be stored in the TrainingSet class. This class is designed to be a container class that could potentially be used for other neural network architectures, as well as the Kohonen neural network. The TrainingSet class is shown in Listing 6.1.

Listing 6.1: Storing Training Sets (TrainingSet.java)

```java
import java.io.*;
import java.util.*;

public class TrainingSet {

  protected int inputCount;
  protected int outputCount;
  protected double input[][];
  protected double output[][];
  protected int trainingSetCount;

  TrainingSet ( int inputCount , int outputCount )
  {
    this.inputCount = inputCount;
    this.outputCount = outputCount;
    trainingSetCount = 0;
  }

  public int getInputCount()
  {
    return inputCount;
  }

  public int getOutputCount()
  {
    return outputCount;
  }

  public void setTrainingSetCount(int trainingSetCount)
  {
    this.trainingSetCount = trainingSetCount;
    input = new double[trainingSetCount][inputCount];
    output = new double[trainingSetCount][outputCount];
    classify = new double[trainingSetCount];
  }

  public int getTrainingSetCount()
  {
```

```
    return trainingSetCount;
}

void setInput(int set,int index,double value)
throws RuntimeException
{
  if ( (set<0) || (set>=trainingSetCount) )
    throw(new RuntimeException("Training set out of range:"
         + set ));
  if ( (index<0) || (index>=inputCount) )
    throw(new RuntimeException(
       "Training input index out of range:" + index ));
  input[set][index] = value;
}

void setOutput(int set,int index,double value)
throws RuntimeException
{
  if ( (set<0) || (set>=trainingSetCount) )
    throw(new RuntimeException("Training set out of range:"
      + set ));
  if ( (index<0) || (set>=outputCount) )
    throw(new RuntimeException(
       "Training input index out of range:" + index ));
  output[set][index] = value;
}

double getInput(int set,int index)
throws RuntimeException
{
  if ( (set<0) || (set>=trainingSetCount) )
    throw(new RuntimeException(
      "Training set out of range:" + set ));
  if ( (index<0) || (index>=inputCount) )
    throw(new RuntimeException(
      "Training input index out of range:" + index ));
  return input[set][index];
}

double getOutput(int set,int index)
throws RuntimeException
{
  if ( (set<0) || (set>=trainingSetCount) )
    throw(new RuntimeException(
      "Training set out of range:" + set ));
  if ( (index<0) || (set>=outputCount) )
```

```
      throw(new RuntimeException(
        "Training input index out of range:" + index ));
    return output[set][index];
  }

  double []getOutputSet(int set)
  throws RuntimeException
  {
    if ( (set<0) || (set>=trainingSetCount) )
      throw(new RuntimeException(
        "Training set out of range:" + set ));
    return output[set];
  }

  double []getInputSet(int set)
  throws RuntimeException
  {
    if ( (set<0) || (set>=trainingSetCount) )
      throw(new RuntimeException("Training set out of range:"
        + set ));
    return input[set];
  }
}
```

As you can see from the above code, the TrainingSet class is managing two variable length arrays. The first is the input vector. The input vector can be made up of one or more double numbers stored in the array. This input array can be accessed by two means.

First, the input training array can be accessed by using the getInputSet and setInputSet methods. These methods allow access to the complete array of the input set. These methods can access an individual training element. To access an individual training set item, you must provide two indexes. The first index specifies which training element should be accessed. In a large training set, there may be many of these. The second index tells the TrainingSet object which indivual input element to access for the specified training item. In addition to the input elements, the TrainingSet class also supports outputs. These outputs are accessed by calling the getOutput and setOutput methods.

The output methods are provided for completeness. These methods are not used by the Kohonen neural network. If the output array had been used, then it would allow supervised training to take place as both the anticipated output and input would be provided.

Internally, the TrainingSet class stores the following variables, which is shown in Table 6.4.

Table 6.4: Training Set Variables

Variable	Purpose
inputCount	The number of input elements there will be for each training sample.
outputCount	The number of output elements there will be for each training sample.

These variables, in Java, are listed below.

```
input[][] - The input training samples.
output[][] - The output training samples.
trainingSetCount - The number of training samples.
```

To use the training set with the Kohonen neural network, the training set must be populated with data. Because the Kohonen neural network is unsupervised, only the input elements need be filled. Once a TrainingSet object has been constructed and properly populated with data, it will be passed to a KohonenNetwork object for training. This process will be explained later in this chapter with an example program.

Reporting Progress

For the Kohonen neural network to be effective, it must be trained. This training process could potiently take awhile. Because of this, the Kohonen classes were designed to support an interface, NeuralReportable, that allows updates to be transmitted between the Kohonen neural network and the external environment. This interface is shown in Listing 6.2.

Listing 6.2: Reporting Process (NeuralReportable.java)

```
public interface NeuralReportable
{
    public void update(int retry,double totalError,
      double bestError);
}
```

A Java interface allows a class to state that it supports a particular set of methods. Any class that implements the NeuralReportable interface must include an update method. This allows the KohonenNetwork class to be able to call an update method from your class, even though the KohonenNetwork class has no other advance knowledge of your class.

The update method will be called for each training epoch. Three parameters are elapsed to the update method to indicate the progress of training. First, a variable named retry is elapsed that tells you how many training cycles have passed. Secondly, two error results are returned. The first error, totalError, indicates the total error for the Kohonen neural network for the epoch that just occurred. The second error, bestError, indicates the best totalError that has occurred so far. Now that you have seen how to prepare training sets and receive status information from the training process, you are ready to see how the Kohonen network classes operate. We will begin by examining the network base class, which implements some basic methods that any neural network, the Kohonen network included, might need.

Network Base Class

We will now examine the Network class. This class is the base class for the Kohonen-Network class, which will ultimately provide the Kohonen neural network. The Network class provides some basic functionality that would be useful for networks other than just the Kohonen neural network. The network class is declared abstract so that it cannot be instantiated by itself. To make use of the Network class, a child class must be derived. The KohonenNetwork class is provided as a child class. The KohonenNetwork class will be examined in the next section. The properties defined in the Network class are shown in Listing 6.3.

Listing 6.3: Network Base Class (Network.java)

```java
import java.util.*;

abstract public class Network {

  public final static double NEURON_ON=0.9;
  public final static double NEURON_OFF=0.1;

  protected double output[];

  protected double totalError;
  protected int inputNeuronCount;
  protected int outputNeuronCount;
  protected Random random = new Random(
    System.currentTimeMillis());
```

Each of these properties, listed below, will be used to hold some attribute of the neural network, or a constant that will be used. The properties are used for the purposes listed in Table 6.5.

Table 6.5: Variables used by the Network Base Class

Variable	Purpose
NEURON_ON	The value that a neuron must be greater than (or equal) to be considered "on".
NEURON_OFF	The value that a neuron must be less than (or equal) to be considered "off".
output[]	The output from the neural network.
totalError	The error from the last epoch. This is the total error, across all training sets.
inputNeuronCount	The number of input neurons.
outputNeuronCount	The number of output neurons.
random	A random number generator, used to initialize the weights to random values.

Earlier, we saw that calculating a vector length is an important part of the recollection process for a Kohonen neural network. The Network class contains a method that calculates the vector length for a given vector, expressed as an array. This method is shown in Listing 6.4.

Listing 6.4: Calculate a Vector Length (Network.java)

```java
/**
 * Calculate the length of a vector.
 *
 * @param v vector
 * @return Vector length.
 */
static double vectorLength( double v[] )
{
  double rtn = 0.0 ;
  for ( int i=0;i<v.length;i++ )
    rtn += v[i] * v[i];
  return rtn;
}
```

As you can see, the vectorLength method sums the squares of the numbers contained in the vector. As discussed previously in this chapter, this is the method used to calculate a vector length. This method will be used by the Kohonen network class, shown in the next section.

Another important function provided by the Network base class, is the calculation of a dot product. The dot product was discussed previously in this chapter. The Kohonen network class, which will be discussed in the next section, makes use of the dot product method to calculate the output of the neural network. The dot product method is shown in Listing 6.5.

Listing 6.5: Calculate a Dot Product (Network.java)

```java
/**
 * Called to calculate a dot product.
 *
 * @param vec1 one vector
 * @param vec2 another vector
 * @return The dot product.
 */

double dotProduct(double vec1[] , double vec2[] )
{
  int k,v;
  double rtn;

  rtn = 0.0;
  k = vec1.length;

  v = 0;
  while ( (k--)>0 ) {
    rtn += vec1[v] * vec2[v];
    v++;
  }

  return rtn;
}
```

As you can see from the listing, the dot product method returns the sum of the products of each element in the vector.

The neuron weights are initially set to random values. These random values are then trained to produce better results. At the beginning of each training cycle, the weights are also initialized to random values. The Network class provides a method to do this. Listing 6.6 shows a method that can be called to randomize the weights used by the neural network.

Listing 6.6: Randomize Weights (Network.java)

```java
/**
 * Called to randomize weights.
 *
 * @param weight A weight matrix.
 */
void randomizeWeights( double weight[][] )
{
  double r ;
```

```
      int temp = (int)(3.464101615 / (2.  * Math.random() ));

   for ( int y=0;y<weight.length;y++ ) {
     for ( int x=0;x<weight[0].length;x++ ) {
       r = (double) random.nextInt(Integer.MAX_VALUE) +
           (double) random.nextInt(Integer.MAX_VALUE) -
           (double) random.nextInt(Integer.MAX_VALUE) -
           (double) random.nextInt(Integer.MAX_VALUE) ;
       weight[y][x] = temp * r ;
     }
   }
 }

}
```

As you can see from the above listing, the program simply loops through the entire weight matrix and assigns a random number. You will also notice that two random numbers are used for each calculation. This is intended to further randomize the weights beyond a single randomly generated number.

The KohonenNetwork Class

We will now examine the KohonenNetwork class. This class implements the Kohonen neural network. The KohonenNetwork class has several properties. These can be seen in Listing 6.7.

Listing 6.7: The Kohonen Network Properties (KohonenNetwork.java)

```
public class KohonenNetwork extends Network {

  double outputWeights[][];
  protected int learnMethod = 1;
  protected double learnRate = 0.5;
  protected double quitError = 0.1;
  protected int retries = 10000;
  protected double reduction = .99;
  protected NeuralReportable owner;
  public boolean halt = false;
  protected TrainingSet train;
```

The variables used by the Kohonen network are summarized in Table 6.6.

Table 6.6: Variables Used by the Kohonen Network

Variable	Purpose
halt	Set this to true to abort training.
learnMethod	The learning method, set to 1 for subtractive or to another value for additive.
learnRate	The initial learning rate.
outputWeights[][]	The weight matrix for the output neurons.
owner	The owner class, which must implement the NeuralReportable interface.
quitError	Once the error rate reaches this level, stop training.
reduction	The amount to reduce the learnRate property by each epoch.
retries	The total number of cycles to allow this places a ceiling on the number of training cycles that can transpire.
train	The training set.

The first of the Kohonen network methods that we will examine, is the constructor. The constructor can be seen in Listing 6.8.

Listing 6.8: The Kohonen network constructor (KohonenNetwork.java)

```java
/**
 * The constructor.
 *
 * @param inputCount Number of input neurons
 * @param outputCount Number of output neurons
 * @param owner The owner object, for updates.
 */
public KohonenNetwork(int inputCount,int outputCount,
  NeuralReportable owner)
{
  int n ;

  totalError = 1.0 ;

  this.inputNeuronCount = inputCount;
  this.outputNeuronCount = outputCount;
  this.outputWeights =
    new double[outputNeuronCount][inputNeuronCount+1];
  this.output = new double[outputNeuronCount];
  this.owner = owner;
}
```

As you can see, the constructor sets up the weight matrix arrays. It also stores the number of input and output neurons in their properties. Management of these weight arrays is a very important aspect of implementing the Kohonen neural network. There are also several utility methods contained in the Network classes used specifically to manipulate these weight matrixes. These weight matrix manipulation utility methods can be seen in Listing 6.9.

Listing 6.9: Weight Utility Methods

```
public static void copyWeights( KohonenNetwork dest ,
  KohonenNetwork source )
{
  for ( int i=0;i<source.outputWeights.length;i++ ) {
    System.arraycopy(source.outputWeights[i],
                     0,
                     dest.outputWeights[i],
                     0,
                     source.outputWeights[i].length);
  }
}

/**
 * Clear the weights.
 */
public void clearWeights()
{
  totalError = 1.0;
  for ( int y=0;y<outputWeights.length;y++ )
    for ( int x=0;x<outputWeights[0].length;x++ )
      outputWeights[y][x]=0;
}

/**
 * Called to initialize the Kononen network.
 */
public void initialize()
{
  int i ;
  double optr[];

  clearWeights() ;
  randomizeWeights( outputWeights ) ;
  for ( i=0 ; i<outputNeuronCount ; i++ ) {
    optr = outputWeights[i];
    normalizeWeight( optr );
  }
}
}
```

First, you will notice that there is a method provided that will copy a weight matrix. It is important to be able to copy a weight matrix because as the Kohonen neural network is training itself, it will need to copy weight matrixes that supplant the current best case weight matrix.

You'll also notice that there is a method provided that is capable of completely blanking the weight matrix. This is done by setting every element in the weight matrix zero. Finally there is also an initialization method provided that will set all of the weight matrices to initial random values. Further, the initialization procedure will also normalize these weights as discussed earlier in the chapter. Weight normalization is performed by a special function named normalizeWeight that will be discussed later in this section.

There are several methods available that are used for normalization. Because normalization is an important part of the Kohonen neural network. Listing 6.10 shows a method is used to normalize the inputs into a Kohonen neural network.

Listing 6.10: Input Normalization (KohonenNetwork.java)

```java
/**
 * Normalize the input.
 *
 * @param input input pattern
 * @param normfac the result
 * @param synth synthetic last input
 */
void normalizeInput(
                    final double input[] ,
                    double normfac[] ,
                    double synth[]
                    )
{
   double length, d ;

   length = vectorLength ( input ) ;
// just in case it gets too small
   if ( length < 1.E-30 )
     length = 1.E-30 ;


   normfac[0] = 1.0 / Math.sqrt ( length ) ;
   synth[0] = 0.0 ;

}
```

The exact process used to normalize an input vector was discussed earlier in this chapter. As you can see from the above code, this method does not actually change the input values and anyway. Rather, a normalization factor is returned after it is calculated. The normalization factor, as discussed earlier, is calculated by taking the reciprocal of the square root of the vector length.

The input vector is not the only thing the must be normalize for Kohonen neural network to function properly. Listing 6.11 shows how the weight matrix is also normalized.

Listing 6.11: Weight Normalization (KohonenNetwork.java)

```java
/**
 * Normalize weights
 *
 * @param w Input weights
 */
void normalizeWeight( double w[] )
{
  int i ;
  double len ;

  len = vectorLength ( w ) ;
  // just incase it gets too small
  if ( len < 1.E-30 )
    len = 1.E-30 ;


  len = 1.0 / Math.sqrt ( len ) ;
  for ( i=0 ; i<inputNeuronCount ; i++ )
    w[i] *= len ;
  w[inputNeuronCount] = 0;
}
```

As you can see from the above code, the weight normalization method begins by calculating the vector length of the weight vector that was passed into it. Using this vector length, a normalization factor is then calculated. The weight normalization method then proceeds by multiplying this normalization factor against all of the weights that were passed and in the weight vector. We've now seen most of the basic utility methods that are provided by the coming neural network. We will now begin to examine some other methods that actually implement the training and recollection processes of the Kohonen neural network. We will begin by examining a method that is used to present an input pattern to the Kohonen neural network. This method, named trial, is shown in Listing 6.12.

Listing 6.12: Input Pattern Trial (KohonenNetwork.java)

```java
/**
 * Try an input pattern.  This can be used to present an
 * input pattern to the network.  Usually its best to call
 * winner to get the winning neuron though.
 *
 * @param input Input pattern.
 */
void trial ( double input[] )
{
  int i ;
  double normfac[]=new double[1], synth[]=new double[1], optr[];

  normalizeInput(input,normfac,synth) ;

  for ( i=0 ; i<outputNeuronCount; i++ ) {
    optr = outputWeights[i];
    output[i] = dotProduct( input , optr ) * normfac[0]
                  + synth[0] * optr[inputNeuronCount] ;
    // Remap to bipolar (-1,1 to 0,1)
    output[i] = 0.5 * (output[i] + 1.0) ;
    // account for rounding
    if ( output[i] > 1.0 )
      output[i] = 1.0 ;
    if ( output[i] < 0.0 )
      output[i] = 0.0 ;
  }
}
```

The exact process used to calculate the output from the Kohonen neural network was discussed earlier in this chapter. As you can see from the above code, the method loops to each of the output neurons, and calculates the value for that output neuron. The value for each output neuron is calculated by taking the dot product of the normalized input their weights. Because of rounding errors, the final output may be greater than 1 or less than 0. To account for these rounding errors, values "less than 0" are treated as 0 and "greater than 1" values are treated as 1. The final output for each neuron is stored in the output array.

As discussed earlier in this chapter, we're not generally concerned with the output of each individual neuron. In the Kohonen neural network, we are only interested in which neuron actually won. The winning neuron is the neuron that determines which class the network recalled the pattern of. Listing 6.13 shows a method that is used to actually present an input pattern to the Kohonen network and receive the winning neuron. This method represents the main entry point into the Kohonen network for pattern classification.

Listing 6.13: Present a Pattern (KohonenNetwork.java)

```java
/**
 * Present an input pattern and get the
 * winning neuron.
 *
 * @param input input pattern
 * @param normfac the result
 * @param synth synthetic last input
 * @return The winning neuron number.
 */
public int winner(double input[] ,double normfac[] ,
  double synth[])
{
  int i, win=0;
  double biggest, optr[];

  // Normalize input

  normalizeInput( input , normfac , synth ) ;

  biggest = -1.E30;
  for ( i=0 ; i<outputNeuronCount; i++ ) {
    optr = outputWeights[i];
    output[i] = dotProduct (input , optr ) * normfac[0]
                + synth[0] * optr[inputNeuronCount] ;
    // Remap to bipolar(-1,1 to 0,1)
    output[i] = 0.5 * (output[i] + 1.0) ;
    if ( output[i] > biggest ) {
      biggest = output[i] ;
      win = i ;
    }

    // account for rounding
    if ( output[i] > 1.0 )
      output[i] = 1.0 ;
    if ( output[i] < 0.0 )
      output[i] = 0.0 ;
  }

  return win ;
}
```

The process executed by the above code was described earlier in this chapter. Much of the code shown here is the same as in the trial method that we just examined. This method will generally be used when you actually want to present a pattern to the neural network for classification. The trial method that we just examined, is generally used only internally by the Kohonen neural network during training. During training, we do care about the actual output of each neuron, whereas during classification, we only care which neuron actually won.

The winner method works by looping through each of the output neurons and calculating the output of that particular neuron. As the method loops through each of these output neurons, indexes are saved to which ever neuron had the highest output. This neuron with the highest output is considered to be the winner. At this point, the winning neuron is returned.

Now that we have examined how the classification phase is implemented, we can begin to examine the training phase. There are several methods that are used to facilitate the training process. The main entry point is the training method. The training method is shown in Listing 6.14.

Listing 6.14: Train the Neural Network (KohonenNetwork.java)

```java
/**
 * This method is called to train the network.  It can run
 * for a very long time and will report progress back to the
 * owner object.
 *
 * @exception java.lang.RuntimeException
 */
public void learn ()
throws RuntimeException
{
  int i, key, tset,iter,n_retry,nwts;
  int won[],winners ;
  double work[],correc[][],rate,best_err,dptr[];
  double bigerr[] = new double[1] ;
  double bigcorr[] = new double[1];
  KohonenNetwork bestnet;   // Preserve best here

  totalError = 1.0 ;

  bestnet = new KohonenNetwork(inputNeuronCount,
    outputNeuronCount,
    owner) ;

  won = new int[outputNeuronCount];
  correc = new double[outputNeuronCount][inputNeuronCount+1];
  if ( learnMethod==0 )
    work = new double[inputNeuronCount+1];
  else
```

```
      work = null ;

   rate = learnRate;

   initialize () ;
   best_err = 1.e30 ;

// main loop:

   n_retry = 0 ;
   for ( iter=0 ; ; iter++ ) {

      evaluateErrors ( rate , learnMethod , won ,
                       bigerr , correc , work ) ;

      totalError = bigerr[0] ;

      if ( totalError < best_err ) {
        best_err = totalError ;
        copyWeights ( bestnet , this ) ;
      }

      winners = 0 ;
      for ( i=0;i<won.length;i++ )
        if ( won[i]!=0 )
          winners++;


      if ( bigerr[0] < quitError )
        break ;


      if ( (winners < outputNeuronCount)  &&
           (winners < train.getTrainingSetCount()) ) {
        forceWin ( won ) ;
        continue ;
      }

      adjustWeights (
        rate ,
        learnMethod ,
        won ,
        bigcorr,
        correc ) ;

      owner.update(n_retry,totalError,best_err);
```

```
    if ( halt ) {
      owner.update(n_retry,totalError,best_err);
      break;
    }
    Thread.yield();

    if ( bigcorr[0] < 1E-5 ) {
      if ( ++n_retry > retries )
        break ;
      initialize () ;
      iter = -1 ;
      rate = learnRate ;
      continue ;
    }

    if ( rate > 0.01 )
      rate *= reduction ;

  }

  // done

  copyWeights( this , bestnet ) ;

  for ( i=0 ; i<outputNeuronCount ; i++ )
    normalizeWeight ( outputWeights[i] ) ;

  halt = true;
  n_retry++;
  owner.update(n_retry,totalError,best_err);
}
```

The training method begins by initializing the weight matrices to random values and setting up other important variables. Once the initialization is complete, the main loop can begin. The main loop presents the training patterns to the neural network and calculates errors based on the results obtained from the neural network. The winning neuron has been determined. Once the winning neuron has been determined, that neuron is trained further consolidates its ability to recognize his particular pattern. At the end of the main loop, it is determined if further training will result in a better weight matrix. This is determined by calculating the improvement in error between this epoch and the previous epoch. If this improvement is negligible, this cycle is considered complete. To begin a new cycle, we initialize the weight matrix to random values and continue with new epochs.

As training progresses, we will likely encounter a situation where certain neurons never win, regardless of which pattern is being presented. We would like all output neurons to participate in the classification of the pattern, so we also execute a method that assists non-winning neurons in better adapting to some of the training data. This process will be discussed later in this section.

As further cycles progress, we keep track of which cycle had best error rate. Once we find a weight matrix that is below the specified desired error level, training is complete. If we never find a weight matrix below the specified error level, then training will be complete when the number of cycles exceeds the maximum number of cycles specified. If this happens, then we will take the best weight matrix that was determined in previous cycles.

The processes of evaluating errors, adjusting weights, and forcing non-winning neurons to win, are all individual processes that are isolated as external methods. We will now examine each of these processes. We will begin by examining how the errors are evaluated. Listing 6.15 shows how errors are evaluated.

Listing 6.15: Evaluate Errors (KohonenNetwork.java)

```java
/**
 * This method does much of the work of the learning process.
 * This method evaluates the weights against the training
 * set.
 *
 * @param rate learning rate
 * @param learn_method method(0=additive, 1=subtractive)
 * @param won a Holds how many times a given neuron won
 * @param bigerr a returns the error
 * @param correc a returns the correction
 * @param work a work area
 * @exception java.lang.RuntimeException
 */
void evaluateErrors (
                  double rate ,
                  int learn_method ,
                  int won[],
                  double bigerr[] ,
                  double correc[][] ,
                  double work[])
throws RuntimeException
{
  int best, size,tset ;
  double dptr[], normfac[] = new double[1];
  double synth[]=new double[1], cptr[], wptr[], length, diff ;


  // reset correction and winner counts
```

```java
for ( int y=0;y<correc.length;y++ ) {
  for ( int x=0;x<correc[0].length;x++ ) {
    correc[y][x]=0;
  }
}

for ( int i=0;i<won.length;i++ )
  won[i]=0;
bigerr[0] = 0.0;

// loop through all training sets to determine correction

for ( tset=0 ; tset<train.getTrainingSetCount(); tset++ ) {
  dptr = train.getInputSet(tset);
  best = winner ( dptr , normfac , synth ) ;
  won[best]++;
  wptr = outputWeights[best];
  cptr = correc[best];
  length = 0.0 ;

  for ( int i=0 ; i<inputNeuronCo the unt ; i++ ) {
    diff = dptr[i] * normfac[0] - wptr[i] ;
    length += diff * diff ;
    if ( learn_method!=0 )
      cptr[i] += diff ;
    else
      work[i] = rate * dptr[i] * normfac[0] + wptr[i] ;
  }
  diff = synth[0] - wptr[inputNeuronCount] ;
  length += diff * diff ;
  if ( learn_method!=0 )
    cptr[inputNeuronCount] += diff ;
  else
    work[inputNeuronCount] = rate * synth[0] +
      wptr[inputNeuronCount] ;
  if ( length > bigerr[0] )
    bigerr[0] = length ;

  if ( learn_method==0 ) {
    normalizeWeight( work ) ;
    for ( int i=0 ; i<=inputNeuronCount ; i++ )
      cptr[i] += work[i] - wptr[i] ;
  }
}
bigerr[0] = Math.sqrt ( bigerr[0] ) ;
}
```

The "evaluateErrors" method is used to evaluate how well the network is training and to create a correction array that contains the corrections that will be made by the adjustWeights method. This method works by presenting each of the training elements to the network. For each of these elements presented, we track which output neuron "won". This winning neuron is then adjusted so that it will respond even better to the training set the next time. This causes neurons to consolidate their win.

An array, named won, is kept which keeps a count of how many times each neuron wins. Later this array will be used to help neurons that failed to ever win. These neurons will be reassigned to remove some of the burden from output neurons that are already winning "too much". This process will be discussed later in this chapter.

Once the correction has been calculated, the weights must be adjusted by this correction. Listing 6.16 shows how the weights are adjusted.

Listing 6.16: Adjust Weights (KohonenNetwork.java)

```
/**
 * This method is called at the end of a training iteration.
 * This method adjusts the weights based on the previous trial.
 *
 * @param rate learning rate
 * @param learn_method method(0=additive, 1=subtractive)
 * @param won holds number of times each neuron won
 * @param bigcorr holds the error
 * @param correc holds the correction
 */
void adjustWeights (
                    double rate ,
                    int learn_method ,
                    int won[] ,
                    double bigcorr[],
                    double correc[][]
                    )

{
  double corr, cptr[], wptr[], length, f ;

  bigcorr[0] = 0.0 ;

  for ( int i=0 ; i<outputNeuronCount ; i++ ) {

    if ( won[i]==0 )
      continue ;

    wptr = outputWeights[i];
    cptr = correc[i];
```

```
      f = 1.0 / (double) won[i] ;
      if ( learn_method!=0 )
        f *= rate ;

      length = 0.0 ;

      for ( int j=0 ; j<=inputNeuronCount ; j++ ) {
        corr = f * cptr[j] ;
        wptr[j] += corr ;
        length += corr * corr ;
      }

      if ( length > bigcorr[0] )
        bigcorr[0] = length ;
    }
    // scale the correction
    bigcorr[0] = Math.sqrt ( bigcorr[0] ) / rate ;
}
```

As you can see from the above code, the correction is scaled by the learning rate. Training occurs by adjusting the winning neuron. Sometimes there will be neurons that fail to ever win. Listing 6.17 shows the process that is used to force a neuron to win.

Listing 6.17: Force a Winning Neuron

```
/**
 * If no neuron wins, then force a winner.
 *
 * @param won how many times each neuron won
 * @exception java.lang.RuntimeException
 */
void forceWin(
              int won[]
              )
throws RuntimeException
{
  int i, tset, best, size, which=0;
  double dptr[], normfac[]=new double[1] ;
  double synth[] = new double[1], dist, optr[];

  size = inputNeuronCount + 1 ;

  dist = 1.E30 ;
  for ( tset=0 ; tset<train.getTrainingSetCount() ; tset++ ) {
    dptr = train.getInputSet(tset);
    best = winner ( dptr , normfac , synth ) ;
    if ( output[best] < dist ) {
```

```
        dist = output[best] ;
        which = tset ;
      }
  }

  dptr = train.getInputSet(which);
  best = winner ( dptr , normfac , synth ) ;

  dist = -1.e30 ;
  i = outputNeuronCount;
  while ( (i--)>0 ) {
    if ( won[i]!=0 )
      continue ;
    if ( output[i] > dist ) {
      dist = output[i] ;
      which = i ;
    }
  }

  optr = outputWeights[which];

  System.arraycopy(dptr,
                   0,
                   optr,
                   0,
                   dptr.length);

  optr[inputNeuronCount] = synth[0] / normfac[0] ;
  normalizeWeight ( optr ) ;
}
```

There are three steps that must be carried out to handle output neurons that are failing to ever learn. First we must loop through the entire training set and find the training set pattern the causes the least activation. This training set is considered to be the least well represented by the current winning neurons.

The second step, is to choose an output neuron that will be modified to better classify the training set identified in the previous step. This is done by looping through every output neuron that did not ever win, and seeing which one has the highest activation for the training pattern identified in step one. Finally, in the third step, we will modify the weight of this neuron so that it will better classify this pattern next time.

You have now seen how the Kohonen neural network was implemented. In the next section, you will be shown a simple example program that tests the classes that were just presented. In Chapter 7 you will be shown a complete example that will recognize hand-written characters.

Using the Kohonen Neural Network

We will now examine a simple program that trains a Kohonen neural network. As the network is trained, you are shown a graphical display of the weights. The output from this program is shown in Figure 6.3.

Figure 6.3: Training a Kohonen Neural Network

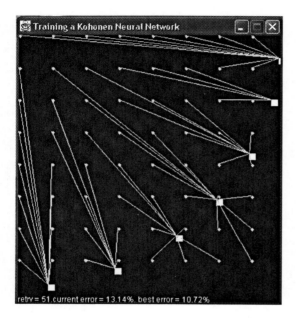

This program contains two input neurons and seven output neurons. Each of the seven output neurons are plotted as white squares. The x-dimension shows their weight to the first input neuron and the y-dimension shows their weight to the second input neuron. You will see the boxes move as training progresses.

You will also see lines from select points on a grid drawn to each of the squares. These identify which output neuron is winning for the x and y coordinates of that point. This shows points with similar x and y coordinates being recognized by the same output neuron.

We will now examine the example program. The program begins by defining certain properties that will be used by the program. This is shown in Listing 6.18.

Listing 6.18: Properties of the Kohonen Example (TestKohonen.java)

```
import java.awt.*;
import javax.swing.*;
import java.text.*;

public class TestKohonen
```

```
extends JFrame
implements NeuralReportable,Runnable {

public static final int INPUT_COUNT=2;
public static final int OUTPUT_COUNT=7;
public static final int SAMPLE_COUNT=100;
protected int unitLength;
protected int retry=1;
protected double totalError=0;
protected double bestError = 0;
protected KohonenNetwork net;
protected TrainingSet ts;
protected Image offScreen;
```

You can modify some of the final constants. You can choose a larger training set by setting the SAMPLE_COUNT variable to other values. You can change the OUTPUT_COUNT to values other than 7 as well. You may not change the INPUT_COUNT due to the fact that the x and y coordinates are tied to the inputs. Since you only have two dimensions, you may not increase or decrease this value.

A constructor is provided to create the window and center it on the screen. This constructor is shown in Listing 6.19.

Listing 6.19: Construct the Example (TestKohonen.java)

```
/**
 * The constructor sets up the position and size of
 * the window.
 */
TestKohonen()
{
  setTitle("Training a Kohonen Neural Network");
  setSize(400,450);
  Toolkit toolkit = Toolkit.getDefaultToolkit();
  Dimension d = toolkit.getScreenSize();
  setLocation(
            (int)(d.width-this.getSize().getWidth())/2,
            (int)(d.height-this.getSize().getHeight())/2 );
  setDefaultCloseOperation(WindowConstants.DISPOSE_ON_CLOSE);
  setResizable(false);
}
```

The update method is provided because we implemented the NeuralReportable interface. The update method will be called for each epoch during training. Here, we record the status values and require that the window be redrawn. This is shown in Listing 6.20.

Listing 6.20: Receive Status Information (TestKohonen.java)

```java
/**
 * Update is called by the neural network as the
 * network is trained.
 *
 * @param retry What the retry number this is.
 * @param totalError The error for this retry.
 * @param bestError The best error so far.
 */
public void update(int retry,double totalError,double bestError)
{
  this.retry = retry;
  this.totalError = totalError;
  this.bestError = bestError;
  this.paint(null);
}
```

This example is a multithreaded program. A background thread is used to train the neural network. Multithreading was discussed in much greater detail in Chapter 5. The background thread is shown in Listing 6.21.

Listing 6.21: The Background Thread (TestKohonen.java)

```java
/**
 * Called to run the background thread.  The background thread
 * sets up the neural network and training data and begins
 * training the network.
 */
public void run()
{
  // build the training set
  ts = new TrainingSet(INPUT_COUNT,OUTPUT_COUNT);
  ts.setTrainingSetCount(SAMPLE_COUNT);

  for ( int i=0;i<SAMPLE_COUNT;i++ ) {
    for ( int j=0;j<INPUT_COUNT;j++ ) {
      ts.setInput(i,j,Math.random());
    }
  }

  // build and train the neural network
  net = new KohonenNetwork(INPUT_COUNT,OUTPUT_COUNT,this);
  net.setTrainingSet(ts);
  net.learn();
}
```

The first thing that the run method does, is to create random training sets. This will give the neural network a random sampling of training items that it must attempt to classify. Next, the learn method of the neural network is called to begin the training process.

As the program runs, a graph must be displayed of the neuron weights. Listing 6.22 shows the method that is responsible for drawing this graph.

Listing 6.22: Graph the Neuron Weights (TestKohonen.java)

```java
/**
 * Display the progress of the neural network.
 *
 * @param g A graphics object.
 */
public void paint(Graphics g)
{
  if ( net==null )
    return;
  if ( offScreen==null ) {
    offScreen = this.createImage(
      (int)getBounds().getWidth(),
      (int)getBounds().getHeight());
  }
  g = offScreen.getGraphics();
  int width = (int)getContentPane().bounds().getWidth();
  int height = (int)getContentPane().bounds().getHeight();
  unitLength = Math.min(width,height);
  g.setColor(Color.black);
  g.fillRect(0,0,width,height);

  // plot the weights of the output neurons
  g.setColor(Color.white);
  for ( int y=0;y<net.outputWeights.length;y++ ) {

    g.fillRect((int)(net.outputWeights[y][0]*unitLength),
               (int)(net.outputWeights[y][1]*unitLength),10,10);

  }

  // plot a grid of samples to test the net with
  g.setColor(Color.green);
  for ( int y=0;y<unitLength;y+=50 ) {
    for ( int x=0;x<unitLength;x+=50 ) {
      g.fillOval(x,y,5,5);
      double d[] = new double[2];
      d[0]=x;
      d[1]=y;
      double normfac[] = new double[1];
```

```
        double synth[] = new double[1];
        int c = net.winner(d,normfac,synth);


        int x2=(int)(net.outputWeights[c][0]*unitLength);
        int y2=(int)(net.outputWeights[c][1]*unitLength);

        g.drawLine(x,y,x2,y2);
    }

}

// display the status info
g.setColor(Color.white);
NumberFormat nf = NumberFormat.getInstance();
nf.setMaximumFractionDigits(2);
nf.setMinimumFractionDigits(2);
g.drawString(
            "retry = "
            + retry
            + ",current error = "
            + nf.format(totalError*100)
            +  "%, best error = "
            + nf.format(bestError*100)
            +"%", 0,
            (int)getContentPane().getBounds().getHeight());
getContentPane().getGraphics().drawImage(offScreen,0,0,this);

}
```

First an off-screen image is created using the createImage method provided by Java. All of our drawing will be to this off-screen image. Once the graph is complete, the off-screen image will be drawn to the window. This prevents flicker as the program constantly redraws itself.

Next, the output neurons are drawn as white rectangles. The x and y coordinates for these neurons are obtained from the weight between the output neuron and one of the two input neurons.

Finally, a grid of samples is drawn onto the screen. This is just a typical grid with each dot being 50 pixels from the other dots. When the network is presented with the x and y coordinates from this grid, lines are then from each of these dots to the winning neuron. To start this program a simple main method is provided as seen in Listing 6.23.

Listing 6.23: Start the program (TestKohonen.java)

```java
/**
 * Startup the program.
 *
 * @param args Not used.
 */
public static void main(String args[])
{
  TestKohonen app = new TestKohonen();
  app.show();
  Thread t = new Thread(app);
  t.setPriority(Thread.MIN_PRIORITY);
  t.start();
}
}
```

This main method begins by displaying the window. Then, a background thread is created.

Summary

In this chapter we learned about the Kohonen neural network. The Kohonen neural network differs from the feedforward backpropagation network in several ways. The Kohonen neural network is trained in an unsupervised way. This means that the Kohonen neural network is given input data but no anticipated output. The Kohonen neural network then begins to map the training samples to each of its output neurons during training.

A Kohonen neural network contains only two levels. The network is presented with an input pattern that is given to the input layer. This input pattern must be normalized to numbers in the range between -1 and 1. The output from this neural network will be one single winning output neuron. The output neurons can be thought of as groups that the Kohonen neural network has classified.

Training a Kohonen neural network is considerably different than the backpropagation algorithm that we examined in Chapter 5. To train the Kohonen neural network we present it with the training elements and see which output neuron "wins". This winning neuron's weights are then modified so that it will activate higher on the pattern that caused it to win.

There is also a case where there may be one or more neurons that fail to ever win. Such neurons are dead-weight to the neural network. We must identify such neurons and cause them to recognize patterns that are already recognized by other more "overworked" neurons. This causes the burden of recognition to fall more evenly over the output neurons.

This chapter presented only a simple example of the Kohonen neural network. In the next chapter we will apply the Kohonen neural network to a more real-world application. We will see how to use the Kohonen neural network to recognize handwriting.

CHAPTER 7: OCR WITH THE KOHONEN NEURAL NETWORK

Chapter Highlights
- **What is OCR**
- **Cropping an Image**
- **Downsampling an Image**
- **Training the Neural Network to Recognize Characters**
- **Recalling Characters**
- **A "Commercial-Grade" OCR Application**

In the previous chapter, you learned how to construct a Kohonen neural network. You learned that a Kohonen neural network can be used to classify samples into several groups. In this chapter, we will closely examine a specific application of the Kohonen neural network. The Kohonen neural network will be applied to Optical Character Recognition (OCR).

OCR programs are capable of reading printed text. This could be text that was scanned in from a document, or hand written text that was drawn on a hand-held device, such as a Personal Digital Assistant (PDA). OCR programs are used widely in many industries. One of the largest users of OCR systems, is the United States Postal Service. In the 1970's and 1980's, the US Postal Service had many Letter Sorting Machines (LSMs). These machines were manned by human clerks that would key the zip codes of sixty letters per minute.

These human letter sorters have now been completely replaced by computerized letter sorting machines. This new generation of letter sorting machines are enabled with OCR technology. These machines scan the incoming letters and read the zip code. Using the ZIP code, these letters can be routed to their correct destination cities.

This chapter will develop an example program that can be trained to recognize human handwriting. We will not create a program that can scan pages of text. Rather, this program will read character by character, as the user draws them. This function will be similar to the handwriting recognition used by many PDA's.

The OCR Application

Once launched, the OCR application will display a simple GUI interface that will allow you both to train and use the neural network. This program is shown in Figure 7.1.

Figure 7.1: The OCR Application

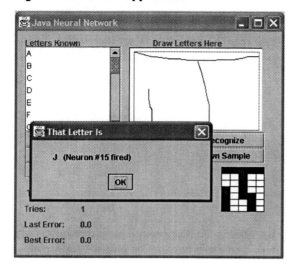

Once started, this program is not immediately ready to recognize letters. This program must first be trained from actual drawn letters before it is able to recognize your input. Letter training files are stored in the same directory as the OCR application. The name of the training sample is "sample.dat".

If you downloaded the "sample.dat" file from Heaton Research, it contains handwriting samples for the author of this book. If you use this "sample.dat" file to recognize your own handwriting your results may be worse than if you had created a training file based on your own handwriting. Creating a sample based on your own handwriting will be covered in the next section. For now, you are probably anxious to see this program recognize handwriting, so we will begin by showing you how to do that.

To make use of the provided "sample.dat" file, you should click the "Load" button on the OCR application. This will attempt to load a handwriting file named "sample.dat". You should see a small message box indicating that the file was loaded successfully. Now that the file has been loaded, you should see all of the letters listed that the program has been trained for. This example training file only contains entries for the capital versions of the 26 letters of the Latin alphabet.

Now that the letters have been loaded, you must train the neural network. By clicking the "Train" button, the application will begin the training process. The training process may take anywhere from a few seconds to several minutes, depending on the speed of your computer. Once training is complete, you will be shown a small message box that will state that training is complete.

Using the Sample Program to Recognize Letters

Now that you have a training set loaded and the neural network has been trained, you are ready to recognize characters. The user interface used to recognize the characters is very easy to use. You simply draw the character that you would like to be recognized in the large rectangular region labeled "Draw Letters Here". Once you have drawn the letter you can select several different options.

The letters that you draw are downsampled before they are recognized. This is because the letter that you have drawn is too high of a resolution to be understood by the neural network. By down sampling the image, the image is mapped into a small grid which is five pixels wide and seven pixels high. If you click the "Downsample" button, you can see the downsampled version of your letter. Clicking the "Clear" button will cause the drawing and downsampled regions to be cleared.

You will also notice that a box is drawn around your letter when you down sample. This is a cropping box. The purpose of the cropping box is to cut out any white space that is not essential to the image. This also has the desirable effect of causing the program to not care about the position of the letter. You could draw the letter in the center, near the top, or some other location, and the program would still recognize the letter the same way.

If you would like to actually recognize a letter, you should use the "Recognize" button. Drawing a letter to the letter input area and clicking the "Recognize" button will cause the application to downsample your letter and then attempt to recognize it using the Kohonen neural network. The advantage of downsampling to such a size is two fold. First, the lower resolution image requires fewer input neurons than would a full-sized image. Secondly, by downsampling everything to a constant size, it does not matter how large, or how small, you draw the image to be trained or recognized. By downsampling the image, the size is neutralized.

The pattern will then be presented to the Kohonen neural network and the winning neuron will be selected. Chapter 7 introduced you to Kohonen neural networks. If you recall from Chapter 7, a Kohonen neural network has several output neurons. One of these output neurons will be selected as a winner for each pattern of data that is entered. The number of output neurons that was chosen for the Kohonen neural network used by this program matches the number of letters that are in the sample set. Because there are 26 letters in the sample set, there will be 26 output neurons.

The input for the neural network comes from the down sampled image. The exact process for how the downsampled image will be presented to the neural network will be discussed in the next section. The program will respond to the letter you entered by telling you both which neuron fired, and also which letter the program believes that you have entered.

I have found that using my own handwriting, this program generally achieves approximately an 80-90% success rate. If the program is not recognizing your letters ensure that you are writing clear capital letters. You may also try training the neural network to recognize your own handwriting, as covered in the next section.

Training the Sample Program to Recognize Letters

You may find that the program does not recognize your handwriting as well as you think that it should. This could be because the program was trained using the author's own handwriting. Perhaps my handwriting is not representative of the entire population. My earlier grade school teachers would surely agree to that. In this section you will learn to train the network to recognize your own handwriting.

You have two choices as to how to train the neural network program. You can choose to start from a blank training set and enter all 26 letters for yourself, or you can also choose to start from my training set. If you start from my training set, you can replace individual letters. This would be a good approach if the network were recognizing most of your characters, but failing on a small set. You could retrain the neural network for the letters that the program was failing to understand.

To delete a letter that the training set already has listed, you should select that letter and press the "Delete" button on the OCR application. Not that this is the GUI's "Delete" button and not the delete button on your computer's keyboard.

To add new letters to the training set, you should draw your letter in the drawing input area. Once your letter is drawn you can click the "Add" button. This will prompt you for the actual letter that you just drew. The character you type for this prompt will be displayed to you when the OCR application recognizes the letter that you just drew.

Now that you have your training set complete, you should save it. This is done by clicking the "Save" button on the OCR application. This will save the training set to the file "sample. dat". If you already have a file named "sample.dat", it will be overwritten. Because of this, it is important to make a copy of your previous training file if you would like to keep it. If you exit the OCR application without saving your training data, it will be lost. When you launch the OCR application again, you can click "Load" to retrieve the data you stored in the "sample. dat" file.

In the previous two sections you learned how to use the OCR application. As you can see, it is adept at recognizing characters that you have entered. This demonstrates a good use of the Kohonen neural network.

Implementing the OCR Program

We will now see how the OCR program was implemented. There are several classes that make up the OCR application. The purposes of each of the files that make up the OCR application are summarized in Table 7.1.

Table 7.1: Classes for the OCR Application

Class	Purpose
Entry	The drawing area that allows the user to draw letters.
KohonenNetwork	The Kohonen neural network (covered in Chapter 6).
MainEntry	The main frame the application, this class starts the OCR application.
Network	Generic neural network functions not specific to the Kohonen neural network(Covered in Chapter 6).
NeuralReportable	The interface that specifies how a neural network reports its progress.
Sample	Used to display a down sampled image.
SampleData	Used to actually hold a down sampled image.
TrainingSet	The training data for a neural network (covered in Chapter 6).

We will now examine each section of the program. We will begin by examining the process by which the user draws an image.

Drawing Images

Though not directly related to neural networks, the process by which the user is allowed to draw the characters is an important part of the OCR application. We will examine that process in this section. The code that allows the user to draw an image is contained in the Sample.java file, which can be seen in Listing 7.1.

Listing 7.1: Drawing Images (Sample.java)

```
import javax.swing.*;
import java.awt.*;
import java.awt.event.*;
import java.awt.image.*;

public class Entry extends JPanel {

  protected Image entryImage;
  protected Graphics entryGraphics;
  protected int lastX = -1;
  protected int lastY = -1;
  protected Sample sample;
  protected int downSampleLeft;
  protected int downSampleRight;
  protected int downSampleTop;
  protected int downSampleBottom;
  protected double ratioX;
```

```
protected double ratioY;
protected int pixelMap[];

Entry()
{
  enableEvents(AWTEvent.MOUSE_MOTION_EVENT_MASK|
               AWTEvent.MOUSE_EVENT_MASK|
               AWTEvent.COMPONENT_EVENT_MASK);
}

protected void initImage()
{
  entryImage = createImage(getWidth(),getHeight());
  entryGraphics = entryImage.getGraphics();
  entryGraphics.setColor(Color.white);
  entryGraphics.fillRect(0,0,getWidth(),getHeight());
}

public void paint(Graphics g)
{
  if ( entryImage==null )
    initImage();
  g.drawImage(entryImage,0,0,this);
  g.setColor(Color.black);
  g.drawRect(0,0,getWidth(),getHeight());
  g.setColor(Color.red);
  g.drawRect(downSampleLeft,
             downSampleTop,
             downSampleRight-downSampleLeft,
             downSampleBottom-downSampleTop);

}

protected void processMouseEvent(MouseEvent e)
{
  if ( e.getID()!=MouseEvent.MOUSE_PRESSED )
    return;
  lastX = e.getX();
  lastY = e.getY();
}

protected void processMouseMotionEvent(MouseEvent e)
{
  if ( e.getID()!=MouseEvent.MOUSE_DRAGGED )
    return;
```

```
    entryGraphics.setColor(Color.black);
    entryGraphics.drawLine(lastX,lastY,e.getX(),e.getY());
    getGraphics().drawImage(entryImage,0,0,this);
    lastX = e.getX();
    lastY = e.getY();
  }

  public void setSample(Sample s)
  {
    sample = s;
  }

  public Sample getSample()
  {
    return sample;
  }

  protected boolean hLineClear(int y)
  {
    int w = entryImage.getWidth(this);
    for ( int i=0;i<w;i++ ) {
      if ( pixelMap[(y*w)+i] !=-1 )
        return false;
    }
    return true;
  }


  public void clear()
  {
    this.entryGraphics.setColor(Color.white);
    this.entryGraphics.fillRect(0,0,getWidth(),getHeight());
    this.downSampleBottom =
    this.downSampleTop =
    this.downSampleLeft =
    this.downSampleRight = 0;
    repaint();
  }
}
```

This class defines a number of properties. These variables are described here in table 7.2.

Table 7.2: Variables for the OCR Application

Variable	Purpose
downSampleBottom	The bottom of the clipping region, used during down sampling.
downSampleLeft	The left side of the cropping region, used during down sampling.
downSampleRight	The right side of the cropping region, used during down sampling.
downSampleTop	The top side of the cropping region, used during down sampling.
entryGraphics	A graphics object that allows drawing to the image that corresponds to the drawing area.
entryImage	The image that holds the character that the user is drawing.
lastX	The last x coordinate that the user was drawing at.
lastY	The last y coordinate that the user was drawing at.
pixelMap	Numeric pixel map that will be actually downsampled. This is taken directly from the entryImage.
ratioX	The downsample ratio for the x dimension.
ratioY	The downsample ratio for the y dimension.
sample	The object that will contain the downsampled image.

Most of the actual drawing is handled by the processMouseMotionEvent. If the mouse is being drug, then a line will be drawn from the last reported mouse drag position to the current mouse position. It is not enough to simply draw a dot. The mouse moves faster than the program has time to accept all values for. By drawing the line, we will cover any missed pixels as best we can. The line is drawn to the off-screen image, and then updated to the users screen. This is done with the following lines of code.

```
entryGraphics.setColor(Color.black);
entryGraphics.drawLine(lastX,lastY,e.getX(),e.getY());
getGraphics().drawImage(entryImage,0,0,this);
lastX = e.getX();
lastY = e.getY();
```

As the program runs, this method is called repeatedly. This causes whatever the user is drawing to be saved to the off-screen image. In the next section you will learn how to downsample an image. You will then see that the off-screen image from this section is accessed as an array of integers, allowing its "image data" to be worked with directly.

Downsampling the Image

Every time a letter is drawn for either training or recognition, it must be downsampled. In this section we will examine the process by which this downsampling occurs. However, before we discuss the downsampling process, we should discuss how these downsampled images are stored.

Storing Downsampled Images

Downsampled images are stored in the SampleData class. The SampleData class is shown in Listing 7.2.

Listing 7.2: Downsampled Image Data

```
public class SampleData implements Comparable,Cloneable {

  protected boolean grid[][];
  protected char letter;

  public SampleData(char letter,int width,int height)
  {
    grid = new boolean[width][height];
    this.letter = letter;
  }

  public void setData(int x,int y,boolean v)
  {
    grid[x][y]=v;
  }

  public boolean getData(int x,int y)
  {
    return grid[x][y];
  }

  public void clear()
  {
    for ( int x=0;x<grid.length;x++ )
      for ( int y=0;y<grid[0].length;y++ )
        grid[x][y]=false;
  }

  public int getHeight()
  {
    return grid[0].length;
  }

  public int getWidth()
```

```java
  {
    return grid.length;
  }

  public char getLetter()
  {
    return letter;
  }

  public void setLetter(char letter)
  {
    this.letter = letter;
  }

  public int compareTo(Object o)
  {
    SampleData obj = (SampleData)o;
    if ( this.getLetter()>obj.getLetter() )
      return 1;
    else
      return -1;
  }

  public String toString()
  {
    return ""+letter;
  }


  public Object clone()

  {
    SampleData obj = new SampleData(
      letter,
       getWidth(),
       getHeight());
    for ( int y=0;y<getHeight();y++ )
      for ( int x=0;x<getWidth();x++ )
        obj.setData(x,y,getData(x,y));
    return obj;
  }

}
```

As you can see, this class represents a grid of 5X7. All downsampled images will be stored in this class. The SampleData class also includes methods to set and get the data associated with the downsampled grid. The SampleData class also contains a method, named clone, that will create an exact duplicate of this image.

Negating Size and Position

All images are downsampled before being used. This prevents the neural network from being confused by size and position. The drawing area is large enough that you could draw a letter at several different sizes. By downsampling the image down to a consistent size, it will not matter how large you draw the letter, as the downsampled image will always remain a consistent size. This section shows you how this is done.

When you draw an image, the first thing that is done is the program draws a box around the boundary of your letter. This allows the program to eliminate all of the white space around your letter. This process is done inside of the "downsample" method of the "Entry" class. As you drew a character, the character was also drawn onto the "entryImage" instance variable of the Entry object. In order to crop this image, and eventually downsample it, we must grab the bit pattern of the image. This is done using a "PixelGrabber" class, as shown here

```
int w = entryImage.getWidth(this);
int h = entryImage.getHeight(this);

PixelGrabber grabber = new PixelGrabber(entryImage,
                                        0,0,w,h,true);
grabber.grabPixels();
pixelMap = (int[])grabber.getPixels();
```

After this code completes, the pixelMap variable, which is an array of int datatypes, contains the bit pattern of the image. The next step is to crop the image and remove any white space. Cropping is implemented by dragging four imaginary lines from the top, left, bottom and right sides of the image. These lines will stop as soon as they cross an actual pixel. By doing this, these four lines snap to the outer edges of the image. The hLineClear and vLineClear methods both accept a parameter that indicates the line to scan, and returns true if that line is clear. The program works by calling hLineClear and vLineClear until they cross the outer edges of the image. The horizontal line method (hLineClear) is shown here:

```
protected boolean hLineClear(int y)
{
  int w = entryImage.getWidth(this);
  for ( int i=0;i<w;i++ ) {
    if ( pixelMap[(y*w)+i] !=-1 )
      return false;
  }
  return true;
}
```

As you can see, the horizontal line method accepts a y coordinate that specifies the horizontal line to check. The program then loops through each x coordinate on that row, checking to see if there are any pixel values. The value of -1 indicates white, so it is ignored. The "findBounds" method uses "hLineClear" and "vLineClear" to calculate the four edges. The beginning of this method is shown here.

```java
protected void findBounds(int w,int h)
{
  // top line
  for ( int y=0;y<h;y++ ) {
    if ( !hLineClear(y) ) {
      downSampleTop=y;
      break;
    }

  }
  // bottom line
  for ( int y=h-1;y>=0;y-- ) {
    if ( !hLineClear(y) ) {
      downSampleBottom=y;
      break;
    }
  }
```

Here, you can see how the program calculates the top and bottom lines of the cropping rectangle. To calculate the top line of the cropping rectangle, the program starts at 0 and continues to the bottom of the image. As soon as the first non-clear line is found, then the program establishes this as the top of the clipping rectangle. The same process, only in reverse, is carried out to determine the bottom of the image. The processes to determine the left and right boundaries are carried out in the same way.

Performing the Downsample

Now that the cropping has taken place, the image must be actually downsampled. This involves taking the image from a larger resolution to a 5X7 resolution. To see how to reduce an image to 5X7, think of an imaginary grid being drawn over top of the high-resolution image. This divides the image into regions, five across and seven down. If any pixel in a region is filled, then the corresponding pixel in the 5X7 downsampled image is also filled it. Most of the work done by this process is accomplished inside of the "downSampleRegion" method. This method is shown here.

```java
protected boolean downSampleRegion(int x,int y)
{
  int w = entryImage.getWidth(this);
  int startX = (int)(downSampleLeft+(x*ratioX));
  int startY = (int)(downSampleTop+(y*ratioY));
  int endX = (int)(startX + ratioX);
```

```
    int endY = (int)(startY + ratioY);

    for ( int yy=startY;yy<=endY;yy++ ) {
      for ( int xx=startX;xx<=endX;xx++ ) {
        int loc = xx+(yy*w);

        if ( pixelMap[ loc ]!= -1 )
          return true;
      }
    }

    return false;
}
```

The "downSampleRegion" method accepts the region number that should be calculated. First, the starting and ending x and y coordinates must be calculated. To calculate the first x coordinate for the specified region, first the "downSampleLeft" is used, this is the left side of the cropping rectangle. Then x is multiplied by "ratioX", which is the ratio of how many pixels make up each region. This allows us to determine where to place "startX". The starting y position, "startY", is calculated by similar means. Next, the program loops through every x and y covered by the specified region. If even one pixel is determined to be filled, then the method returns true, which indicates that this region should be considered filled. The "downSampleRegion" method is called in succession for each region in the image. This results in a sample of the image, stored in the "SampleData" class. The class is a wrapper class that contains a 5X7 array of Boolean values. It is this structure that forms the input for both training and character recognition.

Using the Kohonen Neural Network

There are many different types of neural networks. Most are named after their creators. The neural network that will be used in this chapter is a Kohonen neural network. The character downsampled pattern that is drawn by the user is fed to the input neurons. There is one input neuron for every pixel in the downsampled image. Because the downsampled image is a 5X7 grid, there are 35 input neurons.

The output neurons are how the neural network communicates which letter it thinks the user drew. The number of output neurons always matches the number of unique letter samples that were provided. Since 26 letters were provided in the sample, there will be 26 output neurons. If this program were modified to support multiple samples per individual letter, there would still be 26 output neurons.

In addition to input and output neurons, there are also connections between the individual neurons. These connections are not all equal. Each connection is assigned a weight. The assignment of these weights is ultimately the only factor that will determine what the network will output for a given input pattern. In order to determine the total number of connections, you must multiply the number of input neurons by the number of output neurons. A neural network with 26 output neurons and 35 input neurons would have a total of 910 connection weights. The training process is dedicated to finding the correct values for these weights.

The recognition process begins when the user draws a character and then clicks the "Recognize" button. First the letter is downsampled to a 5X7 image. This downsampled image must be copied from its 2-dimensional array to an array of doubles that will be fed to the input neurons, as seen here.

```
entry.downSample();

double input[] = new double[5*7];
int idx=0;
SampleData ds = sample.getData();
for ( int y=0;y<ds.getHeight();y++ ) {
    for ( int x=0;x<ds.getWidth();x++ ) {
        input[idx++] = ds.getData(x,y)?.5:-.5;
    }
}
```

The above code does this conversion. Neurons require floating point input. As a result, the program feeds it the value of 5 for a black pixel and -5 for a white pixel. The 5X7 array of 35 values is fed to the input neurons. This is done by passing the input array to the Kohonen's "winner" method. This will return which of the 35 neurons won, and is stored in the "best" integer.

```
int best = net.winner ( input , normfac , synth ) ;
char map[] = mapNeurons();

JOptionPane.showMessageDialog(this,
    "  " + map[best] + "    (Neuron #"
    + best + " fired)","That Letter Is",
    JOptionPane.PLAIN_MESSAGE) ;
```

Knowing the winning neuron is not too helpful, because it does not show you which letter was actually recognized. To line the neurons up to their recognized letters, each letter image that the network was trained for must be fed into the network and the winning neuron determined. For example, if you were to feed the training image for "J" into the neural network, and the winning neuron were neuron #4, you would know that neuron #4 is the neuron that had learned to recognize J's pattern. This is done by calling the "mapNeurons" method. The mapNeurons method returns an array of characters. The index of each array element corresponds to the neuron number that recognizes that character.

Most of the actual work performed by the neural network is done in the winner() method. The first thing that the winner method does, is normalize the inputs, then calculate the output value of each output neuron. Whichever output neuron has the largest output value is considered the winner. First, the "biggest" variable is set to a very small number to indicate that there is not yet a winner.

```
biggest = -1.E30;
for ( i=0 ; i<outputNeuronCount; i++ ) {
  optr = outputWeights[i];
  output[i] = dotProduct (input , optr ) * normfac[0]
              + synth[0] * optr[inputNeuronCount] ;
  // Remap to bipolar(-1,1 to 0,1)
  output[i] = 0.5 * (output[i] + 1.0) ;
  if ( output[i] > biggest ) {
    biggest = output[i] ;
    win = i ;
  }
}
```

Each output neuron's weight is calculated by taking the dot product of each of the output neuron weights to the input neurons. The dot product is calculated by multiplying each of the input neuron's input values against the weights between that input neuron and the output neuron. These weights were determined during training, which is discussed in the next section. The output is kept, and if it is the largest output so far, it is set as the "winning" neuron.

As you can see, getting the results from a neural network is a very quick process. Actually determining the weights of the neurons is the complex portion of the this process. Training the neural network is discussed in the following section.

Training the Neural Network

Learning is the process of selecting a neuron weight matrix that will correctly recognize input patterns. A Kohonen neural network learns by constantly evaluating and optimizing a weight matrix. To do this, a starting weight matrix must be determined. This starting weight matrix is chosen by selecting random numbers. Of course, this is a terrible choice for a weight matrix, but it gives a starting point to optimize from.

Once the initial random weight matrix is created the training can begin. First the weight matrix is evaluated to determine what its current error level is. This error is determined by how well the training inputs (the letters that you created) map to the output neurons. The error is calculated by the "evaluateErrors" method of the KohonenNetwork class. When the error level is low, say below 10%, the process is complete.

The training process begins when the user clicks the "Begin Training" button. This begins the training by method calculates the number of input and output neurons. First, the number of input neurons is determined from the size of the downsampled image. Since the height is seven and the width is five, the number of input neurons will be 35. The number of output neurons matches how many characters the program has been given.

This is the part of the program that would be modified if you wanted to cause the program to accept more than one sample per letter to train from. For example, if you wanted to accept 4 samples per letter, you would have to make sure that the output neuron count remained 26, even though 104 input samples were provided to train with–4 for each of the 26 letters.

```
int inputNeuron = MainEntry.DOWNSAMPLE_HEIGHT*
  MainEntry.DOWNSAMPLE_WIDTH;
int outputNeuron = letterListModel.size();
```

Now that the size of the neural network has been determined, the training set and neural network must be constructed. The training set is constructed to hold the correct number of "samples". This will be the 26 letters provided.

```
TrainingSet set = new TrainingSet(inputNeuron,outputNeuron);
set.setTrainingSetCount(letterListModel.size());
```

Next, the downsampled input images are copied to the training set. This is repeated for all 26 input patterns.

```
for ( int t=0;t<letterListModel.size();t++ ) {
  int idx=0;
  SampleData ds = (SampleData)letterListModel.getElementAt(t);
  for ( int y=0;y<ds.getHeight();y++ ) {
    for ( int x=0;x<ds.getWidth();x++ ) {
      set.setInput(t,idx++,ds.getData(x,y)?.5:-.5);
    }
  }
}
```

Finally, the neural network is constructed and the training set is assigned. With a training set assigned, the "learn" method can be called. This will adjust the weight matrix until the network is trained.

```
net = new KohonenNetwork(inputNeuron,outputNeuron,this);
net.setTrainingSet(set);
net.learn();
```

The main loop of the learn method will now be discussed. The learn method will loop up to an unspecified number of iterations. Because this program only has one sample per output neuron it is unlikely that it will take more than one iteration. When the number of training samples matches the output neuron count, training happens very quickly. The while loop begins with "iter" at zero and continues. There is no middle part to the for loop, as the decision to quit is made inside of the while-loop.

```
n_retry = 0 ;
for ( iter=0 ; ; iter++ ) {
```

A method, called "evaluateErrors" is called to evaluate how well the current weights are working. This is determined by looking at how well the training data spreads across the output neurons. If many output neurons are activating for the same training pattern, then the weight set is not a good one. Based on this, an error rate is calculated, which is based on how well the training sets are spreading across the output neurons.

```
evaluateErrors ( rate , learnMethod , won ,
                 bigerr , correc , work ) ;
```

Once the error is determined, we must see if it is below the best error we've seen so far. If it is below that error, then this error is copied to the best error, and the neuron weights are preserved.

```
totalError = bigerr[0] ;
```

```
if ( totalError < best_err ) {
  best_err = totalError ;
  copyWeights ( bestnet , this ) ;
}
```

The total number of winning neurons is then calculated. This will allow us to determine if no output neurons activated. Additionally, if the error is below the accepted quit error (10%), the training stops.

```
winners = 0 ;
for ( i=0;i<won.length;i++ )
  if ( won[i]!=0 )
    winners++;

if ( bigerr[0] < quitError )
  break ;
```

If there is not an acceptable number of winners, one neuron is then forced to win.

```
if ( (winners < outputNeuronCount)  &&
     (winners < train.getTrainingSetCount()) ) {
  forceWin ( won ) ;
  continue ;
}
```

Now that the first weight matrix has been evaluated, it is adjusted based on its error. The adjustment is slight, based on the correction that was calculated when the error was determined. This two-step process of calculating the error and adjusting the weight matrix is continued until the error falls below 10%.

```
adjustWeights(rate , learnMethod , won , bigcorr, correc ) ;
```

This is the process by which a neural network is trained. The method for adjusting the weights and calculating the error is shown in the "KohonenNetwork.java" file.

Beyond this Example

The program presented here is only capable of recognizing individual letters at a time. Also, the sample data provided only includes support for the uppercase letters of the Latin alphabet. There is nothing in this program that would prevent you from using both upper and lower case characters, as well as digits. If you trained the program for two sets of 26 letters and ten digits, the program would use 62 training sets.

You would quickly run into a few problems. The program would have a very hard time determining the difference between the lower case letter "o", the capital letter "O" and the digit zero (0). The problem of discerning between these letters would not be handled by the Kohonen network. For this, you would have to examine the context of the letters around them.

If the program were to be expanded to process entire pages of writing at a time many layers of complexity would be added. Even if the page were only text, it would be necessary for the program to determine where each line begins and ends. Additionally, spaces between letters would need to be located so that the individual characters can be fed to the Kohonen neural network for processing.

If the image being scanned is not pure text, then the job becomes even more complex. It would be necessary for the program to scan around the borders of text and graphics. Some lines may be in different fonts, and thus be of different sizes. All of these issues would need to be considered to extend this program to a commercial grade OCR application.

Another limitation of this example program, is that only one drawing can be defined per character. You might want to take three different handwriting samples for a letter, rather than just one. The underlying Kohonen network classes would easily support this feature. This is something which could be added to the user interface with a few more classes. To do this you would have to allow the program to accept more training data than the number of output neurons.

As you can see, there are many considerations that would have to be made to expand this application into a commercial grade application. You would not be able to use just a single neural network. It would likely be that you would be using several different types of neural networks for the tasks previously mentioned.

Summary

In this chapter you saw a practical application of the Kohonen neural network. You were introduced to the concept of OCR and saw what uses this technology might have. This chapter focused around creating an application that mimics the OCR capabilities of a PDA.

Characters are accepted by allowing the user to draw into a high resolution box. Unfortunately, this resolution is too high to directly present to a neural network. To alleviate this problem we use the techniques of cropping and down sampling. By using these two techniques, the image can be transformed in to a second image that has a much lower resolution.

Once the image has been entered, it must be cropped. Cropping is the process by which extra white space is removed. The program automatically calculates the size of any white space around the image. Then a rectangle is plotted around the boundary between the image and white space. Using cropping also has the effect of removing position dependence. It does not matter where the letter is drawn, since cropping causes only that part of the input area to actually be considered.

Once the image has been cropped, it must be downsampled. Downsampling is the process by which a high resolution image is transformed into a lower resolution image. To downsample the image the high resolution image is broken up into a number of regions that are equal to the number of pixels in the downsampled image. Each pixel in the downsampled image is assigned to the average color of the corresponding region in the high-resolution image.

The resulting downsampled image is then fed to either the training or recollection process of the neural network. The Kohonen neural network used in this example has a number of input neurons that is equal to the pixels in the downsampled image. The neural network has a number of output neurons equal to the number of letters that the application is to recognize.

You have now seen a practical application of the Kohonen neural network. In the next two chapters we will examine two artificial intelligence techniques not related to neural networks. In chapter 8 we will examine simulated annealing, which is a process that simulates a metallurgy technique to remove errors from the weight matrix of a neural network. In Chapter 9 we will examine genetic algorithms that can also be used to eliminate similar areas. Finally, in Chapter 10 you will be shown how to use both techniques together to minimize local minima for neural networks. Local minima will be covered in Chapter 10.

CHAPTER 8: UNDERSTANDING GENETIC ALGORITHMS

Chapter Highlights
- **Introducing the Genetic Algorithm (GA)**
- **Understanding the structure of a Genetic Algorithm**
- **Understanding How a Genetic Algorithm Works**
- **Introducing the Traveling Salesmen Problem**
- **Implementing the Traveling Salesmen Problem**

Up to this point, this book has focused primarily on neural networks. In this chapter and Chapter 9, we will focus on two artificial intelligence technologies not directly related to neural networks. We will begin with the genetic algorithm. In the next chapter you will learn about simulated annealing. Finally, Chapter 10 will apply both of these concepts to neural networks. Please note that at this time, JOONE, which was covered in previous chapters, has no support for GAs' or simulated annealing, so we will create a class to add these capabilities to JOONE.

Genetic Algorithms

Both genetic algorithms and simulated annealing are evolutionary processes that may be utilized to solve search space and optimization problems. The genetic algorithm differs substantially from simulated annealing.

Simulated annealing is based on a thermodynamic evolutionary process, whereas genetic algorithms are based on the principles of Darwin's theory of evolution and the field of biology. Two features introduced by GAs', distinguishing them from simulated annealing, are the inclusion of a population and using a genetic operator composed of two parents called "cross over" or recombination. These features will be discussed in more detail later in this chapter.

A key component of evolution is natural selection. Organisms less suited to their environment tend to die off. Organisms that are more suited to their current environment are most likely to survive. These surviving organisms produce offspring that will have many of the better qualities possessed by their parents. As a result, these children will tend to be "more suited" to their environment. These children will be more likely to survive and to mate in future generations. This is analogous to Darwin's "survival of the fittest" theory. This ongoing process of evolution allows life to continue to improve over time. The same concepts that apply to natural selection apply to genetic algorithms as well.

It is important to note when discussing evolution, sometimes a distinction is made between micro evolution and macro evolution. Micro evolution refers to small changes in the overall genetic makeup of a population that occurs over a small number of generations. These changes are generally small adaptations to an existing species, and not a the introduction of a whole new species. Micro evolution is caused by factors such as natural selection and mutation. Macro evolution refers to significant changes in a population over a long time period. These changes may result in the evolution of a new species. The concepts of genetic algorithms are consistent with micro evolution.

Genetic Algorithm Background

John Holland, a professor at the University of Michigan, performed research with his colleagues and students to develop the concepts for genetic algorithms. In 1975, he published a book, Adaptation in Natural and Artificial Systems, in which he presents the theory behind genetic algorithms and explores practical applications. Holland is considered the father of genetic algorithms.

Another significant contributor in the area of genetic algorithms is David Goldberg. Goldberg studied under Holland at the University of Michigan and has written multiple books including, "Genetic Algorithms in Search", "Optimization and Machine Learning" published in 1989 and more recently, "The Design of Innovation" (2002). Now that you understand the history behind genetic algorithms, we will examine some of their uses.

Uses for Genetic Algorithms

Genetic algorithms are adaptive search algorithms, which can be used for many purposes. GAs' are based upon the principles of evolution and natural selection. GAs' are adept at searching large, non-linear search spaces. A non-linear search space refers to such a large number of potential solutions, that the optimal solution can not be solved by conventional iterative means. GAs' are most efficient and appropriate for situations as:

- Search space is large, complex, or not easily understood
- There is no programmatic method that can be used to narrow the search space
- Traditional optimization methods are not sufficient

Genetic algorithms may be utilized in solving a wide range of problems across multiple fields such as science, business, engineering, and medicine. Table 8.1 shows some examples.

Table 8.1: Common Uses for Genetic Algorithms

Purpose	Common Uses
Optimization	Production scheduling, call routing for call centers, routing for transportation, determining electrical circuit layouts
Design	Machine learning: designing neural networks, designing and controlling robots
Business applications	Utilized in financial trading, credit evaluation, budget allocation, fraud detection

Many optimization problems are non-linear in behavior and are too complex for traditional methods. The set of possible solutions for these problems can be enormous. For example, determining the optimum route for a traveling sales person or determining the optimum design for an electrical circuit layout. Genetic algorithms possess the ability to search large and complex search spaces to efficiently determine near optimal solutions in reasonable time frame by simulating biological evolution. Now that you have been introduced to some of the uses for genetic algorithms, we must examine how to actually construct one.

Understanding Genetic Algorithms

In this section we will review the structure of genetic algorithms. In addition the structure or components of GAs' will be discussed on a technical level. This will allow you to see how GAs' actually work. This section will conclude by providing a general understanding of genetic algorithms, which may be used as a foundation for future chapters and studies.

What is the Structure of a Genetic Algorithm

Genetic algorithms very closely resemble the biological model of chromosomes and genes. Individual organisms in a genetic algorithm are generally composed of single chromosomes. These chromosomes are composed of genes. By manipulating the genes, new chromosomes are created that have different traits. These manipulations occur through cross over and mutation, just as they occur in nature. Cross over is analogous to the biological process of mating. Mutation is a way that new information can be introduced into an existing population.

Understanding Chromosomes

Each organism typically contains only one chromosome. Because of this, these chromosomes represent can be thought of as an "individual" or a solution. Each chromosome is initially assigned a random solution. This solution is used to calculate a "fitness" level. This fitness determines the chromosomes suitability or "fitness" to survive. This is where Darwin's natural selection is applicable. If a chromosome has a higher "fitness" level, it has a higher probability of mating and staying alive. Each chromosome is composed of a collection of parameters to be optimized. These parameters are genes, which you will learn about in the next section.

Understanding Genes

In a genetic algorithm, genes represent individual components of a solution. This is a very important part of the analysis of a problem that is to be used with a genetic algorithm. To effectively solve a problem, you must determine a way to break the problem into related components, or genes.

Later in this chapter, we will examine the traveling salesmen problem. You will be shown how to break up the solution for this problem into individual genes. Additionally, in Chapter 10, you will be shown how you can make the individual weights in a neural network represent the genes in the chromosome.

It is also important to note that there is a finite number of genes that are used. Individual genes are not modified as the organisms evolve. It is the chromosomes that evolve by changing the order and makeup of their genes. Now that you understand genes and chromosomes, we will examine how the genetic algorithm works.

How Genetic Algorithms Work

A genetic algorithm begins by creating an initial population. This population consists of chromosomes that are given a random collection of genes. The steps involved in a genetic algorithm are as follows:

1. Create an initial population of chromosomes.
2. Evaluate the fitness or "suitability" of each chromosome that makes up the population.
3. Based on this fitness, select the chromosomes that will mate, or those that have the "privilege" to mate.
4. Cross over (or mate) the selected chromosomes and produce offspring.
5. Randomly mutate some of the genes of the chromosomes.
6. Repeat steps three through five until a new population is created.
7. The algorithm ends when the best solution has not changed for a preset number of generations.

The steps listed above will be discussed in more detail in the following sections. Genetic algorithms strive to determine the optimal solution to a problem by utilizing three genetic operators. These operators are selection, cross over, and mutation. GAs' search for the optimal solution until specific criteria is met causing termination. These results include providing good solutions as compared to one "optimal" solution for complex (such as "NP hard") problems. NP-hard defers to a problem which cannot be solved in polynomial time. Most problems solved with computers today are not NP-hard and can be solved in polynomial time. A P-Problem, or polynomial problem, is a problem where the number of steps to complete the answer is bounded by a polynomial. A polynomial is a mathematical expression involving exponents and variables. A NP-hard problem does not increase exponentially. An NP-hard problem often increases at a much greater rate, often described by the factorial operator (n!). One example of an NP-hard problem is the traveling salesman problem. The traveling salesman problem will be discussed later in this chapter.

Initial Population

In a genetic algorithm, the population is comprised of organisms. Each of these organisms is usually composed of a single chromosome. Each chromosome represents one complete solution to the defined problem. The genetic algorithm must create the initial population which is comprised of multiple chromosomes or solutions. Chromosomes are comprised of genes and these genes are usually initialized to random values based on the boundaries defined.

Each chromosome in the initial population must be evaluated. This is done by evaluating the "fitness" of each chromosome which represents the quality of the solution. The fitness is determined by a function and is specific to the defined problem the genetic algorithm is designed to solve.

Suitability and the Privilege to Mate

The purpose of mating, in a genetic algorithm, is to create a new improved population. The "suitability" to mate refers to how we determine those chromosomes that are qualified to mate, or those that have the "privilege" to mate.

Determining the specific chromosomes that will mate is based upon each individual chromosome's fitness. The chromosomes are selected from the old population, mate, and produce children or new chromosomes. These new children are joined with the existing population. In subsequent generations, combined generation will be the base for selection of the mating population.

Mating

We will now examine the cross over process that allows genetic algorithms to mate. Mating works by taking two parents and taking a "splice" from their gene sequence. This splice effectively divides the chromosome into three gene sequences. The children will be built based on genes from each of these three sections.

The process of mating simply jumbles the genes from two parents into a new offspring chromosome. This is useful in that it allows the new chromosomes to take traits from each parent. This method can also lead to the problem of no new genetic material being introduced. To introduce new genetic material, the process of mutation is used. Mutation will be discussed in the next section.

Mutation

Without mutation, the only genetic material that will be used is that which comes from the parents. Mutation allows new genetic patterns to be introduced that were not already contained in the population. This mutation can be thought of as natural experiments. These experiments introduce a new, somewhat random, sequence of genes into a chromosome. It is completely unknown if this mutation will produce a desirable or undesirable attribute.

It does not matter if the mutation produces a desirable or undesirable feature. Natural selection will determine the fate of the mutated chromosome. If the fitness of the mutated chromosome is higher than the general population, it will survive and likely be allowed to mate with other chromosomes. If the genetic mutation produces a undesirable feature, then natural selection will ensure that the chromosome does not live to mate.

An important consideration for any genetic algorithm is the mutation level that will be used. The mutation level is generally expressed as a percent. The example program that will be examined later in this chapter will use a mutation level of 10%. There are many ramifications that are directly tied to this mutation level. If you choose too high of a mutation level, you will be performing nothing more than a random search. There will be no adaptation; simply a completely new solution will be tried until no better solution can be found. Now that you understand the general structure of a genetic algorithm, we will examine a common problem that genetic algorithms are often applied to. In the next section you will be introduced to the traveling salesmen problem (TSP).

The Traveling Salesmen Problem

In this section you will be introduced to the traveling salesman problem (TSP). The traveling salesman problem is a common choice for algorithms such as the genetic algorithm. The TSP is popular because it is an NP-Hard problem that cannot generally be solved by traditional iterative programming.

The traveling salesman problem will be revisited in Chapter 9, "Simulated Annealing". This chapter shows how find solutions for the TSP using a genetic algorithm. As we will learn in Chapter 9, this is not the only way that this can be done. Of course the ultimate goal of this book is programming neural networks in Java. Though neither this chapter nor chapter 9 teach you anything specifically about neural networks, the algorithms of genetic algorithms and simulated annealing will form the foundation for optimization of a neural network. Chapter 11 will show you how simulated annealing and genetic algorithms can be used to optimize the weight matrix of a neural network. Now you will be shown exactly what the traveling salesman problem is.

Understanding the Traveling Salesman Problem

The traveling salesman problem involves a "traveling salesman" who must visit a certain number of cities. The shortest route that the salesman will travel is what is being sought. The salesman is allowed to begin and end at any city. The only requirement, is that the traveling salesmen visit each city once. The salesman may not visit a city more than once.

This may seem like an easy enough task for a normal iterative program, however, consider the magnitude with which the number of possible combinations grows as the number of cities increases. If there is one or two cities, only one step is required. Three increases this to six. Table 8.2 shows how quickly these combinations grow.

Table 8.2: Number of Steps to Solve TSP with a Conventional Program

Number of Cities	Number of Steps
1	1
2	1
3	6
4	24
5	120
6	720
7	5,040
8	40,320
9	362,880
10	3,628,800
11	39,916,800
12	479,001,600
13	6,227,020,800
...	...
50	$3.041 * 10^{64}$

The formula behind the above table is the factorial. The number of cities, n, is calculated using the factorial operator (!). The factorial of some arbitrary n value is given by n * (n-1) * (n-2) * ... * 3 * 2 * 1. As you can see from the above table, these values become incredibly large when a program must do a "brute force" search. The example program that we will examine in the next section, finds a solution to a fifty city problem in a matter of minutes. This is done by using a genetic algorithm, rather than a normal brute-force search.

Implementing the Traveling Salesmen Problem

So far we have discussed the basic principles of what genetic algorithms are and how they are used. Now it is time to examine a Java example. In this section, you will be shown a complete application that is capable of finding solutions to the TSP. As this program is examined, you will be shown how the user interface is constructed, and also how the genetic algorithm itself is implemented. We will begin by introducing the example program and showing you how to use it.

Using the Traveling Salesmen Program

The traveling salesmen program itself is very easy to use. This program displays the cities, shown as dots, and the current best solution. The number of generations and the mutation percentage are also shown. As the program runs, these values are updated. The final output from the program is shown in Figure 8.1.

Figure 8.1: The Traveling Salesman Program

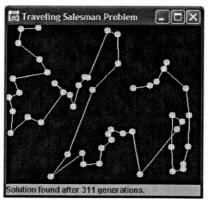

As the program is running, you will see white lines change between the green cities. The path currently being displayed is close to the shortest path in the entire population. As the program runs you will see a path begin to emerge.

When the program is nearly finished, you will notice that new patterns are not introduced, and the program seems to stabilize. Yet, you will also notice that additional generations are still being calculated. This is an important part of the genetic algorithm. Knowing when its done! This is not as straightforward as it might seem. You do not know how many steps are required, nor do you know what the shortest distance actually is.

Some criteria must be specified so that the program knows when to stop. This program stops when the optimal solution does not change for 100 generations. Once this has happened, the program indicates that it has found a solution after the number of generations that it actually took, which includes the 99 generations that did not change the solution. Now that you have seen how the GA program works, we will examine how it was constructed. We will begin by examining the user interface.

Overall Structure

The traveling salesman program uses four Java classes. In this section we will examine how the individual classes of the traveling salesman program fit together. Subsequent sections will examine each of these classes in detail. The overall structure of this program is shown as a UML diagram in Figure 8.2.

Figure 8.2: The Traveling Salesman Program

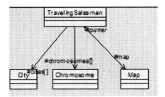

It is important to understand the relationship between the individual classes that make up the traveling salesman program. These classes, and their functions, are summarized in Table 8.3.

Table 8.3: Classes Used for the GA Version of Traveling Salesman

Class	Purpose
Map	This class assists the TravelingSalesman class by drawing the map of cities.
City	This class stores individual city coordinates. This class also contains methods that are used to calculate the distance between cities.
Chromosome	This class implements the chromosome. This is the most complex class of the program, as it implements most of the functionality of the genetic algorithm.
TravelingSalesman	This class implements the user interface and performs general initiliazation.

The User Interface

The first part of the program that we will examine is the TravelingSalesman.java file. This file implements the user interface and is responsible for setting up the city locations. This file will be reused considerably in the next chapter.

The TravelingSalesman class extends the Java class JFrame. This means that it is a fully functional window. The TravelingSalesman class implements the main application window that the user interacts with. The complete listing for this class is shown in Listing 8.1.

Listing 8.1: The User Interface (TravelingSalesman.java)

```java
import javax.swing.*;
import java.awt.*;
import java.awt.event.*;
import java.text.*;

public class TravelingSalesman
 extends JFrame
 implements Runnable,ComponentListener {

 public static final int CITY_COUNT = 50;
 public static final int POPULATION_SIZE = 1000;
 public static final double MUTATION_PERCENT = 0.10;
 protected int matingPopulationSize = POPULATION_SIZE/2;
 protected int favoredPopulationSize = matingPopulationSize/2;
 protected Map map = null;
 protected JLabel status;
 protected int cutLength = CITY_COUNT/5;
 protected int generation;
 protected Thread worker = null;

 protected boolean started = false;
 protected City [] cities;
 protected Chromosome [] chromosomes;

 public TravelingSalesman() {
  addComponentListener(this);
  setSize(300,300);
  setTitle("Traveling Salesman Problem");
 }

 /**
  * Used to add necessary components.
  *
  * @param e The event.
  */
 public void componentShown(ComponentEvent e)
 {
  getContentPane().setLayout(new BorderLayout());

  if ( map == null ) {
   map = new Map(this);
```

```
    getContentPane().add(map,"Center");
    status = new JLabel("Starting up");
    getContentPane().add(status,"South");
  }
  start();

}

/**
 * Start the background thread.
 */
public void start() {
// create a random list of cities

  cities = new City[TravelingSalesman.CITY_COUNT];
  for ( int i=0;i<TravelingSalesman.CITY_COUNT;i++ ) {
   cities[i] = new City(
     (int)(Math.random()*(getBounds().width-10)),
     (int)(Math.random()*(getBounds().height-60)));
  }


  // create the initial chromosomes

  chromosomes = new Chromosome[TravelingSalesman.POPULATION_SIZE];
  for ( int i=0;i<TravelingSalesman.POPULATION_SIZE;i++ ) {
   chromosomes[i] = new Chromosome(cities);
   chromosomes[i].setCut(cutLength);
   chromosomes[i].setMutation(TravelingSalesman.MUTATION_PERCENT);
  }
  Chromosome.sortChromosomes(chromosomes,
    TravelingSalesman.POPULATION_SIZE);

// start up the background thread
  started = true;
  map.update(map.getGraphics());

  generation = 0;

  if ( worker != null )
    worker = null;
  worker = new Thread(this);
  worker.setPriority(Thread.MIN_PRIORITY);
  worker.start();
  }
```

```java
/**
 * The main loop for the background thread.
 * It is here that most of the work i s orchestrated.
 */
public void run() {

  double thisCost = 500.0;
  double oldCost = 0.0;
  double dcost = 500.0;
  int countSame = 0;

  map.update(map.getGraphics());

  while(countSame<100) {

   generation++;

   int ioffset = matingPopulationSize;
   int mutated = 0;


   // Mate the chromosomes in the favored population
   // with all in the mating population
   for ( int i=0;i<favoredPopulationSize;i++ ) {
    Chromosome cmother = chromosomes[i];
    // Select partner from the mating population
    int father = (int) ( 0.999999*Math.random()*
      (double)matingPopulationSize);
    Chromosome cfather = chromosomes[father];

    mutated += cmother.mate(cfather,
      chromosomes[ioffset],
      chromosomes[ioffset+1]);
    ioffset += 2;
   }

   // The new generation is in the matingPopulation area
   // move them to the correct area for sort.
   for ( int i=0;i<matingPopulationSize;i++ ) {
    chromosomes[i] = chromosomes[i+matingPopulationSize];
    chromosomes[i].calculateCost(cities);
   }


   // Now sort the new mating population
   Chromosome.sortChromosomes(chromosomes,matingPopulationSize);
```

```java
    double cost = chromosomes[0].getCost();
    dcost = Math.abs(cost-thisCost);
    thisCost = cost;
    double mutationRate = 100.0 * (double) mutated /
      (double) matingPopulationSize;

    NumberFormat nf = NumberFormat.getInstance();
    nf.setMinimumFractionDigits(2);
    nf.setMinimumFractionDigits(2);

    status.setText("Generation "+generation+
      " Cost "+(int)thisCost+" Mutated "+
      nf.format(mutationRate)+"%");


    if ( (int)thisCost == (int)oldCost ) {
     countSame++;
    } else {
     countSame = 0;
     oldCost = thisCost;
    }
    map.update(map.getGraphics());


  }
  status.setText(
    "Solution found after "+generation+" generations.");
}

/**
 * The main method.
 *
 * @param args Not used
 */
public static void main(String args[])
{
  (new TravelingSalesman()).show();
}

}
```

There are two very important methods inside of the TravelingSalesman class. The first, is the start method which initializes the cities and other data structures and begins the background thread. Once the background thread is started, the run () method is called to actually execute the background thread. As is consistent with other Java programs, the run method makes up the background thread, and once the run method returns the thread ends. The background thread will remain running until a solution is found. We will begin by examining how the start method is constructed.

The first thing that the start method does, is to create the list of cities. These cities are assigned random x and y coordinates so that the cities are placed differently each time the program is run. The City class, which will be described later in this section, is used to hold the x and y coordinates of each city. The following lines of code create an array of random cities.

```
cities = new City[TravelingSalesman.CITY_COUNT];
for ( int i=0;i<TravelingSalesman.CITY_COUNT;i++ ) {
 cities[i] = new City(
  (int)(Math.random()*(getBounds().width-10)),
  (int)(Math.random()*(getBounds().height-60)));
}
```

Once the cities have been created, the organisms (or chromosomes) must be created. The POPULATION_SIZE variable defines how many organisms will be created. Each of these chromosomes will be assigned a random path through the cities. Therefore, each of these chromosomes represents a potential path, or solution. Each leg in this journey can be thought of as a gene. Each chromosome is also given a mutation percentage. This defines the percent of the offspring of this chromosome that will undergo mutation. The cut-length determines how where the chromosome will be "cut" when it mates.

```
chromosomes = new Chromosome[TravelingSalesman.POPULATION_SIZE];
for ( int i=0;i<TravelingSalesman.POPULATION_SIZE;i++ ) {
 chromosomes[i] = new Chromosome(cities);
 chromosomes[i].setCut(cutLength);
 chromosomes[i].setMutation(TravelingSalesman.MUTATION_PERCENT);
}
```

Finally, the chromosomes must be sorted. This allows natural selection to occur. Calling the following line of code will sort each of the chromosomes according to their suitability. In the case of the traveling salesman problem, the suitability refers to the length of the path through the cities. The shorter the distance, the more suited the chromosome.

```
Chromosome.sortChromosomes(chromosomes,
  TravelingSalesman.POPULATION_SIZE);
```

Next, the program starts up the background thread. This background thread will run until a solution is found.

```
// start up the background thread
  started = true;
  map.update(map.getGraphics());

  generation = 0;

  if ( worker != null )
    worker = null;
  worker = new Thread(this);
  worker.setPriority(Thread.MIN_PRIORITY);
  worker.start();
}
```

The run method of the TravelingSalesman class implements the background thread. The run method begins by updating the map. The map is what is displayed to the user. This class will be discussed in a subsequent section. The program then begins a while loop that will continue until the same solution has been found for 100 generations in a row.

```
map.update(map.getGraphics());

while(countSame<100) {

  generation++;

  int ioffset = matingPopulationSize;
  int mutated = 0;
```

The run method begins by mating all of the chromosomes that are in the favored population with partners in the mating population. The favored population is the top 25% and the mating population is the top 50%. A mother and father are selected. The mother comes from the favored population and may choose a father from any of the mating population. The terms mother and father are purely arbitrary. Any organism can play any role.

```
for ( int i=0;i<favoredPopulationSize;i++ ) {
  Chromosome cmother = chromosomes[i];
  // Select partner from the mating population
```

```
int father = (int) ( 0.999999*Math.random()*
   (double)matingPopulationSize);
Chromosome cfather = chromosomes[father];
```

The actual mating occurs by calling the mate method of the mother organism. This method will be explained in a later section.

```
mutated += cmother.mate(cfather,chromosomes[ioffset],
   chromosomes[ioffset+1]);
ioffset += 2;
}
```

The newly created children are moved to the bottom 50% of the population. This effectively kills the lower 50% of organisms that are not well suited.

```
for ( int i=0;i<matingPopulationSize;i++ ) {
 chromosomes[i] = chromosomes[i+matingPopulationSize];
 chromosomes[i].calculateCost(cities);
}
```

Now the new children, which are likely superior to many of the parents, are at the bottom. We must resort the entire list of organisms so that new "classes" may be formed. This is done by using the sortChromosomes method of the Chromosome class.

```
Chromosome.sortChromosomes(chromosomes,matingPopulationSize);
```

Finally, the statistics are calculated and displayed to the user.

```
double cost = chromosomes[0].getCost();
dcost = Math.abs(cost-thisCost);
thisCost = cost;
double mutationRate = 100.0 * (double) mutated /
   (double) matingPopulationSize;

NumberFormat nf = NumberFormat.getInstance();
nf.setMinimumFractionDigits(2);
nf.setMinimumFractionDigits(2);

status.setText("Generation "+generation+
   " Cost "+(int)thisCost+" Mutated "+
  nf.format(mutationRate)+"%");
```

```
if ( (int)thisCost == (int)oldCost ) {
 countSame++;
} else {
 countSame = 0;
 oldCost = thisCost;
}
map.update(map.getGraphics());

}
```

Once the main loop exits, the final solution is displayed.

```
status.setText("Solution found after "+generation+" genera-
tions.");
}
```

The TravelingSalesman class makes up most of the user interface. Next, we will examine the City class, which stores the coordinates of cities and also calculates the distance between cities.

Handling Cities

The City class is used to hold the x and y coordinates for each city. The City class is shown in Listing 8.2.

Listing 8.2: Cities (City.java)

```
class City {

 int xpos;
 int ypos;

 /**
  * Constructor.
  *
  * @param x The city's x position
  * @param y The city's y position.
  */
 City(int x, int y) {
  xpos = x;
  ypos = y;
 }
```

```java
/**
 * Return's the city's x position.
 *
 * @return The city's x position.
 */
int getx() {
 return xpos;
}

/**
 * Returns the city's y position.
 *
 * @return The city's y position.
 */
int gety() {
 return ypos;
}

/**
 * Returns how close the city is to another city.
 *
 * @param cother The other city.
 * @return A distance.
 */
int proximity(City cother) {
 return proximity(cother.getx(),cother.gety());
}

/**
 * Returns how far this city is from a specific point.
 * This method uses the pythagorean theorum to calculate
 * the distance.
 *
 * @param x The x coordinate
 * @param y The y coordinate
 * @return The distance.
 */
int proximity(int x, int y) {
 int xdiff = xpos - x;
 int ydiff = ypos - y;
 return(int)Math.sqrt( xdiff*xdiff + ydiff*ydiff );
}
}
```

The City class serves mainly as a holder for the x and y coordinates of a city. Collections of these cities will make up the paths that will be represented by the chromosomes. Another useful function of the City class is the proximity method. This method is used to calculate how far the city is from another x and y coordinate or another city. The proximity method works by using the Pythagorean theorem. The Pythagorean theorem specifies that for a right triangle, the sum of the squares of the two legs is equal to the square of the hypotenuse. Now that you have seen how individual cities are stored, we will examine how the output from the program is displayed.

Display the Map

The Map class is a simple component that can be placed onto a Java window. This class displays the path of cities contained in a chromosome. This class is used to display the path used by the current best chromosome. The Map class is shown in Listing 8.3.

Listing 8.3: Display the Map (Map.java)

```java
import javax.swing.*;
import java.awt.*;

public class Map extends JPanel {

  /**
   * The TravelingSalesman object that owns this object.
   */
  protected TravelingSalesman owner;

  /**
   * Constructor.
   *
   * @param owner The TravelingSalesman object that owns
   * this object.
   */
  Map(TravelingSalesman owner)
  {
   this.owner = owner;
  }

  /**
   * Update the graphical display of the map.
   *
   * @param g The graphics object to use.
   */
  public void paint(Graphics g) {
   update(g);
  }

  /**
```

```
 * Update the graphical display of the map.
 *
 * @param g The graphics object to use.
 */
public void update(Graphics g) {
  int width = getBounds().width;
  int height = getBounds().height;

  g.setColor(Color.black);
  g.fillRect(0,0,width,height);

  if ( !owner.started ) return;

  g.setColor(Color.green);
  for ( int i=0;i<TravelingSalesman.CITY_COUNT;i++ ) {
   int xpos = owner.cities[i].getx();
   int ypos = owner.cities[i].gety();
   g.fillOval(xpos-5,ypos-5,10,10);
  }

  g.setColor(Color.white);
  for ( int i=0;i<TravelingSalesman.CITY_COUNT;i++ ) {
   int icity = owner.chromosomes[0].getCity(i);
   if ( i!=0 ) {
    int last = owner.chromosomes[0].getCity(i-1);
    g.drawLine(
        owner.cities[icity].getx(),
        owner.cities[icity].gety(),
        owner.cities[last].getx(),
        owner.cities[last].gety());
   }
  }
 }
}
```

Most of the work performed by this class is done by the paint method. This method is called by the TravelingSalesman class to display the list in a graphical form. The paint method is fairly simple. The paint method loops through the list of cities for the best chromosome, displays each city as a dot, and displays paths as lines connecting the dots.

Now that you understand how the user interface works with this program, we will examine the actual genetic algorithm. The genetic algorithm is implemented primarily in the Chromosome class. The Chromosome class will be examined in the next section.

Implementing the Chromosomes

The Chromosome class implements most of the genetic algorithm. This class is responsible for mating the chromosomes, performing mutations and sorting a list of chromosomes, by their suitability. Listing 8.4 shows the Chromosome class.

Listing 8.4: Display the Chromosomes (Chromosome.java)

```
class Chromosome {

protected int [] cityList;
protected double cost;
protected double mutationPercent;
protected int cutLength;

Chromosome(City [] cities) {
  boolean taken[] = new boolean[cities.length];
  cityList = new int[cities.length];
  cost = 0.0;
  for ( int i=0;i<cityList.length;i++ ) taken[i] = false;
  for ( int i=0;i<cityList.length-1;i++ ) {
   int icandidate;
   do {
    icandidate = (int) ( 0.999999* Math.random() *
                 (double) cityList.length );
   } while ( taken[icandidate] );
   cityList[i] = icandidate;
   taken[icandidate] = true;
   if ( i == cityList.length-2 ) {
    icandidate = 0;
    while ( taken[icandidate] ) icandidate++;
    cityList[i+1] = icandidate;
   }
  }
  calculateCost(cities);
  cutLength = 1;
 }

void calculateCost(City [] cities) {
  cost=0;
  for ( int i=0;i<cityList.length-1;i++ ) {
   double dist = cities[cityList[i]].proximity(
     cities[cityList[i+1]]);
   cost += dist;
  }
 }
```

```java
double getCost() {
  return cost;
 }

int getCity(int i) {
  return cityList[i];
 }

void setCities(int [] list) {
  for ( int i=0;i<cityList.length;i++ ) {
   cityList[i] = list[i];
  }
 }

void setCity(int index, int value) {
  cityList[index] = value;
 }

void setCut(int cut) {
  cutLength = cut;
 }

void setMutation(double prob) {
  mutationPercent = prob;
 }

int mate(Chromosome father, Chromosome offspring1,
   Chromosome offspring2) {
  int cutpoint1 = (int) (0.999999*Math.random()*(double)
    (cityList.length-cutLength));
  int cutpoint2 = cutpoint1 + cutLength;

  boolean taken1 [] = new boolean[cityList.length];
  boolean taken2 [] = new boolean[cityList.length];
  int off1 [] = new int[cityList.length];
  int off2 [] = new int[cityList.length];

  for ( int i=0;i<cityList.length;i++ ) {
   taken1[i] = false;
   taken2[i] = false;
  }

  for ( int i=0;i<cityList.length;i++ ) {
   if ( i<cutpoint1 || i>= cutpoint2 ) {
    off1[i] = -1;
    off2[i] = -1;
```

```
   } else {
    int imother = cityList[i];
    int ifather = father.getCity(i);
    off1[i] = ifather;
    off2[i] = imother;
    taken1[ifather] = true;
    taken2[imother] = true;
   }
  }
 }

 for ( int i=0;i<cutpoint1;i++ ) {
  if ( off1[i] == -1 ) {
   for ( int j=0;j<cityList.length;j++ ) {
    int imother = cityList[j];
    if ( !taken1[imother] ) {
     off1[i] = imother;
     taken1[imother] = true;
     break;
    }
   }
  }
  if ( off2[i] == -1 ) {
   for ( int j=0;j<cityList.length;j++ ) {
    int ifather = father.getCity(j);
    if ( !taken2[ifather] ) {
     off2[i] = ifather;
     taken2[ifather] = true;
     break;
    }
   }
  }
 }
 for ( int i=cityList.length-1;i>=cutpoint2;i-- ) {
  if ( off1[i] == -1 ) {
   for ( int j=cityList.length-1;j>=0;j-- ) {
    int imother = cityList[j];
    if ( !taken1[imother] ) {
     off1[i] = imother;
     taken1[imother] = true;
     break;
    }
   }
  }
  if ( off2[i] == -1 ) {
   for ( int j=cityList.length-1;j>=0;j-- ) {
    int ifather = father.getCity(j);
```

```
      if ( !taken2[ifather] ) {
       off2[i] = ifather;
       taken2[ifather] = true;
       break;
      }
     }
    }
   }

   offspring1.setCities(off1);
   offspring2.setCities(off2);

   int mutate = 0;
   if ( Math.random() < mutationPercent ) {
    int iswap1 = (int) (0.999999*Math.random()*(double)
      (cityList.length));
    int iswap2 = (int) (0.999999*Math.random()*(double)
      cityList.length);
    int i = off1[iswap1];
    off1[iswap1] = off1[iswap2];
    off1[iswap2] = i;
    mutate++;
   }
   if ( Math.random() < mutationPercent ) {
    int iswap1 = (int) (0.999999*Math.random()*
      (double)(cityList.length));
    int iswap2 = (int) (0.999999*Math.random()*
      (double)cityList.length);
    int i = off2[iswap1];
    off2[iswap1] = off2[iswap2];
    off2[iswap2] = i;
    mutate++;
   }
   return mutate;
  }

 public static void sortChromosomes(Chromosome chromosomes[],
   int num) {
  Chromosome ctemp;
  boolean swapped = true;
  while ( swapped ) {
   swapped = false;
   for ( int i=0;i<num-1;i++ ) {
    if ( chromosomes[i].getCost() > chromosomes[i+1].getCost() ) {
     ctemp = chromosomes[i];
     chromosomes[i] = chromosomes[i+1];
```

```
      chromosomes[i+1] = ctemp;
      swapped = true;
    }
   }
  }
 }
}
```

The most important method provided by the Chromosome class, is the mate method. This method will cause a father, which is passed in as a parameter, to mate with the mother class. We will now examine this method and see the algorithm used to combine the genetic material from two chromosomes to produce two offspring.

First a random cut point is chosen that will determine what percent of the genes, which are legs in the journey from city to city, will be taken from each parent.

```
int cutpoint1 = (int) (0.999999*Math.random()*(double)(cityList.
length-cutLength));
int cutpoint2 = cutpoint1 + cutLength;
```

Next, two boolean arrays are setup so that we can remember which genes were taken from each parent. This array is initialized to false.

```
boolean taken1 [] = new boolean[cityList.length];
boolean taken2 [] = new boolean[cityList.length];
int off1 [] = new int[cityList.length];
int off2 [] = new int[cityList.length];

for ( int i=0;i<cityList.length;i++ ) {
 taken1[i] = false;
 taken2[i] = false;
}
```

The mating process is a relatively straightforward process. The mother and father chromosomes are both "cut" at two points. This divides each into three sections. These three sections are then selectively spliced back together to form two offspring. First we will handle the middle component. The following lines of code do this:

```
for ( int i=0;i<cityList.length;i++ ) {
 if ( i<cutpoint1 || i>= cutpoint2 ) {
  off1[i] = -1;
  off2[i] = -1;
 } else {
```

```
      int imother = cityList[i];
      int ifather = father.getCity(i);
      off1[i] = ifather;
      off2[i] = imother;
      taken1[ifather] = true;
      taken2[imother] = true;
    }
  }
```

The middle component will be taken from the father for child one and the mother for child two. Each of the genes used for this section are marked as taken. Next we will loop through the left section of the chromosome. The following lines of code do this:

```
for ( int i=0;i<cutpoint1;i++ ) {
 if ( off1[i] == -1 ) {
  for ( int j=0;j<cityList.length;j++ ) {
   int imother = cityList[j];
   if ( !taken1[imother] ) {
    off1[i] = imother;
    taken1[imother] = true;
    break;
   }
  }
 }
 if ( off2[i] == -1 ) {
  for ( int j=0;j<cityList.length;j++ ) {
   int ifather = father.getCity(j);
   if ( !taken2[ifather] ) {
    off2[i] = ifather;
    taken2[ifather] = true;
    break;
   }
  }
 }
}
```

For the left section, child one will take available genes from the mother and child two will take available genes from the father. Finally, the program must handle the right section. The right section works similar to the left section. The main difference is, child one will take available genes from the father and child two will take available genes from the mother. The following lines of code do this:

```
for ( int i=cityList.length-1;i>=cutpoint2;i-- ) {
 if ( off1[i] == -1 ) {
  for ( int j=cityList.length-1;j>=0;j-- ) {
   int imother = cityList[j];
   if ( !taken1[imother] ) {
    off1[i] = imother;
    taken1[imother] = true;
    break;
   }
  }
 }
 if ( off2[i] == -1 ) {
  for ( int j=cityList.length-1;j>=0;j-- ) {
   int ifather = father.getCity(j);
   if ( !taken2[ifather] ) {
    off2[i] = ifather;
    taken2[ifather] = true;
    break;
   }
  }
 }
}
```

The two new paths are copied to the new children. The following lines of code do this:

```
offspring1.setCities(off1);
offspring2.setCities(off2);
```

Now that the parents have successfully created two offspring we may want to mutate these children slightly. The following lines of code handles the mutation process.

```
int mutate = 0;
if ( Math.random() < mutationPercent ) {
 int iswap1 = (int) (0.999999*Math.random()*
   (double)(cityList.length));
 int iswap2 = (int) (0.999999*Math.random()*
   (double)cityList.length);
```

```
   int i = off1[iswap1];
   off1[iswap1] = off1[iswap2];
   off1[iswap2] = i;
   mutate++;
 }
 if ( Math.random() < mutationPercent ) {
   int iswap1 = (int) (0.999999*Math.random()*
     (double)(cityList.length));
   int iswap2 = (int) (0.999999*Math.random()*
     (double)cityList.length);
   int i = off2[iswap1];
   off2[iswap1] = off2[iswap2];
   off2[iswap2] = i;
   mutate++;
 }
```

The mutation process is completely random. Two random genes are chosen, and then swapped as part of the mutation process. The random mutation counters the very methodical mating process that is used.

The other major component of the Chromosome class, is the sortChromosomes method. This method is used to sort the chromosomes according to their suitability to the problem. This allows the less desirables to be kept to the bottom of the list. The top of this list will make up the mating and preferred classes.

You have now seen a simple application of genetic algorithms. If you consider the traveling salesmen problem you will see that it is actually very similar to a neural network. There are just too many combinations to try every path in the Traveling Salesman Problem. Likewise, in a neural network, there are just too many synaptic connections to track all of them. To optimize the neural network weight matrix, we can also apply a genetic algorithm.

Summary

In this chapter, you were introduced to genetic algorithms. Genetic algorithms are one of the ways that programs can find potential solutions to complex NP-hard problems. A NP-hard problem is a problem where the number of steps required to solve the problem increases at a very high rate as the number of units in the program increases.

An example of an NP-hard problem, which was examined in this chapter, is the traveling salesman problem. The traveling salesmen problem attempts to seek the shortest path that a salesman would travel if he needed to visit a certain number of cities. The number of possible paths that a program would have to search increases factorially as the number of cities increases.

To solve such a problem, a genetic algorithm is used. The genetic algorithm creates a population of chromosomes. Each of these chromosomes is one path through the cities. Each leg in that journey is a gene. The best chromosomes are determined, and they are allowed to "mate". This mating process combines the genes of the two parents. The chromosomes that have longer, less desirable, paths are not allowed to mate. Because the population has a fixed size, the less desirable chromosomes are purged from memory. As the program continues, natural selection causes the better suited chromosomes to mate and produce better and better solutions.

The actual process of mating occurs by splitting the parent chromosomes into three splices. These three splices are then used to build a new chromosome. The result of all of this will be two child chromosomes. Unfortunately, the mating process does not introduce new genetic material. New genetic material is introduced by mutation.

Mutation is also introduced to help find a optimal solution. One problem that arises from using only mating, is that the only genetic material that will be used is that which is already in the population. Mutation randomly changes the genes of some of the newly created offspring. This introduces new traits. Many of these mutations will not be well suited and will be purged from memory. However, others can be used to move on an otherwise stagnated population.

Genetic algorithms will be used to optimize the weight matrixes of neural networks. In the next chapter you will learn another technique, to solve NP-hard problems, called simulated annealing. Finally, in Chapter 10, we will apply both genetic algorithms and simulated annealing to neural network optimization.

CHAPTER 9: UNDERSTANDING SIMULATED ANNEALING

Chapter Highlights
- **What is Simulated Annealing**
- **What is Simulated Annealing Used For**
- **Implementing Simulated Annealing in Java**
- **Applying Simulated Annealing to the Traveling Salesman Problem**

In this chapter we will examine another technique that allows you to train neural networks. In Chapter 8, you were introduced to using genetic algorithms to train a neural network. This chapter will show you how you can use another popular algorithm, which is named simulated annealing. Simulated annealing has become a popular method of neural network training. As you will see in this chapter, it can be applied to other uses as well.

This chapter will show you how simulated annealing can be used to solve problems. The example program that is presented in this chapter solves the traveling salesman problem, just like the genetic algorithm in Chapter 8 did. This time, however, simulated annealing will be used in place of the genetic algorithm. This will allow you to see some of the advantages that simulated annealing offers over a genetic algorithm.

This chapter will begin by giving you a general background of the simulated annealing process. Next, we will construct a class that is capable of using simulated annealing to solve the traveling salesman problem. Both Chapter 8 and 9 are leading up to Chapter 10, which is where you will see how both simulated annealing and genetic algorithms can be used to train a neural network. We will begin this chapter by introducing the simulated annealing algorithm.

Simulated Annealing Background

Simulated annealing was developed in the mid 1970's by Scott Kirkpatric, along with a few other researchers. Simulated annealing was originally developed to better optimized the design of integrated circuit (IC) chips. Simulated annealing simulates the actual process of annealing.

Annealing is the metallurgical process of heating up a solid and then cooling it slowly until it crystallizes. The atoms of this material have high energies at very high temperatures. This gives the atoms a great deal of freedom in their ability to restructure themselves. As the temperature is reduced, the energy of these atoms decreases.

If this cooling process is carried out too quickly many irregularities and defects will be seen in the crystal structure. The process of cooling too rapidly, is known as rapid quenching.

Ideally, the temperature should be deceased at a slower rate. A slower fall to the lower energy rates will allow a more consistent crystal structure to form. This causes a more stable crystal form will allow the metal to be much more durable.

Simulated annealing seeks to emulate this process. Simulated annealing begins at a very high temperature where the input values are allowed to assume a great range of random values. As the training progresses, the temperature is allowed to fall. This restricts the degree to which the inputs are allowed to vary. This often leads the simulated annealing algorithm to a better solution, just as a metal achieves a better crystal structure through the actual annealing process.

What is Simulated Annealing Used for

Simulated annealing can be used to find the minimum of an arbitrary equation that has a specified number of inputs. Simulated annealing will find the inputs to the equation that will produce a minimum value. In the case of the traveling salesman, this equation is the calculation of the total distance that the salesman must travel. In the case of a neural network, as we will learn in Chapter 10, this equation is the error function of the neural network.

When simulated annealing was first introduced, the algorithm was very popular for integrated circuit (IC) chip design. Most IC chips are composed internally of many logic gates. These gates allow the chip to perform tasks that the chips were designed to perform. Just as algebraic equations can often be simplified, so too can the IC chip layouts. Simulated annealing is often used to find a IC chip design that has fewer logic gates than the original. This causes the chip to generate less heat and run faster.

The weight matrix of a neural network makes for an excellent set of inputs for the simulated annealing algorithm to minimize. Different sets of weights are used for the neural network, until one is found that produces a sufficiently low return from the error function.

Understanding Simulated Annealing

The previous sections showed you where the simulated annealing algorithm came from, as well as what applications it is used for. In this section you will be shown how to implement the simulated annealing algorithm. You will first be presented with the algorithm. In the next section we will develop a genetic algorithm class that can be used to solve the traveling salesman problem, which was introduced in Chapter 8.

What is the Structure of a Simulated Annealing Algorithm

We will now examine the structure of the simulated annealing algorithm. There are several distinct steps that the simulated annealing process goes through as the temperature is decreased, and randomness is applied to the input values. Figure 9.1 shows this process as a flowchart.

Figure 9.1: Overview of the Simulated Annealing Process

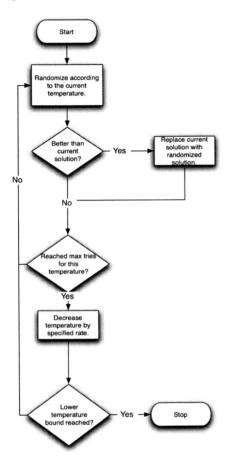

As you can see from Figure 9.1, there are two major processes that are occurring during the simulated annealing algorithm. First, for each temperature, the simulated annealing algorithm runs through a number of cycles. This number of cycles is predetermined by the programmer. As the cycle runs, the inputs are randomized. In the case of the traveling salesman problem, these inputs are the order of the cities that the traveling salesman will visit. Only randomizations which produce a better suited set of inputs will be kept.

Once the specified number of training cycles has been completed, the temperature can be lowered. Once the temperature is lowered, it is determined if the temperature has reached the lowest allowed temperature. If the temperature is not lower than the lowest allowed temperature, then the temperature is lowered and another cycle of randomizations will take place. If the temperature is lower than the minimum temperature allowed, the simulated annealing algorithm is complete.

At the core of the simulated annealing algorithm is the randomization of the input values. This randomization is ultimately what causes simulated annealing to alter the input values that the algorithm is seeking to minimize. This randomization process must often be customized for different problems. In this chapter we will discuss randomization methods that can be used both for the traveling salesman problem and neural network training. In the next section we will examine how this randomization occurs.

How are the Inputs Randomized

An important part of the simulated annealing process is how the inputs are randomized. This randomization process takes the previous values of the inputs and the current temperature as inputs. The input values are then randomized according to the temperature. A higher temperature will result in more randomization, a lower temperature will result in less randomization.

There is no exact method defined by the simulated annealing algorithm for how to randomize the inputs. The exact nature by which this is done often depends on the nature of the problem being solved. When comparing the methods used in simulated annealing for both the traveling salesman and neural network weight optimization, we can see some of these differences.

Simulated Annealing and Neural Networks

The method used to randomize the weights of a neural network is somewhat simpler than the traveling salesman's simulated annealing algorithm. A neural network's weight matrix can be thought of as a linear array of floating point numbers. Each weight is independent of the others. It does not matter if two weights contain the same value. The only major constraint is that there are ranges that all weights must fall within.

Because of this the process generally used to randomize the weight matrix of a neural network is relatively simple. Using the temperature, a random ratio is applied to all of the weights in the matrix. This ratio is calculated using the temperature and a random number. The higher the temperature, the more likely the ratio will cause a larger change in the weight matrix. A lower temperature will most likely produce a smaller ratio. This is the method that is used for the simulated annealing algorithm that will be presented in Chapter 10.

Simulated Annealing and the Traveling Salesman Problem

The method used to randomize the path of the traveling salesman is somewhat more complex than randomizing the weights of a neural network. This is because there are constraints that exist on the path of the traveling salesman problem that do not exist when optimizing the weight matrix of the neural network. The biggest difference is that the traveling salesman cannot visit the same city more than once during his trip. The randomization of the path must be controlled enough that it does not cause the traveling salesman to visit the same city more than once. By the same token, the traveling salesman must visit each city once. No cities may be skipped. The randomization algorithm must also be careful to not to drop any cities.

You can think of the traveling salesman randomization as simply moving elements of a fixed sized list. This fixed size list is the path that the traveling salesman must follow. Because the traveling salesman can neither skip nor revisit cities, the path of the traveling salesman will always have the same number of "stops" as there are cities.

Because of the constraints imposed by the traveling salesman problem, most randomization methods used with the traveling salesman problem work simply by jumbling the order of the previous path through the cities. By simply jumbling the data, and not modifying original values, we can be assured that the final result of this jumbling will neither skip, nor revisit, cities.

This is the method that is used to randomize traveling salesman's path in this chapter. Using a combination of the temperature and distance between two cities, the simulated annealing algorithm determines if the positions of these two cities should be changed. You will see the actual Java implementation of this method later in this chapter.

The final portion of the simulated annealing algorithm that we will explore in this section, is temperature reduction. Temperature reduction will be discussed in the next section.

Temperature Reduction

There are several different methods that can be used for temperature reduction. In this chapter we will examine two methods. The most common is to simply reduce the temperature by a fixed amount through each cycle. This is the method that is used in this chapter for the traveling salesman problem example.

Another method is to specify a beginning and ending temperature. This is the method that will be used by the simulated annealing algorithm that is shown in Chapter 10. To do this we must calculate a ratio at each step in the simulated annealing process. This is done by using an equation that guarantees that the step amount will cause the temperature to fall to the ending temperature in the number of cycles requested. The following equation shows how to logarithmically decrease the temperature between a beginning and ending temperature.

```
    double ratio = Math.exp(Math.log(stopTemperature/
startTemperature)/(cycles-1));
```

The above line calculates a ratio that should be multiplied against the current temperature. This will produce a change that will cause the temperature to reach the ending temperature in the specified number of cycles. This method is used in Chapter 10 when simulated annealing is applied to neural network training.

Implementing Simulated Annealing

Now that you have been shown how the simulated annealing process functions, we will implement this algorithm as a Java example. This section will begin by developing a simulated annealing class that will contain the code necessary to perform the simulated annealing algorithm.

The following section will apply this simulated annealing class to the traveling salesman problem. This will result in the completed program that you see in Figure 9.2.

Figure 9.2: The Simulated Annealing Example

As you can see, the program displays the path that the traveling salesman will take through the cities. The cities are shown as large dots, and the path of the traveling salesman is shown by the lines. The current best solution to the traveling salesman problem is shown with the lines. As the simulated annealing progresses, you will see the path stabilize. Ultimately the program will stop when the best solution has remained the same for 50 consecutive cycles. In this program, there are buttons to control the settings. The program begins seeking a solution as soon as it is run. The program will continue until a solution is found. If you wish to abort the program before a solution is found, you may click the close box for the program's window. We will begin examining how the program was constructed by examining the class "SimulatedAnnealing".

The Simulated Annealing Class

All of the code necessary to perform the simulated annealing specific functions is encapsulated inside of the SimulatedAnnealing class. This source code to this class is shown in Listing 9.1.

Listing 9.1: Simulated Annealing Class (SimulatedAnnealing.java)

```
public class SimulateAnnealing extends Thread {

  protected TravelingSalesman owner;
  protected double temperature;
  protected double pathlength;
  protected double minimallength;
  protected int order[];
  protected int minimalorder[];
```

```
/**
 * Constructor
 *
 * @param owner The TravelingSalesman class that owns this
 * object.
 */
SimulateAnnealing(TravelingSalesman owner)
{
  this.owner = owner;
  order = new int[TravelingSalesman.CITY_COUNT];
  minimalorder = new int[TravelingSalesman.CITY_COUNT];
}

/**
 * Called to determine if annealing should take place.
 *
 * @param d The distance.
 * @return True if annealing should take place.
 */
public boolean anneal(double d)
{
  if (temperature < 1.0E-4) {
    if (d > 0.0)
      return true;
    else
      return false;
  }
  if (Math.random() < Math.exp(d / temperature))
    return true;
  else
    return false;
}

/**
 * Used to ensure that the passed in integer is within thr
 * city range.
 *
 * @param i A city index.
 * @return A city index that will be less than CITY_COUNT
 */
public int mod(int i)
{
  return i % TravelingSalesman.CITY_COUNT;
}
```

```java
/**
 * Called to get the distance between two cities.
 *
 * @param i The first city
 * @param j The second city
 * @return The distance between the two cities.
 */
public double distance(int i, int j)
{
  int c1 = order[i%TravelingSalesman.CITY_COUNT];
  int c2 = order[j%TravelingSalesman.CITY_COUNT];
  return owner.cities[c1].proximity(owner.cities[c2]);
}


/**
 * Run as a background thread.  This method is called to
 * perform the simulated annealing.
 */
public void run()
{
  int cycle=1;
  int sameCount = 0;
  temperature = TravelingSalesman.START_TEMPERATURE;

  initorder(order);
  initorder(minimalorder);

  pathlength = length();
  minimallength = pathlength;

  while (sameCount<50) {
    // update the screen
    owner.paint();
    owner.setStatus("Cycle=" + cycle + ",Length=" +
      minimallength + ",Temp=" + temperature );

    // make adjustments to city order(annealing)
    for (int j2 = 0; j2 < TravelingSalesman.CITY_COUNT *
      TravelingSalesman.CITY_COUNT; j2++) {
      int i1 = (int)Math.floor((double)
        TravelingSalesman.CITY_COUNT * Math.random());
      int j1 = (int)Math.floor((double)
      TravelingSalesman.CITY_COUNT * Math.random());
      double d = distance(i1, i1 + 1) +
        distance(j1, j1 + 1) -
        distance(i1, j1) - distance(i1 + 1, j1 + 1);
```

```
      if (anneal(d)) {
        if (j1 < i1) {
          int k1 = i1;
          i1 = j1;
          j1 = k1;
        }
        for (; j1 > i1; j1--) {
          int i2 = order[i1 + 1];
          order[i1 + 1] = order[j1];
          order[j1] = i2;
          i1++;
        }
      }
    }

    // See if this improved anything
    pathlength = length();
    if (pathlength < minimallength) {
      minimallength = pathlength;
      for (int k2 = 0; k2 < TravelingSalesman.CITY_COUNT; k2++)
        minimalorder[k2] = order[k2];
      sameCount=0;
    } else
      sameCount++;
    temperature = TravelingSalesman.TEMPERATURE_DELTA *
      temperature;
    cycle++;
  }

  // we're done
  owner.setStatus("Solution found after " + cycle +
    " cycles." );
}

/**
 * Return the length of the current path through
 * the cities.
 *
 * @return The length of the current path through the cities.
 */
public double length()
{
  double d = 0.0;
  for (int i = 1; i <= TravelingSalesman.CITY_COUNT; i++)
    d += distance(i, i - 1);
  return d;
```

```
}

/**
 * Set the specified array to have a list of the cities in
 * order.
 *
 * @param an An array to hold the cities.
 */
public void initorder(int an[])
{
  for (int i = 0; i < TravelingSalesman.CITY_COUNT; i++)
    an[i] = i;
}
}
```

There are several variables that will be used by the class. These variables, and their purpose, are listed here in Table 9.1.

Table 9.1: Simulated Annealing Variables

Variable	Purpose
owner	The TravelingSalesman object that owns this object.
temperature	The current temperature.
pathlength	The length of the current path.
minimallength	The length of the best path.
order	The current order of cities.
minimalorder	The best order of cities.

As you can see, this class contains several attributes that are specific to the traveling salesman problem. This is because a different variant of the simulated annealing algorithm is used for the traveling salesman, just as was done with genetic algorithms. In Chapter 10, we will develop a simpler version of the simulated annealing algorithm, which is designed to work with neural networks. The simulated annealing algorithm must be able to determine the degree to which it has improved the input values. In the case of the traveling salesman, this is done using a simple distance formula between the two cities, as shown here.

```
public double distance(int i, int j)
{
  int c1 = order[i%TravelingSalesman.CITY_COUNT];
  int c2 = order[j%TravelingSalesman.CITY_COUNT];
  return owner.cities[c1].proximity(owner.cities[c2]);
}
```

This is unique to the traveling salesman problem. In Chapter 10, you will see that the error function of the entire neural network will be used to provide such feedback. The above method uses the proximity method, which is contained in the City class. We will not review the City class in this chapter, as it was discussed in Chapter 8. The proximity function is able to calculate the distance between two cities using the Pythagorean theorem, as discussed in Chapter 8.

The SimulatedAnnealing class is designed to run as a background thread. We will now examine what work is performed by this background thread. This is covered in the next section.

The Background Thread

The SimulatedAnnealing class, named SimulatedAnnealing, is a subclass of the Thread class contained in Java. This allows the simulated annealing class to run as a background thread. Just like the thread class in Java, you can call the "start" method to begin the thread's execution.

The simulated annealing class contains a "run" method that performs the simulated annealing algorithm. We will now examine the contents of the run class in greater detail. The "run" method begins by initializing a few variables to starting values.

```
int cycle=1;
int sameCount = 0;
temperature = TravelingSalesman.START_TEMPERATURE;
```

As you can see from the above code, we are setting the cycle to start at one, because we are on the first cycle, and the temperature to the starting temperature. We also maintain a variable, named sameCount, which counts the number of times that we have found the same solution.

Keeping track of the number of times the same path through the cities has been determined is a good way for the traveling salesman program to determine when processing is complete. This is a method which only works for the traveling salesman problem. The neural network based simulated annealing algorithm that we will examine in Chapter 10, will use a different method to determine when it is complete.

There are two sets of cities that we keep during the run of the simulated annealing algorithm. First, we keep a set that holds the best order of cities that we have found yet. This is the set of cities that produces the shortest path. This set of cities is stored in the "minimal-order" property. The second set of cities we keep is the current working set. This is the set of cities that the algorithm is currently "randomizing" according to the current temperature. If the working set of cities produces a path that is better than the current best set of cities, the working set will be copied to the best set. This allows the program to always keep track of the best path that has been determined.

When the genetic algorithm first begins, we simply set the working set and the best path set to the numeric order of the cities (i.e. city one first, then city two). This order is most likely not the optimal order, but it is as good of a starting point as any. The code that sets these two paths is shown here.

```
initorder(order);
initorder(minimalorder);
```

Now that we have a current best set and working set, we must calculate their lengths. This is done using the following lines of code.

```
pathlength = length();
minimallength = pathlength;
```

At this point we can set the "minimallenght" property equal to the "pathlength" property because both the working set and current best set have the same order of cities, and thus will have the same length.

We are now ready to begin the main loop of the simulated annealing algorithm. The following line begins the main loop.

```
while (sameCount<50) {
```

As you can see, we will continue looping so long as "sameCount" is less than 50. As you recall, "sameCount" holds the number of times the same solution has been found. At the beginning of the loop the simulated annealing algorithm updates its "owner object" as to the status of the algorithm. In the case of the traveling salesman example shown in this chapter, the "owner object" is the main window of the application. This update is performed with the following lines of code.

```
// update the screen
owner.paint();
owner.setStatus("Cycle=" + cycle + ",Length=" +
  minimallength + ",Temp=" + temperature );
```

We are now ready to cycle through a number of iterations at the current temperature. This will allow us to determine if we would like to perform annealing for each city in the current working set. If we do perform annealing for a city, that city will be swapped with another city.

This process method for simulated annealing is very much fine tuned to the traveling salesman problem. We take extra care to make sure cities are not duplicated as the annealing algorithm progresses. This is because the traveling salesman will never visit the same city more than once. You will see that the annealing process used in Chapter 10 will be someone different, as a neural network weight matrix does not have this issue.

```
// make adjustments to city order(annealing)
for (int j2 = 0; j2 < TravelingSalesman.CITY_COUNT *
  TravelingSalesman.CITY_COUNT; j2++) {
```

For this city, we calculate two random numbers. Each random number can be up to the city count. Because this is basically a random index we use the "floor" method of the "Math" class to convert to a integer.

```
int i1 = (int)Math.floor((double)TravelingSalesman.CITY_COUNT *
  Math.random());
int j1 = (int)Math.floor((double)TravelingSalesman.CITY_COUNT *
  Math.random());
```

We then produce a variable, named d, which holds the difference in the distances between these two cities. This distance will be fed to the annealing decision function. A greater distance will cause a greater chance modification to take place.

```
double d = distance(i1, i1 + 1) + distance(j1, j1 + 1) -
  distance(i1, j1) - distance(i1 + 1, j1 + 1);
```

Next, we will use this distance to determine if we should anneal. This is determined by the "anneal" method, which will be described in the next section. The anneal method takes into consideration both the temperature and the distance. Greater distance and greater temperatures cause a greater likelihood for a modification to the inputs to take place.

```
if (anneal(d)) {
```

If it is determined that we should anneal ("j1" is less than "i1"), then we swap the values of the "j1" and "i1".

```
if (j1 < i1) {
   int k1 = i1;
   i1 = j1;
   j1 = k1;
}
```

Now, we loop between "i1" and "j1" and swap the values as we progress. This reorders the path. This also has the effect of not introducing additional cities that have the same index.

```
for (; j1 > i1; j1--) {
   int i2 = order[i1 + 1];
   order[i1 + 1] = order[j1];
   order[j1] = i2;
   i1++;
```

The last part of the main loop must check to see if the annealing, that we just performed actually improved anything or not. To do this we calculate the length of the current working set. If the length is an improvement over the current best set, the current working set will be copied to the current best set. First we calculate the length of the current working set.

```
// See if this improved anything
pathlength = length();
```

Now, we must check to see if this length is better than the current best set.

```
if (pathlength < minimallength) {
```

If this length is greater than the current best set, then we will copy the working set to the current best set. The following lines of code perform this copy.

```
minimallength = pathlength;
for (int k2 = 0; k2 < TravelingSalesman.CITY_COUNT; k2++)
   minimalorder[k2] = order[k2];
```

We also set the "sameCount" variable to zero, since we have found a different solution.

```
      sameCount=0;
   } else
```

We must also handle the case where no improvement was made to the path that the salesman must travel. If this is the case, we increase the cycle count and decrease the temperature. The following lines of code do this.

```
   sameCount++;
   temperature = TravelingSalesman.TEMPERATURE_DELTA *
     temperature;
   cycle++;
 }
```

If the loop exits, then we know that we have reached 50 cycles that contained the same solution. We are now done. We report this to the main window and terminate the thread. The thread is terminated by simply returning from the "run" method, as is consistent with Java thread processing. The following lines of code perform this final report.

```
  // we're done
  owner.setStatus("Solution found after " + cycle +
    " cycles." );
```

This completes the "run" method. This loop, that we just examined, is what performs the simulated annealing process. When stepping through the statements that make up this loop we mentioned that the "anneal" method was used to determine if we should perform annealing or not. This method will be examined in the next section.

To Modify or not to Modify

In the previous section we looked at the main loop for the simulated annealing process. At each stage through the loop we had to make a decision as to if we would modify the inputs or not. This decision was made by a method named "anneal". We will now examine how the "anneal" method makes this determination. The "anneal" method is shown here.

```
public boolean anneal(double d)
{
  if (temperature < 1.0E-4) {
    if (d > 0.0)
      return true;
    else
```

```
      return false;
    }
  if (Math.random() < Math.exp(d / temperature))
    return true;
  else
    return false;
}
```

As you can see, we first see if the temperature is below a specified threshold. If the temperature is below this amount, then the temperature plays no role in determining if annealing will take place or not. If the temperature is below this threshold then we simply check to see if the distance is greater than 0. If the distance is greater than zero we return true to specify that annealing should take place.

If the temperature is above the threshold then we will use the distance and temperature to make a determination as to whether a modification should occur to the inputs. To calculate this, the ratio of the temperature and distance is raised to the power of the natural base (e). This is done using the "Math.exp()" method.

Now that you have seen how the simulated annealing class works, we are ready to see it adapted to the traveling salesman problem. The traveling salesman user interface is identical to the traveling salesman problem that was presented in Chapter 8. The underlying user interface code is somewhat different than Chapter 8. You will be shown how the user interface to the traveling salesman problem was constructed in the next section.

Application to the Traveling Salesman

Now that you have seen how the simulated annealing class was constructed you will see how to put it to use. In this section we will examine the main window of the traveling salesman problem. This window contains the code that begins the simulated annealing problem and displays the results to the user. The main window is contained in the class Traveling-Salesman. Listing 9.2 shows the source code to this class.

Listing 9.2: The Traveling Salesman Problem (TravelingSalesman.java)

```
import javax.swing.*;
import java.awt.*;
import java.awt.event.*;
import java.text.*;

public class TravelingSalesman
  extends JFrame {

  public static final int CITY_COUNT = 50;
  public static final double START_TEMPERATURE = 10;
  public static final double TEMPERATURE_DELTA = 0.99;
  protected Map map = null;
  protected JLabel status;
```

```java
public SimulateAnnealing worker = null;
protected boolean started = false;
public City [] cities;

/**
 * The constructor
 */
public TravelingSalesman() {
  setSize(300,300);
  setTitle("Traveling Salesman Problem2");

  getContentPane().setLayout(new BorderLayout());

  if ( map == null ) {
    map = new Map(this);
    getContentPane().add(map,"Center");
    status = new JLabel("Starting up");
    getContentPane().add(status,"South");
  }
  start();

}

/**
 * Start the background thread.
 */
public void start() {
// create a random list of cities

  cities = new City[TravelingSalesman.CITY_COUNT];
  for ( int i=0;i<TravelingSalesman.CITY_COUNT;i++ ) {
    cities[i] = new City(
      (int)(Math.random()*(getBounds().width-10)),
      (int)(Math.random()*(getBounds().height-60)));
  }

// start up the background thread
  started = true;
  map.update(map.getGraphics());

  if ( worker != null )
    worker = null;
  worker = new SimulateAnnealing(this);
  worker.setPriority(Thread.MIN_PRIORITY);
  worker.start();
}
```

```
public void paint()
{
  map.update(getGraphics());
}

/**
 * Display the current status
 *
 * @param status The current status.
 */
public void setStatus(String status)
{
  this.status.setText(status);
}

/**
 * The main method.
 *
 * @param args Not used
 */
public static void main(String args[])
{
  (new TravelingSalesman()).show();
}
}
```

As you can see the traveling salesman program contains several properties and constants that are used for various purposes. You can change the three constants to adjust the number of cities, starting temperature, and the rate at which the temperature decreases. These variables are summarized in Table 9.2.

Table 9.2: Traveling Salesman Variables for Simulated Annealing

Variable	Purpose
CITY_COUNT	How many cities to use.
START_TEMPERATURE	Starting temperature for simulated annealing.
TEMPERATURE_DELTA	The temperature delta for simulated annealing
map	A Map object that will display the city map.
status	The current status. Used to display the current status to the user.
worker	The background worker thread.
started	Is the thread started.
cities	The list of cities.

The three constant values are given default values that provide a good environment to test the program in. A city count of 50 cities is used because this will take the program a few minutes to solve, yet does not overload the program. A starting temperature of 10, along with a temperature decrease rate of 0.99 also seems to work well.

The traveling salesman main window class contains a method named "start" that will begin the simulated annealing process. We will now examine the tasks that are completed by this method. The first thing that the "start" method does is creates a random list of cities. The code the assigns the cities to random locations is shown here.

```
// create a random list of cities
   cities = new City[TravelingSalesman.CITY_COUNT];
   for ( int i=0;i<TravelingSalesman.CITY_COUNT;i++ ) {
     cities[i] = new City(
       (int)(Math.random()*(getBounds().width-10)),
       (int)(Math.random()*(getBounds().height-60)));
   }
```

Now that the cities are in random locations, we must start up the background thread. This is done by instantiating an object of the SimulatedAnnealing class. Because the simulated annealing class is a subclass of "Thread", you begin the simulated annealing background thread just as you would begin any other thread in Java. This is done by calling the thread's start method. We will now examine how the background thread is started up.

First, we set the started property to true, so that the rest of the program knows that the background thread has started. Next, we call the Map class to display the Map of cities to the user. Because the Map class is so similar to the Map class used in Chapter 8, the Map class will not be reviewed in this chapter. For more information about the Map class refer to Chapter 8. The following lines of code complete this initialization.

```
// start up the background thread
   started = true;
   map.update(map.getGraphics());
```

Now, we are ready to begin the background thread. This is done by instantiating the simulated annealing class. We pass in the current object to the simulated annealing class's constructor. The current object is needed by the simulated annealing class so that it knows which object to send update information to.

```
worker = new SimulateAnnealing(this);
```

We must also set the thread's priority to minimum. This is so that the thread does not consume so many processor cycles that the user no longer has access to the operating system. The following line of code does this.

```
worker.setPriority(Thread.MIN_PRIORITY);
```

This will be especially important on a Windows platform. Using both Windows XP and Windows 2000, the operating system be in a nearly locked up state without the thread priority setting. The simulated annealing program would continue to run.

Finally, we call the start method. This begins the background thread.

```
worker.start();
```

As you can see, the "driver program" for the simulated annealing implementation of the traveling salesman problem is very similar to the genetic algorithm. You can easily run the two programs and compare the relative performance of each. I conducted some test cases on my own computer system. In nearly every case, the simulated annealing algorithm outperforms the genetic algorithm. The gap will become even wider when applied to neural network optimization. In Chapter 10 you will be shown one single program that is able to use both genetic algorithms and simulated annealing to attempt to optimize the weight matrix of a neural network. You will also be able to compare the relative performance of backpropagation to both genetic algorithms and simulated annealing.

Summary

In this chapter you learned about the simulated annealing algorithm. The simulated annealing algorithm is based on the actual process of annealing. The annealing process says that a metal which is allowed to cool more slowly will form more consistent, and therefore stronger, crystal structures. This is because higher temperatures result in higher energy levels for the atoms that make up the metal. At the higher energy levels, the atoms that make up the metal are allowed a much greater freedom of movement. As the metal cools, this freedom of movement is curtailed. This allows the atoms to settle into consistent crystal patterns.

The process of simulated annealing is very similar to the actual annealing process. A series of input values are presented to the simulated annealing algorithm. The simulated annealing algorithm wants to optimize these input values so that an arbitrary equation can be minimized. Examples of the equation that is to be minimized might be the error function for a neural network, or the distance that the traveling salesman travels. The input values, which drive the simulated annealing algorithm, could be such things as the weight matrix of a neural network or the current route of cities that the traveling salesman is traveling.

To see a relatively simple example of how to use simulated annealing, this chapter once again turned to the traveling salesman problem. The traveling salesman problem was also used in Chapter 8 in conjunction with genetic algorithms. Reusing the traveling salesman problem allows you to easily compare the performance of genetic algorithms, when compared to simulated annealing.

In the next chapter, we will see how to apply both genetic algorithms and simulated annealing to neural network training. We will develop an application that allows either of these training methods to be used.

CHAPTER 10: HANDLING LOCAL MINIMA

Chapter Highlights
- **Understanding Local Minima**
- **Finding the Global Minimum**
- **Why Backpropagation is Prone to Local Minima**
- **Using Genetic Algorithms to Evade Local Minima**
- **Using Simulated Annealing to Evade Local Minima**

In Chapter 5, backpropagation was introduced. Backpropagation is a very effective means of training a neural network. However, there are some inherent flaws in the backpropagation training algorithm. One of the most fundamental flaws is the tendency for the backpropagation training algorithm to fall into a "local minima". A local minima is a false optimal weight matrix that prevents the backpropagation training algorithm from seeing the true solution.

In this chapter you will see how you may use other training techniques to supplement backpropagation and elude local minima. In the previous two chapters, you learned about two net optimization techniques that were used to find the minimal path that a traveling salesman might travel. This chapter will begin by introducing you to exactly what a local minima is. Then, the genetic and simulated annealing algorithms will be used to allow the backpropagation training algorithm to escape a local minima, and seek a more optimal solution, if one does exist. We will begin by examining global and local minima.

Understanding Minima

To understand the significance of global and local minima, we must first establish exactly what is meant by the term "minima". Minima are the bottoms of curves on a graph. Figure 10.1 shows a graph that contains several minima.

Figure 10.1: Several Minima

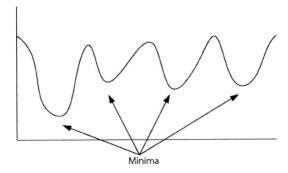

Minima

Local Minima

The function that we are seeking the minimum to is not nearly as simple as the graph shown in Figure 10.1. We are seeking the minimum of the error function chosen for the neural network. Because the entire weight matrix serves as input to this function it produces a far more complex graph than the one shown in Figure 10.1.

Local minima are any points that form the bottom of a selected region of the graph. This region can be of any arbitrary size. Backpropagation has a tendency to find these local minima. Once the backpropagation learning algorithm settles into one of these local minima it is very difficult for the algorithm to continue its search to find the global minimum. The global minimum is the absolute lowest point that the graph of the error function will ever attain.

The Search for the Global Minimum

The objective of training a neural network is the minimization of the error function. Supervised training, using a backpropagation based learning algorithm, can become trapped in a local minima of the error function. The reason this can occur is the fact that steepest descent and conjugate gradient backpropagation based training methods are local minimization algorithms. There is no mechanism that allows them to escape such a local minima.

Simulated annealing and genetic algorithms are two algorithms that have the capability to move out of regions near local minima. Though there is no guarantee that it will find the true global minimum, these algorithms can often help to find a more suitable local minima. That is a local minima with a lower error score. Figure 10.2 shows the chart of an arbitrary function that has several local minima and a global minimum.

Figure 10.2: The Global Minimum

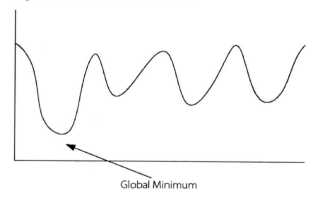

Global Minimum

Escaping Local Minima

In this chapter you will be shown how you can use simulated annealing and genetic algorithms to escape the local minima issues inherent with backpropagation. This chapter will focus primarily on the use of simulated annealing. Simulated annealing has become a very popular training algorithm, as it generally finds a better solution than backpropagation. We will begin by examining how simulated annealing will be used.

Using Simulated Annealing

As you recall from Chapter 9, simulated annealing works by simulating the cooling process of a metal. To apply this to a neural network we simply treat the weights and tolerances of the neural network as the individual ions in the metal. As the temperature falls, the weights of the neural network will achieve less excited states. As this process progresses, the most optimal weight matrix is chosen, based on the error of the neural network. The error, as was discussed in chapter 3, is how well the neural network is recognizing the sample input. In the case of the example program in this chapter, that is the XOR problem.

Using Genetic Algorithms

Genetic algorithms seem to be less popular than simulated annealing for neural network training. Genetic algorithms take considerably more processing time, and memory than simulated annealing. This is because the genetic algorithm must keep a population of weight matrixes. Because of this, thousands of weight matrixes must be kept through successive generations. For this reason, this chapter will focus on simulated annealing as a training method.

Nevertheless, this chapter does show an example of using a genetic algorithm. The genetic algorithm shown in this chapter is designed to work using the neural network class that was presented in Chapter 3. This algorithm is presented primarily for demonstrative purposes and executes considerably slower than the simulated annealing example.

Implementing Local Minima Escape

We will now examine an example that uses both simulated annealing and genetic algorithms to help find the most optimal weight matrix. For this example we will revisit the XOR example that was shown in Chapter 3. This example program used a multilayer feedforward backpropagation neural network to solve the XOR logic gate. This application can also be applied to other logic gates simply by modifying its training grid. For this example we will assume that you are using the XOR training grid provided with this book.

The example program looks similar to the example program from Chapter 3. This program is shown in Figure 10.3.

Figure 10.3: The Genetic/Annealing XOR Example Program

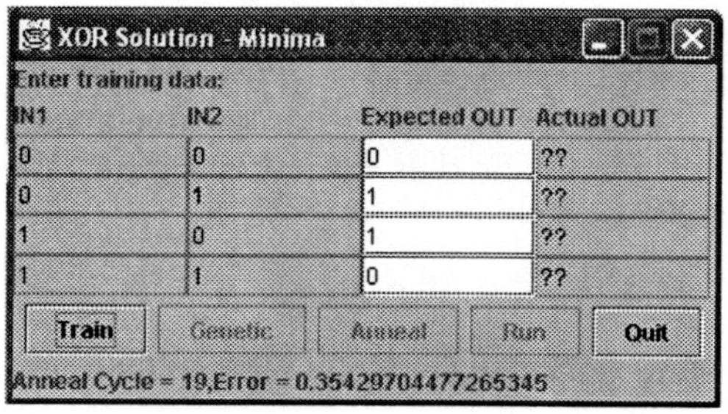

The primary difference is two additional regions just below the top of the application. These areas allow you to control the simulated annealing and genetic algorithm portions of the program.

Just as with the XOR example program from Chapter 3, you are able to begin a training cycle. Once you begin a training cycle, by clicking the "Train" button, the program will begin training the neural network. As the neural network is trained, you will see the current error for the neural network. This error should decrease as the program runs.

Usually this error number will decrease to well below 10%. Once this happens, you have a sufficiently trained neural network. If this happens you should click the "Randomize" button and begin training again. In this particular case we are looking for a weight matrix that will get stuck in a local minima and not decrease below 10%.

In addition to the backpropagation training that was provided in Chapter 3, this neural network can also be trained in other ways. Clicking on the "Anneal" button will begin training the neural network using the simulated annealing algorithm. Clicking on the "Genetic" button will begin training the neural network using a genetic algorithm.

If you run both the simulated annealing and genetic algorithms you will notice a considerable difference in the outputs of each. The simulated annealing routine will execute much faster. Usually within a few seconds, a weight matrix will be established. This weight matrix will almost always be lower in error than the weight matrix determined by the backpropagation algorithm. This is because the simulated annealing algorithm was not caught up by local minima.

Executing the genetic algorithm will take a considerably longer time than simulated annealing. If you examine the process list for your computer, while the genetic algorithm is running, you will also notice the genetic algorithm takes up considerably more memory than the simulated annealing algorithm. Because of its quick execution and low memory requirements, simulated annealing has become a very popular means of training neural networks.

The example program remains similar to the XOR problem from Chapter 3, however, additional user interface elements have been added for simulated annealing and genetic algorithm. We will now examine how this example program was constructed. The UML diagram for this example program is shown in Figure 10.4.

Figure 10.4: Genetic/Annealing XOR UML Diagram

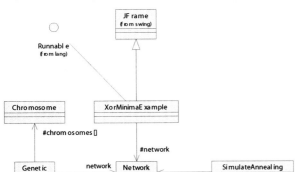

You will now be shown how this program was constructed. We will begin with the user interface. The user interface for the simulated annealing and genetic algorithms version of the XOR problem adds some user interface elements to the XOR example shown in Chapter 3. The additional user interface elements are discussed in the next section.

The User Interface

This program has essentially the same user interface as the XOR example shown in Chapter 3. Because of this we will not examine the complete source code of the user interface. We will now highlight some of the differences between the user interface source code and what was already presented in Chapter 3.

The user interface code is contained in the file XorMinimaExample.java. Rather than just having the "Train" and "Run" buttons, the minima example also contains buttons to allow the program to train using simulated annealing and a genetic algorithm. When the user selects to train using simulated annealing the following method is called.

```
/**
 * Train the neural network with simulated
 * annealing.
 */
protected void anneal()
{
  double xorData[][] = getGrid();
  double xorIdeal[][] = getIdeal();
  int update=0;

  status.setText("Starting...");
  btnRun.setEnabled(false);
  btnGenetic.setEnabled(false);
  btnAnneal.setEnabled(false);
```

```
SimulateAnnealing anneal = new SimulateAnnealing(network);
anneal.start(10,2,100);
anneal.setInput(xorData);
anneal.setIdeal(xorIdeal);

for (int x=0;x<100;x++) {
  anneal.anneal();
  status.setText("Anneal Cycle = " + x + ",Error = " +
    anneal.getGlobalError());
}

btnRun.setEnabled(true);
btnGenetic.setEnabled(true);
btnAnneal.setEnabled(true);
}
```

None of the actual simulated annealing algorithm is actually contained in this method. Rather, this method simply serves as a bridge between the user interface code and the SimulateAnnealing class that actually performs the simulated annealing.

As you can see, the method begins by disabling the buttons so that the user does not accidentally initiate two training sessions simultaneously. Then the simulated annealing class is instantiated and passed a few parameters. The following line does this:

```
SimulateAnnealing anneal = new SimulateAnnealing(network);
anneal.start(10,2,100);
```

The "ten" and "two" arguments specify the beginning and ending temperatures. The 100 value specified how many cycles will be used. It is necessary for the algorithm to know how many cycles will be used so that the temperature is decreased in a way that will cause it to end at the "specified ending temperature".

The starting and ending temperatures can be altered if the network is not being trained well. Higher values for the starting temperature will cause greater deviations in the weight matrix. This may be necessary in order to reach acceptable error levels with certain neural networks. Lower ending temperatures often allow the algorithm to fine tune the weight matrix more before the algorithm completes. Some degree of experimentation is generally required to find a optimal set of parameters.

Next, the genetic algorithm is given the training data so that the error of the neural network can be determined at each cycle.

```
anneal.setInput(xorData);
anneal.setIdeal(xorIdeal);
```

Finally the method runs through 100 cycles and applies the annealing algorithm at each cycle. The global error is reported to the user interface at each cycle.

```
for (int x=0;x<100;x++) {
  anneal.anneal();
  status.setText("Anneal Cycle = " + x + ",Error = " +
    anneal.getGlobalError());
}
```

The method that is used to train the neural network with a genetic algorithm is very similar to the method just examined. The genetic algorithm method is shown here:

```
/**
 * Train the neural network with a genetic algorithm.
 */
protected void genetic()
{
  double xorData[][] = getGrid();
  double xorIdeal[][] = getIdeal();
  int update=0;
  status.setText("Starting...");
  Genetic genetic = new Genetic(network);
  genetic.setInput(xorData);
  genetic.setIdeal(xorIdeal);
  genetic.start();

  btnRun.setEnabled(false);
  btnGenetic.setEnabled(false);
  btnAnneal.setEnabled(false);

  int x=0;
  while (genetic.getGlobalError()>.1) {
    x++;
    genetic.generation();
    status.setText("Genetic Cycle = " + x + ",Error = " +
      genetic.getGlobalError());
  }

  btnRun.setEnabled(true);
  btnGenetic.setEnabled(true);
```

```
    btnAnneal.setEnabled(true);
}
```

Just as was the case with the simulated annealing method, the genetic method is merely an interface between the user interface and the class that actually handles the genetic algorithm. It is the Genetic class that actually implements the genetic algorithm.

The Neural Network

Only minor changes were made to the neural network class to support genetic algorithms and simulated annealing. Two methods were added to the Network class that allows better access to the weight matrix and threshold values of the neural network.

The simulated annealing and genetic algorithms work best when the weight matrix and thresholds are presented as a linear array of doubles. To do this, two new method were added. The "fromArray" method will copy an array to the weight matrix and thresholds of the neural network. The "toArray" method is provided to convert the weight matrixes and thresholds to a simple array. The "toArray" method is shown here:

```
/**
 * Convert to an array.  This is used with some training
 * algorithms that require that the "memory" of the
 * neuron(the weight and threshold values) be expressed
 * as a linear array.
 *
 * @return The memory of the neuron.
 */
public double []toArray()
{
  double result[] = new double[matrix.length+thresholds.length];
  for (int i=0;i<matrix.length;i++)
    result[i] = matrix[i];
  for (int i=0;i<thresholds.length;i++)
    result[matrix.length+i] = thresholds[i];
  return result;
}
```

As you can see, the "toArray" method does nothing more than allocate a new array that is large enough to hold both the weight matrix and thresholds of the neural network. Then the weight matrix and threshold values are copied to this new array. The "fromArray" method does the opposite. The "fromArray" method is shown here:

```
/**
 * Use an array to populate the memory of the neural network.
```

```
 *
 * @param array An array of doubles.
 */
public void fromArray(double array[])
{
  for (int i=0;i<matrix.length;i++)
    matrix[i] = array[i];
  for (int i=0;i<thresholds.length;i++)
    thresholds[i] = array[matrix.length+i];
}
```

As you can see, the "fromArray" method copies an array, which was created by "toArray", back into the weight matrix and threshold values of the neural network.

These two methods will allow more direct access to the weight matrix and threshold values that will be needed by the simulated annealing and genetic algorithms. We will now examine the classes that implement the simulated annealing and genetic algorithm classes. You were already introduced to these classes back in Chapters 8 and 9. These classes were modified somewhat to be adapted for use with neural networks.

These changes were necessary due to some inherent differences in neural network training and the traveling salesman problem. In the traveling salesman problem, the order of cities is what is changing. In neural network training, it is the weights that are changing in value. Also, where it was illegal for the traveling salesman to visit a city more than once, there is no such constraint on neural network training. In the next two sections you will be shown exactly how this training is done. We will begin with simulated annealing.

Simulated Annealing

You will now be shown how the simulated annealing learning algorithm was implemented. The simulated annealing algorithm fits completely in the SimulatedAnnealing class. This file is shown in Listing 10.1.

Listing 10.1: Simulated Annealing (SimulateAnnealing.java)

```
public class SimulateAnnealing {

  protected Network network;
  protected double input[][];
  protected double ideal[][];
  protected double startTemperature;
  protected double stopTemperature;
  protected int cycles;
  protected double globalError;

  /**
   * The constructor.
   *
```

```
 * @param network The neural network that is to be trained.
 */
public SimulateAnnealing(Network network)
{
  this.network = network;
}
/**
 * Set the training input.
 *
 * @param input The data that is to be used to train the
 * neural network.
 */
public void setInput(double input[][])
{
  this.input = input;
}

/**
 * Set the ideal results for the training data.
 *
 * @param ideal The ideal results for the training data.
 */
public void setIdeal(double ideal[][])
{
  this.ideal = ideal;
}

/**
 * The current temperature.
 */
protected double temperature;

/**
 * Randomize the weights and thresholds.  This function
 * does most of the work of the class.  Each call to this
 * class will randomize the data according to the current
 * temperature.  The higher the temperature the more randomness.
 */
protected void randomize()
{
  double ratio = temperature * Math.sqrt(12);

  double array[] = network.toArray();

  for (int i=0;i<array.length;i++) {
    double add = 0.5 - (Math.random());
```

```
    add /= startTemperature;
    add *= temperature;
    array[i] = array[i] + add;
  }

  network.fromArray(array);
}

/**
 * Determine the error of the current weights and
 * thresholds.
 */
protected double determineError()
{
  for (int i=0;i<input.length;i++) {
    network.computeOutputs(input[i]);
    network.calcError(ideal[i]);
  }
  return network.getError(input.length);
}

/**
 * Initialize the simulated annealing class.
 *
 * @param startTemp The starting temperature.
 * @param stopTemp The ending temperature.
 * @param cycles The number of cycles to use.
 */
public void start(double startTemp,double stopTemp,int cycles)
{
  temperature = startTemp;
  this.cycles = cycles;
  this.startTemperature = startTemp;
  this.stopTemperature = stopTemp;
}

/**
 * Called to perform one cycle of the annealing process.
 */
public void anneal()
{
  double bestArray[];

  globalError = determineError();
  bestArray = network.toArray();
```

```java
    for (int i=0;i<100;i++) {
      double curError;
      randomize();
      curError = determineError();
      if (curError<globalError) {
        bestArray = network.toArray();
        globalError = curError;
      }
    }

    network.fromArray(bestArray);
    double ratio = Math.exp(
      Math.log(stopTemperature/startTemperature)/(cycles-1));
    temperature*=ratio;
  }

  /**
   * Get the current temperature.
   *
   * @return The current temperature.
   */
  public double getTemperature()
  {
    return temperature;
  }

  /**
   * Get the global error.
   *
   * @return The global error.
   */
  public double getGlobalError()
  {
    return globalError;
  }

}
```

To understand this class we will begin by looking at the properties. The properties of this class are listed in Table 10.1.

Table 10.1: Simulated Annealing Variables

Variable	Purpose
network	The neural network that is being trained.
input	Training data that will be used to determine the error for the neural network.
ideal	Holds the ideal results from the neural network for the training sets.
startTemperature	The beginning temperature.
stopTemperature	The ending temperature. This value should be reached once the number of cycles, specified by the cycles property, has passed.
cycles	The total number of cycles that the simulated annealing algorithm is to be run for.
globalError	The current error of the neural network. This value is to be minimized.

To begin the process of simulated annealing, the start method must be called. The start method accepts the network to be optimized and sets up the other properties based on that network.

Most of the work is done by the "randomize" method. This method will randomize the weights and tolerances to a degree specified by the current temperature. The algorithm works by repeatedly calling the randomize method, as the temperature drops. This allows an optimal weight matrix and threshold values to be gradually created.

The algorithm used to randomize the weight matrix and threshold values is not complex. The "randomize" method works by looping across all of the weight matrix and threshold values and multiplying each by a ratio. This ratio is derived directly from the current temperature.

The main entry point for external class is the anneal method. The anneal method is responsible for actually calling the "randomize" method. The anneal method begins by looping through 100 iterations at the current temperature. This is done by calling the "randomize" method 100 times. Each time through the iteration, the new version of the weight matrix, which was created by the "randomize" method, is evaluated. If it is better than the previous "best matrix", then it is replaced. At the end of these 100 iterations, you will be left with the best weight matrix with all considered.

Once the 100 iterations have been completed, the "anneal" method must decrease the temperature. The temperature is decreased in a way so that the temperature will reach the ending temperature by the time that program has reached the maximum number of cycles. Each time the "anneal" method is called, it is considered one cycle. The total number of cycles was specified when the simulated annealing class was instantiated. To allow the temperature to be decreased in this way, the following method is used. First, a ratio is calculated that determines how much to decrease the temperature by.

```
    double ratio = Math.exp(Math.log(stopTemperature/
startTemperature)/(cycles-1));
```

Next, this ratio is multiplied against the current temperature.

```
    temperature*=ratio;
```

Now that you have seen how the simulated annealing class was implemented, you will be shown the class that allows genetic algorithms.

Genetic Algorithms

Unlike the simulated annealing algorithm, the genetic algorithm is implemented in more than one class. The Chromosome class is provided to hold one individual chromosome. A chromosome is one life form. In this case, the life form represents the weight matrix and threshold values of a neural network. The chromosomes are processed by the GeneticAlgoritm class. We will begin by examining the Chromosome class.

Chromosome class

All life forms in the genetic algorithm, that we are using, have on single chromosome. Because of this, the Chromosome class implements the individual life forms that will be used for the genetic algorithm. The complete listing for this class is shown in Listing 10.2.

Listing 10.2: Chromosomes (Chromosome.java)

```java
class Chromosome {

  protected static final int GENE_SIZE = 64;
  protected int [] gene;
  protected double cost;
  protected double mutationPercent;
  protected int cutLength;
  double matrix[];

  /**
   * The constructor, takes a list of cities to
   * set the initial "genes" to.
   *
   * @param cities The order that this chromosome would
   * visit the
   * cities.  These cities can be thought of as the
   * genes of this chromosome.
```

```java
  */
Chromosome(Network network) {
  matrix = network.toArray();
  gene = new int[matrix.length*GENE_SIZE];
  cost = 0.0;
  fromMatrix();
  cutLength = gene.length/2;
}


/**
 * Copy the genes to a weight matrix.
 */
public void toMatrix()
{
  int idx = 0;

  for (int i=0;i<matrix.length;i++) {
    long l = 0;
    long or = 1;
    for (int j=0;j<GENE_SIZE;j++) {
      if ( gene[idx++]!=0 )
        l = l | or;
      or+=or;
    }
    matrix[i] = Double.longBitsToDouble(l);
  }

}

/**
 * Copy the weight matrix to the genes.
 */
public void fromMatrix()
{
  int idx = 0;
  for (int i=0;i<matrix.length;i++) {
    long l = Double.doubleToLongBits(matrix[i]);
    long and = 1;
    for (int j=0;j<GENE_SIZE;j++) {
      gene[idx++] = (l & and)!=0?1:0;
      and+=and;
    }
  }
}

/**
```

```
  * Calculate the cost of this solution.  This is
  * the error of this weight matrix against the
  * sample data.
  *
  * @param network The neural network to use to calculate
  * the cost.
  * @param trial
  * @param ideal
  */
public void calculateCost(
  Network network,
  double trial[][],
  double ideal[][])
{
  toMatrix();
  network.fromArray(matrix);
  for (int i=0;i<trial.length;i++) {
    network.computeOutputs(trial[i]);
    network.calcError(ideal[i]);
  }
  cost = network.getError(trial.length);
}


/**
  * Get the cost for this chromosome.  Note that
  * the cost must be calculated first.
  *
  * @return The cost of this chromosome's solution.
  */
double getCost() {
  return cost;
}


/**
  * Get the ith gene in this chromosome.
  *
  * @param i The city you want.
  * @return The ith city.
  */
int getGene(int i) {
  return gene[i];
}

/**
  * Set all genes.
  *
```

```
 * @param list A list of genes.
 */
void setGenes(int [] list) {
  for ( int i=0;i<gene.length;i++ ) {
    gene[i] = list[i];
  }
}


/**
 * Set the cut value.
 *
 * @param cut The new cut value.
 */
void setCut(int cut) {
  cutLength = cut;
}


/**
 * Set the percent of new births that will be mutated.
 *
 * @param prob The probability that a mutation will occur.
 */
void setMutation(double prob) {
  mutationPercent = prob;
}
/**
 * Assuming this chromosome is the "mother" mate with
 * the passed in "father".
 *
 * @param father The father.
 * @param offspring1 Returns the first offspring
 * @param offspring2 Returns the second offspring.
 * @return The amount of mutation that was applied.
 */
int mate(
  Chromosome father,
  Chromosome offspring1,
  Chromosome offspring2) {
  int cutpoint = (int) (0.999999*Math.random()*
    (double)(gene.length-cutLength));

  int off1 [] = new int[gene.length];
  int off2 [] = new int[gene.length];

// mate
```

```java
    int n1 = gene.length/2;
    int n2 = gene.length-n1;
    int c = cutpoint;

    while ((n1--)>0) {
      c = (c+1)%gene.length;
      off1[c] = this.getGene(c);
      off2[c] = father.getGene(c);
    }

    while ((n2--)>0) {
      c = (c+1)%gene.length;
      off2[c] = this.getGene(c);
      off1[c] = father.getGene(c);
    }

    int mutate = 0;
    if ( Math.random() < mutationPercent ) {
      int iswap1 = (int) (0.999999*Math.random()*
        (double)(gene.length));
      int iswap2 = (int) (0.999999*Math.random()*
        (double)gene.length);
      int i = off1[iswap1];
      off1[iswap1] = off1[iswap2];
      off1[iswap2] = i;
      mutate++;
    }
    if ( Math.random() < mutationPercent ) {
      int iswap1 = (int) (0.999999*Math.random()*
        (double)(gene.length));
      int iswap2 = (int) (0.999999*Math.random()*
        (double)gene.length);
      int i = off2[iswap1];
      off2[iswap1] = off2[iswap2];
      off2[iswap2] = i;
      mutate++;
    }

    // copy results
    offspring1.setGenes(off1);
    offspring1.toMatrix();
    offspring2.setGenes(off2);
    offspring2.toMatrix();

    return mutate;
  }
```

```
/**
 * Sort the chromosomes by their cost.
 *
 * @param chromosomes An array of chromosomes to sort.
 * @param num How much of the chromosome list to sort.
 */
public static void sortChromosomes(
    Chromosome chromosomes[],
    int num) {
  Chromosome ctemp;
  boolean swapped = true;
  while ( swapped ) {
    swapped = false;
    for ( int i=0;i<num-1;i++ ) {
      if ( chromosomes[i].getCost() >
           chromosomes[i+1].getCost() ) {
        ctemp = chromosomes[i];
        chromosomes[i] = chromosomes[i+1];
        chromosomes[i+1] = ctemp;
        swapped = true;
      }
    }
  }
}

/**
 * Get the weight matrix associated with this chromosome.
 *
 * @return The weight matrix associated with this chromosome.
 */
public double[] getMatrix()
{
  return matrix;
}
}
```

There are several properties that are contained by the chromosome class. They are defined in Table 10.2.

Table 10.2: Chromosome Variables

Variable	Purpose
GENE_SIZE	The size of an individual gene. In this case it is 64 because each double has 8 bytes, and each of those bytes has 8 bits.
gene	An array of the genes. In this case, the genes contain the binary representation of the weight matrix and threshold values of the neural network.
cost	The error that this chromosome gives when evaluated.
mutationPercent	The percent of genes that should be mutated.
cutLength	Where to cut the chromosome during mating.
matrix	The weight matrix and threshold values that this chromosome corresponds to.

The genetic algorithm prefers that data be expressed as one long stream of genes. This allows these genes to be cut at certain intervals and spliced back together during the process of reproduction, or crossover. To do this, an important question becomes, "how, exactly, we represent the weight matrix and thresholds of the neural network as one long stream of information?"

This is similar to the process of converting the weight matrix and thresholds to a single array of doubles, as was done for simulated annealing. Thought the process is similar, there are some very important differences. Breaking the weight matrix and threshold values into individual numbers is far too coarse of a granularity for a genetic algorithm. If the individual weights were the genes, then the weights would simply be swapped about, and not actually modified. This is because a genetic algorithm does not actually modify the genes themselves. Rather the genes are simply recombined from the parents to produce the child. Because of this we need a finer level of granularity for the genes.

Storing the Gene Sequence

The binary representation of numbers is often chosen as the level of granularity required for an individual gene. This causes the individual binary digit to become the gene. This works well as "strips" of this binary information can be taken from both mother and father to produce the child. This level of detail is also below the individual weight number, so the weights will change as mating occurs.

To represent this binary stream of information, we need to choose a Java data type. To maintain some degree of similarity to the traveling salesman version of the genetic algorithm, the Java int type was chosen. This also allows marginal changes to the encode and decode routines to change the level of grandularity. For example, you may choose to modify the program so that individual digits of the weight and threshold values become the genes.

To encode and decode between binary and the weight matrix array, two data structures are provided by the Chromosome class. First, a variable named "matrix" is provided that holds the matrix and threshold values from the neural network. This data structure holds the data in the same format as is returned from the "toArray" method of the Network class. The binary representation of the genes is stored in the "gene" array. Two methods are provided that allow you to move data between the gene array and the matrix. These methods are named "toMatrix" and "fromMatrix", The "toMatrix" method is shown here.

```
public void toMatrix()
{
  int idx = 0;

  for (int i=0;i<matrix.length;i++) {
    long l = 0;
    long or = 1;
    for (int j=0;j<GENE_SIZE;j++) {
      if ( gene[idx++]!=0 )
        l = l | or;
      or+=or;
    }
    matrix[i] = Double.longBitsToDouble(l);
  }

}
```

As you can see, this method loops through each double value that is in the matrix. For each of these values, a corresponding value is built from the gene array. Because the gene array stores its information in binary, and the size of a double is 8 bytes, it takes 64 bits to create a single double value. As these bits are read, they are concatenated to a long value. Once the long value is full, the Java method "Double.longBitsToDouble" is called to actually create the double value.

Because Java is a high-level language you cannot simply access the bytes that make up a type, such as double. Yet the designers of Java realized that there are cases where the programmer will need access to the individual bits of number format such as double. To solve this issue, two Java methods were added. The "Double.longBitsToDouble" method is provided to convert individual bits to a double type. Additionally, the "Double. Double.double-ToLongBits " method is provided to convert a double to the bits that make up that value.

In addition to the "toMatrix" method, which converts the gene binary sequence to a weight matrix and threshold array, the "fromMatrix" method is also provided to do the reverse. The "fromMatrix" method will take the weight matrix and threshold values and fill the "gene" array with the binary representation. The "fromMatrix" method is shown here.

```
public void fromMatrix()
{
  int idx = 0;
  for (int i=0;i<matrix.length;i++) {
    long l = Double.doubleToLongBits(matrix[i]);
    long and = 1;
    for (int j=0;j<GENE_SIZE;j++) {
      gene[idx++] = (l & and)!=0?1:0;
      and+=and;
    }
  }
}
```

As you can see from the above code, the "fromMatrix" method begins by looping through each of the matrix values. For each matrix value, 64 bits are generated. The GENE_SIZE constant shown above holds the value of 64. The logical "and" operator is used to determine if each bit position is active or not.

The Mating Process

The "mate" method of the Chromosome class is provided to allow the chromosome to mate with another chromosome. Two offspring are always produced as a result of this mating. You will notice that the mate method, as seen in Listing 10.3 is somewhat different than the mate algorithm used in traveling salesman problem of Chapter 8.

The main difference between the mating algorithm of the traveling salesman problem and neural network training lies in one constraint that the traveling salesman problem has that neural network training does not. In the case of the traveling salesman problem, it is illegal to use the same gene more than once. If the same gene were used more than once, this would mean that the traveling salesman were visiting the same city more than once. This is a basic requirement of the traveling salesman problem.

When the genetic algorithm is applied to neural network training, no such constraint is present. Because the individual genes for the neural network are made up of binary bits, there really are only two gene types. It would not be possible to require a unique gene at each position on the chromosome. This makes the process of cutting the gene of the parents to produce the outputs much simpler than the process that was used in Chapter 8 for the traveling salesman problem. We will now examine the mating process.

First a random cut point is chosen. This cut point should be somewhere within the cut-length specified earlier.

```
    int cutpoint = (int) (0.999999*Math.random()*(double)(gene.
length-cutLength));
```

Two arrays are then allocated to hold the two offspring.

```
int off1 [] = new int[gene.length];
int off2 [] = new int[gene.length];
```

Next, the number of genes that will be in each area of the cut is determined. These two numbers will always be within one unit of each other. This is because the gene cut will wrap around the gene sequence. If you thought of the gene sequence as a circle, each cut would have 180 degrees. The only thing that varies is the starting point of the cut.

```
int n1 = gene.length/2;
int n2 = gene.length-n1;
int c = cutpoint;
```

Then, the program loops through and assigns the mother's DNA for the first cut to offspring one and the father's DNA to offspring two.

```
while ((n1--)>0) {
  c = (c+1)%gene.length;
  off1[c] = this.getGene(c);
  off2[c] = father.getGene(c);
}
```

The same process is completed for the second cut, except the mother and father are switched. The program loops through and assigns the mother's DNA for the first cut to offspring two and the father's DNA to offspring one.

```
while ((n2--)>0) {
  c = (c+1)%gene.length;
  off2[c] = this.getGene(c);
  off1[c] = father.getGene(c);
}
```

Finally, mutations may be allowed to occur. A random number is selected based on the mutation percent. If mutation is to occur, then two of the genes in the offspring will be switched. This simple alteration provides some variety to the population that might otherwise become stagnant with no new genetic material being introduced. The mutation process for the first offspring is shown below.

```
int mutate = 0;
```

```
if ( Math.random() < mutationPercent ) {
  int iswap1 = (int) (0.999999*Math.random()*
    (double)(gene.length));
  int iswap2 = (int) (0.999999*Math.random()*
    (double)gene.length);
  int i = off1[iswap1];
  off1[iswap1] = off1[iswap2];
  off1[iswap2] = i;
  mutate++;
}
```

The same mutation algorithm is then carried out on the second offspring. Now that you have seen how the individual chromosomes function, we must take a look at the main class for the genetic algorithm, the "Genetic" class. The Genetic class holds all of the chromosomes and regulates the mating process. The "Genetic" class will be discussed in the next section.

The Genetic Algorithm Class

We will now examine the controller class for the genetic algorithm. Most of the work is done in the Chromosome class that we just discussed. The controller class for the genetic algorithm is shown in Listing 10.3.

Listing 10.3: Genetic Algorithm (Genetic.java)

```
public class Genetic {

  public double globalError = 0;
  public static final int POPULATION_SIZE = 5000;
  public static final double MUTATION_PERCENT = 0.10;
  protected int matingPopulationSize = POPULATION_SIZE/2;
  protected int favoredPopulationSize = matingPopulationSize/2;
  protected double input[][];
  protected double ideal[][];
  protected Chromosome [] chromosomes;
  Network network;

  /**
   * Get the error for the best chromosome.
   *
   * @return The error for the best chromosome.
   */
  public double getGlobalError()
  {
```

```
    return globalError;
}

/**
 * Construct a new genetic algorithm class.
 *
 * @param network The neural network that is to be optimized.
 */
public Genetic(Network network)
{
  this.network = network;
}

/**
 * Init the genetic algorithm.
 */
public void start()
{
  chromosomes = new Chromosome[POPULATION_SIZE];
  for (int i=0;i<POPULATION_SIZE;i++) {
    network.reset();
    chromosomes[i] = new Chromosome(network);
    chromosomes[i].calculateCost(network,input,ideal);

    Chromosome c = chromosomes[i];
    c.fromMatrix();
    c.toMatrix();

  }
  Chromosome.sortChromosomes(chromosomes,chromosomes.length);
}


/**
 * Set the training data that will be used to evaluate the
 * error level of the weight matrixes.
 *
 * @param input The training data.
 */
public void setInput(double input[][])
{
  this.input = input;
}

/**
 * Set the idea results for the training data.
```

```
   *
 * @param ideal The ideal results for the training data.
 */
public void setIdeal(double ideal[][])
{
  this.ideal = ideal;
}

/**
 * Process one generation.
 */
public void generation()
{

  int ioffset = matingPopulationSize;
  int mutated = 0;
  double thisCost = 500.0;
  double oldCost = 0.0;
  double dcost = 500.0;
  int countSame = 0;

  // Mate the chromosomes in the favored population
  // with all in the mating population
  for ( int i=0;i<favoredPopulationSize-1;i++ ) {
    Chromosome cmother = chromosomes[i];
    // Select partner from the mating population
    int father = (int) ( 0.999999*Math.random()*
      (double)matingPopulationSize);
    Chromosome cfather = chromosomes[father];

    mutated += cmother.mate(
      cfather,
      chromosomes[ioffset],
      chromosomes[ioffset+1]);
    ioffset += 2;
  }

  // The new generation is in the matingPopulation area
  // move them to the correct area for sort.
  for ( int i=0;i<matingPopulationSize;i++ ) {
    chromosomes[i] = chromosomes[i+matingPopulationSize];
    chromosomes[i].calculateCost(network,input,ideal);
  }


  // Now sort the new mating population
```

```
Chromosome.sortChromosomes(chromosomes,matingPopulationSize);

double cost = chromosomes[0].getCost();
dcost = Math.abs(cost-thisCost);
thisCost = cost;
double mutationRate = 100.0 *
  (double) mutated /
  (double) matingPopulationSize;
globalError = thisCost;
chromosomes[0].toMatrix();
network.fromArray(chromosomes[0].getMatrix());

  }
}
```

There are several properties that are used by the genetic algorithm controller class. These properties are listed in Table 10.3.

Table 10.3: Genetic Algorithm Variables

Variable	Purpose
globalError	The error of the current best chromosome.
POPULATION_SIZE	A constant that holds the total size of the population.
MUTATION_PERCENT	The percent of new-born chromosomes that are mutated.
matingPopulationSize	The size of the mating population. This is half of the total population. This the favored population will select partners from this population.
favoredPopulationSize	The size of the favored population. This is half of the size of the mating population.
input	The training data that is used to determine the error for a given chromosome.
ideal	The ideal results from the training data.
chromosomes	The chromosomes that make up the total population.
network	The neural network that is to be trained.

Most of the work that is done by the genetic algorithm's controller class occurs in the methods "start" and "generation". The start method prepares the genetic algorithm for execution. The generation method is then called successively for each generation that is to be processed.

The "start" method is relatively simple. It begins by initializing some of the properties that will be used as the genetic algorithm executes. The "start" method then continues by creating the required number of chromosomes. Each chromosome is created and set to a random gene sequence. Obviously, these chromosomes will not be well suited. This will be corrected by successive generations as evolution occurs.

The "generation" method involves more steps. The "generation" method begins by looping through the favored population and mating each chromosome with a random selection from the preferred population. The following loop does this:

```java
for ( int i=0;i<favoredPopulationSize-1;i++ ) {
  Chromosome cmother = chromosomes[i];
  // Select partner from the mating population
  int father = (int) ( 0.999999*Math.random()*
    (double)matingPopulationSize);
  Chromosome cfather = chromosomes[father];

  mutated += cmother.mate(cfather,chromosomes[ioffset],
    chromosomes[ioffset+1]);
  ioffset += 2;
}
```

The children that are created from these matings are stored in the bottom half of the population array.

```java
for ( int i=0;i<matingPopulationSize;i++ ) {
  chromosomes[i] = chromosomes[i+matingPopulationSize];
  chromosomes[i].calculateCost(network,input,ideal);
}
// Now sort the new mating population
Chromosome.sortChromosomes(chromosomes,matingPopulationSize);
```

As you can see, there are quite a number of steps involved in the genetic algorithm. The genetic algorithm also consumes a considerable amount of memory, as each chromosome's patterns and weight matrixes must be stored. The genetic algorithm also takes considerably longer to execute than a comparable solution from simulated annealing. That is why simulated annealing is generally preferred to genetic algorithms. That is not to say that genetic algorithms have no place. Genetic algorithms are frequently other non-neural network projects.

Summary

In this chapter we saw how simulated annealing and genetic algorithms can be used to help backpropagation escape from a local minima. A local minima is a dip in the error function that backpropagation can easily become stuck on. By not evaluating beyond the crest of the local minima the backpropagation algorithm loses a chance to find other minima that may be more suited than the current local minima. The lowest point that the error curve will ever reach is called the global minimum. The optimal training process will find the global minimum.

Simulated annealing can be used to further optimize a neural network. To use the simulated annealing algorithm, the weights must be aligned in a linear structure such as an array. Then the simulated annealing process begins by "randomizing" these weight values taking into consideration the current "temperature" and the suitability of the current weight matrix. The temperature is decreased and the weight matrix ideally converges on an ideal solution. This process continues until the temperature reaches zero or no improvements have occurred for a specifies number of cycles. The simulated annealing algorithm executes relatively quickly.

Likewise, genetic algorithms can be used to further optimize a neural network. To use a genetic algorithm, the weights must be aligned in a linear structure such as an array. This array will be used as a chromosome. Then, the genetic algorithm proceeds to splice the genes of this weight matrix with other suitable weight matrixes. Through subsequent generations the suitability of the neural network should increase as less fit weight matrixes are replaced with better suited ones. This process continues until no improvements have occurred for a specified number of generations. The genetic algorithm generally takes up a great deal of memory and executes much slower than simulated annealing. Because of this, simulated annealing has become a popular method of neural network training.

Of course the process of simulated annealing and genetic algorithms may produce a less suitable weight matrix than what was started with. This can happen when a simulated annealing or a genetic algorithm is used against an already trained network. This lack of improvement is not always a bad thing, as the weight matrix may have moved beyond the local minima. Further backpropagation training may allow the neural network to now converge on a better solution. However, it is still always best to remember the previous local minima in case a better solution simply cannot be found.

This chapter showed you how to use simulated annealing and backpropagation to produce a weight matrix that is better suited to the problem the neural network is being trained for. This process only changes the weights of the synaptic connections. In the next chapter, we will see how we can further optimize the structure of the neural network. Chapter 11 will introduce the topic of pruning, which allows us to remove synaptic connections that do not contribute to the output of the neural network. This results in neural network that will take less time to execute.

CHAPTER 11: PRUNING NEURAL NETWORKS

Chapter Highlights
- **What is Pruning**
- **Incremental Pruning**
- **Selective Pruning**
- **Pruning Example**

In chapter 10 we saw that you could use simulated annealing and genetic algorithms to better train a neural network. These two techniques employ various algorithms to better fit the weights of the neural network to the problem that the neural network is being applied to. However, these techniques do nothing to adjust the structure of the neural network.

In this chapter, we will examine several algorithms that can be used to actually modify the structure of the neural network. This structural modification will not generally improve the error rate of the neural network, but can make it more efficient. This is done by analyzing how much each neuron contributes to the actual output of the neural network. If a particular neuron's connection to other neurons does not significantly affect the output of the neural network, the connection will be pruned. By this process, connections, and even entire neurons that have only a marginal impact on the output, are removed.

This process is called pruning. In this chapter, we will examine how pruning is accomplished. We will begin by examining the pruning process in greater detail and discuss some of the popular methods used to prune. Finally, this chapter will conclude by adding pruning capabilities to the neural network example given in Chapter 10.

Understanding Pruning

Pruning is a process where the neural network is made more efficient. Unlike genetic algorithms or simulated annealing, pruning does not increase the effectiveness of the neural network. The primary goal of pruning is to decrease the amount of processing required to use the neural network.

Pruning can be especially effective when used with a large neural network that is taking too long to execute. By pruning unneeded connections, the neural network can be made to execute faster. This allows the neural network to perform more work in a given amount of time.

Pruning works by analyzing the connections of the neural network. The pruning algorithm is looking for individual connections and neurons that can be clipped from the neural network to make the operation of the neural network more efficient. Both neurons and connections can be pruned from the neural network. In the next two sections we will examine how to prune both connections and neurons.

Pruning Connections

Connection pruning is central to most pruning algorithms. The individual connections between the neurons are analyzed to determine which connections have the least impact to the effectiveness of the neural network. One of the methods that we will examine will remove all connections that have a weight below a certain threshold value. The second method evaluates the effectiveness of the neural network as certain weights are considered for removal.

Connections are not the only thing that can be pruned. By analyzing which connections were pruned we can also prune individual neurons. This process will be discussed in the next section.

Pruning Neurons

Pruning focuses primarily on the connections between the individual neurons of the neural network. This is not to say that individual neurons can not be pruned as well. One of the pruning algorithms that we will examine later in this chapter will prune neurons as well as connections.

To prune individual neurons, the connections between each neuron and the other neurons must be examined. If one particular neuron is surrounded entirely by weak connections to the other neurons, there is no reason to keep that neuron. If we apply the criteria discussed in the previous section to the neural network, we can end up with neurons that have no connections. This is because all of the neuron's connections were pruned. Such a neuron can then be pruned itself.

Improving or Degrading Performance

It is possible that pruning a neural network may improve performance. Any modifications to the weight matrix of a neural network will always have some impact on the accuracy of the recognitions made by the neural network. A connection that has little or no impact on the neural network may actually be slightly degrading the accuracy of the neural network's recognitions. Removing such weak connections may improve the overall output of the neural network.

Unfortunately, it is also possible to decrease the effectiveness of the neural network through pruning. Because of this, it is always important to analyze the effectiveness of the neural network before and after pruning. Because efficiency is the primary benefit to pruning you must be careful to evaluate whether the improvement in the processing time of the neural network is worth the decrease in the neural networks effectiveness. The example program that we will examine later in this chapter will evaluate the overall effectiveness of the neural network both before and after pruning. This will give us an idea of what effect the pruning process had on the effectiveness of the neural network.

Pruning Algorithms

We will now review exactly how pruning takes place. In this section we will examine two different methods for pruning. These two methods work in somewhat opposite ways. The first method, incremental pruning, works by gradually increasing the number of hidden neurons until an acceptable error rate has been obtained. The second method, selective pruning, works by taking an existing neural network and decreasing the number of hidden neurons so long as the error rate remains acceptable. In this section we will examine both methods. We will begin with incremental pruning.

Incremental Pruning

Incremental pruning is a trial and error approach to finding an appropriate number of hidden neurons. This method is summarized in Figure 11.1.

Figure 11.1: Flowchart of the Incremental Pruning Algorithm

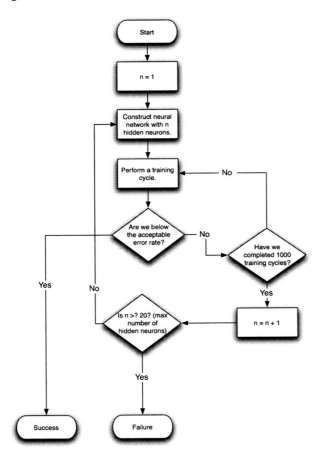

Incremental pruning begins with an untrained neural network. The incremental pruning algorithm will attempt to train the neural network many times. Each of these times, the incremental training process will use a different set of hidden neurons.

The incremental training algorithm must be supplied with a minimal acceptable error rate. The incremental training algorithm is looking for the neural network, with the fewest number of hidden neurons possible that will cause the error rate to fall below the desired level. Once a neural network that can be trained to fall below this rate is found, the algorithm is complete.

As you saw in Chapter 3, it is often necessary to train for many cycles before a solution can be found. The incremental pruning algorithm requires the entire training session to be completed many times. Each time a new neuron is added to the hidden layer, the neural network must be retrained. Because of this, it can take a while for the incremental pruning algorithm to run.

The neural network will train for many different numbers of hidden neurons, beginning initially with a single neuron. Because the error rate does not drop sufficiently fast, the single hidden neuron neural network will be quickly abandoned. Any number of methods can be used to determine when to abandon a neural network. The method that will be used in this chapter, is to check the current error rate in 1,000 cycle intervals. If the error does not decrease by a single percentage point, then the search will be abandoned. This allows us to quickly abandon hidden layer sizes that are too small for the intended task.

One advantage to the incremental pruning algorithm, is that it usually will create neural networks with fewer hidden neurons than the other methods. The biggest disadvantage is the amount of processor time that it takes to run this algorithm. Now that you have seen how the incremental pruning algorithm works, we will examine the selective pruning algorithm.

Selective Pruning

The selective pruning algorithm differs from the incremental pruning algorithm in several important ways. One of the most notable differences is the beginning state of the neural network. No training was required before beginning the incremental pruning algorithm. This is not the case with the selective pruning algorithm. The selective pruning algorithm works by examining the weight matrixes of a previously trained neural network. The selective training algorithm will then attempt to remove neurons without disrupting the output of the neural network. The algorithm used for selective pruning is shown in Figure 11.2.

Figure 11.2: Flowchart of the Selective Pruning Algorithm

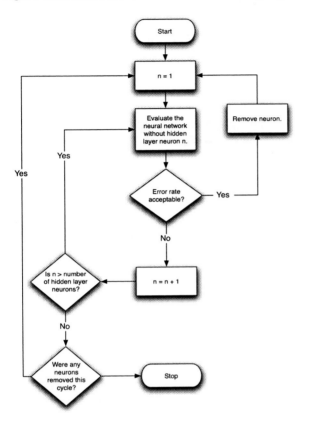

As you can see the selective pruning algorithm is something of a trial and error approach as well. The selective pruning algorithm attempts to remove neurons from the neural network until no more neurons can be removed without degrading the performance of the neural network.

To begin this process, the selective pruning algorithm loops through each of the hidden neurons. For each hidden neuron encountered, the error level of the neural network is evaluated both with and without the specified neuron. If the error rate jumps by more than a predefined level, the neuron will be left and the next neuron evaluated. If the error rate does not jump by much, the neuron will be removed.

Once the program has evaluated all neurons, the program repeats the process. This cycle continues until the program has made one pass through the hidden neurons without being able to remove a single neuron. Once this process is complete, a new neural network is achieved that performs acceptably close to the original, yet has fewer hidden neurons.

The major advantage of the selective pruning algorithm, is the fact that it takes very little processing time to complete. The example program that will be shown later in this chapter, will take under a second to prune a neural network with 10 hidden layer neurons. This is considerably less time than the incremental pruning algorithm in the previous section.

Implementing Pruning

Now that you have been shown how the pruning algorithms work, you will be shown how to implement them in Java. In this section, we will examine a general class that is designed to prune feedforward neural networks. The name of this class will simply be "Prune". This class will accept a "Network" class and perform either incremental or selective pruning. We will begin by examining the prune class, then we will examine the incremental and selective algorithms within the class.

The Prune Class

The Prune class contains all of the methods and properties that are required to prune a feedforward neural network. We will fist examine the structure of the entire class, then we will examine how the incremental and selective pruning algorithms were constructed. This class, named "Prune," is shown in Listing 11.1.

Listing 11.1: The prune Class (Prune.java)

```java
public class Prune {

  protected Network currentNetwork;
  protected double train[][];
  protected double ideal[][];
  protected double rate;
  protected double momentum;;
  protected double minError;
  protected double error;
  protected double markErrorRate;
  protected int sinceMark;
  protected int cycles;
  protected int hiddenNeuronCount;
  protected boolean done;

  /**
   * Constructor used to setup the prune object for an
   * incremental prune.
   *
   * @param rate The desired learning rate.
   * @param momentum The desired momentum.
   * @param train The training data.
   * @param ideal The ideal results for the training data.
   * @param minError The minimum error that is acceptable.
   */
```

```java
public Prune(
  double rate,
  double momentum,
  double train[][],
  double ideal[][],
  double minError)
{
  this.rate = rate;
  this.momentum = momentum;
  this.train = train;
  this.ideal = ideal;
  this.minError = minError;
}

/**
 * Constructor that is designed to setup for a selective
 * prune.
 *
 * @param network The neural network that we wish to prune.
 * @param train
 * @param ideal
 */
public Prune(Network network,double train[][],double ideal[][])
{
  this.currentNetwork = network;
  this.train = train;
  this.ideal = ideal;
}

/**
 * Method that is called to start the incremental prune
 * process.
 */
public void startIncremental()
{
  hiddenNeuronCount = 1;
  cycles = 0;
  done = false;
  currentNetwork = new Network(
                              train[0].length,
                              hiddenNeuronCount,
                              ideal[0].length,
                              rate,
                              momentum);
}
```

```java
/**
 * Internal method that is called at the end of each
 * incremental cycle.
 */
protected void incrament()
{
  boolean doit = false;

  if (markErrorRate==0) {
    markErrorRate = error;
    sinceMark = 0;
  } else {
    sinceMark++;
    if (sinceMark>10000) {
      if ( (markErrorRate-error)<0.01 )
        doit = true;
      markErrorRate = error;
      sinceMark = 0;
    }
  }


  if (error<minError)
    done = true;

  if (doit) {
    cycles = 0;
    hiddenNeuronCount++;
    currentNetwork = new Network(
                          train[0].length,
                          hiddenNeuronCount,
                          ideal[0].length,
                          rate,
                          momentum);

  }
}

/**
 * Method that is called to prune the neural network
 * incrementally.
 */
public void pruneIncremental()
{
  if (done)
    return;
```

```java
  for (int i=0;i<train.length;i++) {
    currentNetwork.computeOutputs(train[i]);
    currentNetwork.calcError(ideal[i]);
    currentNetwork.learn();
  }
  error = currentNetwork.getError(train.length);
  cycles++;
  incrament();
}


/**
 * Called to get the current error.
 *
 * @return The current error.
 */
public double getError()
{
  return error;
}


/**
 * Get the number of hidden neurons.
 *
 * @return The number of hidden neurons.
 */
public double getHiddenNeuronCount()
{
  return hiddenNeuronCount;
}


/**
 * Called to get the current number of cycles.
 *
 * @return The current number of cycles.
 */
public int getCycles()
{
  return cycles;
}


/**
 * Called to determine if we are done in an incremental prune.
 *
 * @return Returns true if we are done, false otherwise.
 */
```

```java
public boolean getDone()
{
  return done;
}

/**
 * Get the current neural network.
 *
 * @return The neural network.
 */
public Network getCurrentNetwork()
{
  return currentNetwork;
}

/**
 * Internal method used to clip the hidden neurons.
 *
 * @param neuron The neuron to clip.
 * @return Returns the new neural network.
 */
protected Network clipHiddenNeuron(int neuron)
{
  Network result = new Network(
                              currentNetwork.getInputCount(),
                              currentNetwork.getHiddenCount()-1,
                              currentNetwork.getOutputCount(),
                              currentNetwork.getLearnRate(),
                              currentNetwork.getMomentum());

  double array1[] = currentNetwork.toArray();
  double array2[] = new double[array1.length];
  int index1 = 0;
  int index2 = 0;

  // weight matrix

  for (int i=0;i<currentNetwork.getInputCount();i++) {
    for (int j=0;j<currentNetwork.getHiddenCount();j++) {
      if (j!=neuron) {
        array2[index2] = array1[index1];
        index2++;
      }
      index1++;
    }
  }
}
```

```java
  for (int i=0;i<currentNetwork.getHiddenCount();i++) {
    for (int j=0;j<currentNetwork.getOutputCount();j++) {
      if (i!=neuron) {
        array2[index2] = array1[index1];
        index2++;
      }
      index1++;
    }
  }


  // threshold

  int neuronCount =
  currentNetwork.getInputCount()+
  currentNetwork.getHiddenCount()+
  currentNetwork.getOutputCount();
  for (int i=0;i<neuronCount;i++) {
    if (i!=currentNetwork.getInputCount()+neuron) {
      array2[index2] = array1[index1];
      index2++;
    }
    index1++;
  }

  result.fromArray(array2);
  return result;
}

/**
 * Internal method to determine the error for a neural network.
 *
 * @param network The neural network that we are seeking a
 * error rate for.
 * @return The error for the specified neural network.
 */
protected double determineError(Network network)
{
  for (int i=0;i<train.length;i++) {
    network.computeOutputs(train[i]);
    network.calcError(ideal[i]);
    network.learn();
  }
  return network.getError(train.length);
```

```java
}

/**
 * Internal method that will loop through all hidden neurons and
 * prune them if pruning the neuron does not cause too great
 * of an increase in error.
 *
 * @return True if a prune was made, false otherwise.
 */
protected boolean findNeuron()
{
  double e1 = determineError(currentNetwork);

  for (int i=0;i<currentNetwork.getHiddenCount();i++) {
    Network trial = this.clipHiddenNeuron(i);
    double e2 = determineError(trial);
    if ( Math.abs(e1-e2)<0.2 ) {
      currentNetwork = trial;
      return true;
    }
  }
  return false;
}


/**
 * Called to complete the selective pruning process.
 *
 * @return The number of neurons that were pruned.
 */
public int pruneSelective()
{
  int i = currentNetwork.getHiddenCount();
  while (findNeuron());
  return(i-currentNetwork.getHiddenCount());
}
}
```

There are several properties that are used internally by many of the methods that make up the "Prune" class. These properties are summarized in Table 11.1.

Table 11.1: Variables Used for the Prune Process

Variable	Purpose
currentNetwork	The neural network that is currently being processed.
train	The training set.
ideal	The ideal results from the training set.
rate	The desired learning rate.
momentum	The desired momentum.
minError	The minimum acceptable error.
error	The current error.
markErrorRate	Used to determine if training is still effective. Holds the error level the last time the error level was tracked. This is 1000 cycles ago. If no significant drop in error occurs for 1000 cycles, training ends.
sinceMark	Used with markErrorRate. This is the number of cycles since the error was last marked.
cycles	The number of cycles used.
hiddenNeuronCount	The number of hidden neurons.
done	Flag to indicate if the incremental prune process is done or not.

You will now be shown how the selective and incremental pruning algorithms were implemented. We will begin with incremental pruning.

Incremental Pruning

As you will recall from earlier in this chapter, the process of incremental pruning simply involves increasing the number of neurons in the hidden layer until the neural network is able to be trained sufficiently well. This should automatically lead us to a good number of hidden neurons. The constructor used to implement incremental pruning is very simple. It collects the required parameters and stores them in the class's properties. The constructor for the incremental prune can be seen in Listing 11.1.

The parameters required by the incremental prune constructor are the usual parameters needed to perform backpropagation training of a feedforward neural network. The learning rate and momentum are both required. These backpropagation constants are discussed in greater detail in Chapter 5. Additionally, a training set, along with the ideal outputs for the training set, is also required.

The final parameter that is required by the incremental prune constructor is the minimum acceptable error. This is the error rate that is sufficient for a neural network to attain. As the incremental pruning algorithm progresses, it will try to train neural networks with various numbers of hidden neurons. The final number of hidden neurons will be determined by the neural network with the fewest number of hidden neurons that was able to be trained to reach this error level.

Starting the Incremental Pruning Process

To begin the process of incremental pruning, you must call the start method for the incremental prune. This sets up the Prune class for a new pruning run. First, some of the properties are set to their initial values. One such property is the number of neurons that will be in the hidden layer. Initially we will begin with one single neuron in the hidden layer.

```
hiddenNeuronCount = 1;
cycles = 0;
done = false;
```

Next, we must create a new neural network that will be of the correct size. Initially this neural network will have only one neuron in the hidden layer. This will be incremented as the algorithm progresses.

```
currentNetwork = new Network(
                    train[0].length,
                    hiddenNeuronCount,
                    ideal[0].length,
                    rate,
                    momentum);
```

Now the incremental prune algorithm is ready to begin. In the next section, you will see how the main loop of the incremental algorithm was constructed.

Main Loop of the Incremental Algorithm

The incremental pruning algorithm is processor intensive and may take some time to run. This is because the incremental algorithm is literally trying different numbers of hidden neurons, in a trial and error fashion, until the least number of neurons can be found that produces an acceptable error level.

The incremental pruning algorithm is designed so that a background thread will call the "pruneIncremental" method rapidly until the "getDone" method indicates that the algorithm is done. The "pruneIncremental" method begins by first checking to see if it is already done. If the algorithm is already done, the "pruneIncremental" method simply returns.

```
if (done)
  return;
```

The next step is to attempt a single training cycle for the neural network. The program loops through all of the training sets and calculates the error based on the ideal outputs. The neural network is allowed to learn, using backpropagation, by calling the "learn" method of the "Network" class.

```
for (int i=0;i<train.length;i++) {
  currentNetwork.computeOutputs(train[i]);
  currentNetwork.calcError(ideal[i]);
  currentNetwork.learn();
}
```

Once the training set has been presented, the root mean square (RMS) error is calculated. RMS error was discussed in Chapter 3. This will allow the pruning algorithm to determine if the error has reached the desired level.

```
error = currentNetwork.getError(train.length);
cycles++;
increment();
```

Each time a training cycle is executed, the neural network must check to see if the number of hidden neurons should be increased, or if training should continue with the current neural network. This process is discussed in the next section.

Incrementing the Number of Neurons

To determine if the number of hidden neurons should be increased or not, a helper method named "increment" is provided. The increment method keeps track of training progress for the neural network. If the training improvement for each cycle falls below a constant value, further training is deemed futile. In this case we increment the number of hidden neurons and continue training.

The "increment" method begins by setting up a flag that indicates if the increment method should increment the number of hidden neurons. The default is false, which means do not increment the number of neurons.

```
boolean doit = false;
```

The algorithm that this class uses to determine if further training is futile, works by examining the amount of improvement every 10,000 cycles. If the error rate does not change by more than a percent, within 10,000 cycles, further training is deemed futile, and the number of neurons in the hidden layer is incremented.

The following lines of code evaluate this. First, when the "markErrorRate" is zero, it means that we are just starting up and have not yet sampled the error rate. In this case we initialize the "markErrorRate" and "sinceMark" variables.

```
if (markErrorRate==0) {
  markErrorRate = error;
  sinceMark = 0;
} else {
```

If the "markErrorRate" is not zero then we are tracking errors. We should increase the "sinceMark" cycle counter and determine if more than 10,000 cycles have passed since we last sampled the error rate.

```
sinceMark++;
if (sinceMark>10000) {
```

If more than 10,000 cycles have passed, we check to see if the improvement between the "markErrorRate" and current error rate is less than a single percent. If this is the case, then we set the flag to indicate that the number of hidden neurons should be incremented.

```
if ( (markErrorRate-error)<0.01 )
  doit = true;
```

Next the error rate is resampled.

```
markErrorRate = error;
sinceMark = 0;
```

If the error rate is below the acceptable error, then we have found the number of neurons we will recommend for the neural network. We can now set the done flag to true.

```
if (error<minError)
  done = true;
```

If the flag is set that indicates that we should increment the number of neurons, the following lines of code handle this.

```
if (doit) {
  cycles = 0;
  hiddenNeuronCount++;
  currentNetwork = new Network(
                       train[0].length,
                       hiddenNeuronCount,
                       ideal[0].length,
                       rate,
                     momentum);
}
```

As you can see, a new neural network is constructed after the number of hidden neurons is increased. The cycle count is also set back to zero because we are now training a new neural network.

You should now be familiar with how the incremental pruning algorithm was implemented. Later in this chapter, we will construct a example program that makes use of this algorithm. For now, we will cover the implementation of the second pruning algorithm, the selective pruning algorithm.

Selective Pruning

Now that you have seen how the incremental pruning algorithm was implemented, we will examine the implementation of the selective pruning algorithm. In some ways, the selective pruning algorithm works in reverse of the incremental pruning algorithm. Where the incremental pruning algorithm starts small and grows, the selective pruning algorithm starts with a large, already trained neural network, and selects neurons for removal.

To use selective pruning, you can make use of a simplified version of the constructor. Selective pruning does not need to know anything about the learning rate or momentum of the backpropagation process. This is because the selective pruning algorithm does not involve the backpropagation algorithm. The simplified version of the constructor is shown below.

```
public Prune(Network network,double train[][],double ideal[][])
```

As you can see, you are only required to pass a neural network training sets and the ideal results, for the selective pruning algorithm to function. The constructor is very simple and merely stores the values that it was passed. We will now examine the implementation of the selective pruning methods. We will begin by examining the main loop of the selective pruning algorithm.

Selective Pruning Main Loop

The main loop of the selective pruning algorithm is much less processor intense than the incremental pruning algorithm. The incremental pruning algorithm that we examined in the previous section, was designed to run as a background thread due to the large number of cycles that might be required to find a solution. This is not the case with the selective pruning algorithm.

The selective pruning algorithm is designed to attempt to remove each of the hidden neurons and evaluate the performance of the neural network. If the performance of the neural network does not degrade too substantially with the removal of a neuron, that neuron will permanently be removed. This process will continue until no more neurons can be removed without substantially degrading the neural network performance. Because of this, the selective pruning algorithm is designed to perform the entire algorithm from one method call. There is no reason for a background thread, as this method should be able to perform its task nearly instantaneously.

The method that should be called to prune a neural network selectively, is the "pruneSelective" method. We will now examine how this method performs. This short method is shown here.

```java
public int pruneSelective()
{
  int i = currentNetwork.getHiddenCount();
  while (findNeuron());
  return(i-currentNetwork.getHiddenCount());
}
```

As you can see from the above code, the current number of hidden neurons is remembered, by storing it into the "i" variable. We then enter a loop until no more neurons can be removed. Finally, the "pruneSelective" method returns the number of neurons that were removed from the neural network. The new optimized neural network is stored in the "currentNetwork" property of the Prune class and can be accessed using the "getCurrentNetwork" method.

The real work performed by the selective pruning algorithm is done by the "findNeuron" method. It is the "findNeuron" method that actually identifies and removes neurons that will not affect the error rate too adversely. The "findNeuron" method will remove a neuron if possible, and return true. If no neuron was able to be removed, the "findNeuron" method will return false. As you can see from the above code in the "pruneSelective" method, the "findNeuron" method is called so long as the return value is true.

We will now examine the contents of the findNeuron method. This method begins by calculating the current error rate.

```
double e1 = determineError(currentNetwork);
```

We will not examine the "determineError" method. We have already seen the algorithm used in Chapter 3. Once the current error is determined, we must loop through all of the hidden neurons.

```
for (int i=0;i<currentNetwork.getHiddenCount();i++) {
```

We will create a trial neural network that will remove the current neuron.

```
Network trial = this.clipHiddenNeuron(i);
```

Now the error rate will be recalculated, and we will see what effect this had on the quality of the neural network. So long as the quality does not change by more than 20%, we will continue pruning. This rate does not degrade the performance of the XOR problem. For other problems, you may need to adjust the error tolerance.

```
double e2 = determineError(trial);
if ( Math.abs(e1-e2)<0.2 ) {
```

If we have an acceptable network, with the neuron removed, we can exit the method and return true. The value of true indicates that the neuron was removed, and we should attempt to remove further neurons.

```
    currentNetwork = trial;
    return true;
  }
}
```

If no neurons were removed, we can return false. This indicates, to the selective pruning algorithm, that no further processing will be of any value.

```
return false;
```

You will now be shown the process by which neurons are removed from the neural network.

Removing Neurons

Removing a neuron from the "Network" structure shown in Chapter 3 is a relatively straightforward process. The task of removing an individual hidden neuron is encapsulated inside the "clipHiddenNeuron" method of the "Prune" class. The first thing that the "clipHiddenNeuron" method does is to create a new neural network with one less neuron.

```
Network result = new Network(
                        currentNetwork.getInputCount(),
                        currentNetwork.getHiddenCount()-1,
                        currentNetwork.getOutputCount(),
                        currentNetwork.getLearnRate(),
                        currentNetwork.getMomentum());
```

All other neural network parameters will remain the same. We will now use the "toArray" and "fromArray" methods that were introduced in Chapter 10. These methods allow us to direct access to the weight matrix of the neural network. By removing all of the links between the target neuron and other neurons, we are able to remove the intended neuron. The first step is to obtain the current neural network's array and allocate a new array that will be at least large enough to hold the new weights and thresholds.

```
double array1[] = currentNetwork.toArray();

double array2[] = new double[array1.length];
```

Now that "array1" and "array2" have been created, we are ready to copy "array1" into "array2". We will only copy the weights and thresholds that relate to neurons that are not being removed. To do this we will maintain two indexes.

```
int index1 = 0;
int index2 = 0;
```

The index variable, "index1", will hold the current index into array1. Likewise, the second index variable, "index2", will hold the current index into "array2".

We are now ready to copy the weight matrix between the input and hidden layers. The following loop will accomplish this.

```
for (int i=0;i<currentNetwork.getInputCount();i++) {
  for (int j=0;j<currentNetwork.getHiddenCount();j++) {
```

```
    if (j!=neuron) {
      array2[index2] = array1[index1];
      index2++;
    }
    index1++;
  }
}
```

As you can see, we simply copy everything except the neuron that we are seeking to delete. The index of the neuron that we are deleting is stored in the variable "neuron". Now that we have removed any links between the hidden neuron and the input layer, we must also address the output layer. This is because the hidden layer is sandwiched between the input and output layer, and has connections to both. The process for removing the links between the hidden layer and the output layer is nearly identical to the process that was used to remove the links between the hidden layer and the input layer. The loop that removes these connections is shown here.

```
for (int i=0;i<currentNetwork.getHiddenCount();i++) {
  for (int j=0;j<currentNetwork.getOutputCount();j++) {
    if (i!=neuron) {
      array2[index2] = array1[index1];
      index2++;
    }
    index1++;
  }
}
```

We must also remove the threshold value for the neuron that we are removing. There is only one threshold value per neuron. As a result there is only one threshold value that we must remove. This causes the threshold removal to be considerably faster than the removal of connections among the input, hidden and output layers. The code that is used to remove the threshold value for the targeted neuron is shown below.

The first step that we must accomplish, is determining the total number of neurons in the neural network.

```
int neuronCount =
currentNetwork.getInputCount()+
currentNetwork.getHiddenCount()+
currentNetwork.getOutputCount();
```

We are now ready to loop through every threshold value that is contained in the neural network.

```
for (int i=0;i<neuronCount;i++) {
```

For each neuron we compare its value to the target neuron. Skipping the target neuron, the threshold value of every other neuron will be copied to the new array.

```
if (i!=currentNetwork.getInputCount()+neuron) {
  array2[index2] = array1[index1];
  index2++;
}
index1++;
}
```

We are now done pruning the neuron from the neural network. We can now copy the array from "array2" into the resulting neural network that will be returned.

```
result.fromArray(array2);
return result;
```

You have now been shown how the Prune class was constructed. We covered both incremental and selective pruning. We will now see how to make use of this class in a Java program. In the next section, you will see how to create two example programs to demonstrate both selective and incremental pruning.

Using the Prune Class

Now that you have seen how the prune class was implemented you are ready to see how you can make use of it in a Java program. There are two example programs that are provided to demonstrate the use of the prune class. These examples demonstrate the two pruning methods that we discussed in this chapter. We will examine both examples in this section, beginning with the incremental prune example.

The Incremental Prune Example

The incremental prune example is based on the XOR problem that was shown in Chapter 3. Because of this, the complete code to the incremental prune example will not be shown here. Rather, we will show you the additional code that was added to the XOR example in Chapter 3 to support pruning. You can see the output from the incremental prune example in Figure 11.3.

Figure 11.3: The incremental prune example

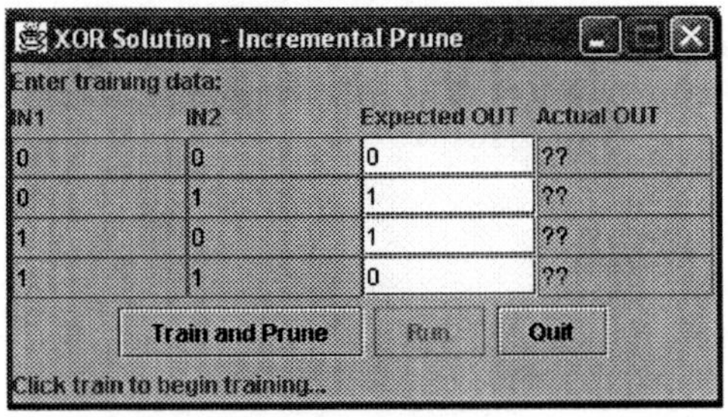

When the "Prune/Train" button is pressed, a background thread is created. This background thread will execute the prune example's run method. We will now examine the contents of this run method.

The run method begins by reading the data that the user may have entered. Both the training sets and the ideal results are read from the window. The code that reads this data is shown below.

```
public void run()
  {
    double xorData[][] = getGrid();
    double xorIdeal[][] = getIdeal();
    int update=0;
```

We are now ready to construct a prune object. We also pass in the training data and the acceptable weight error level.

```
Prune prune = new Prune(0.7,0.5,xorData,xorIdeal,0.05);
```

We are now ready to call the "startIncremental" method to begin the process.

```
prune.startIncremental();
```

For the main loop of this thread, we will call the "pruneIncremental" method until the "getDone" method returns true.

```
    while (!prune.getDone()) {
      prune.pruneIncremental();
```

As the loop progresses, we would like to display status information to the user. This lets the user know how far along the prune process has completed. Because Java's GUI components are somewhat slow, we do not want to update the GUI for each cycle. Updating the user interface through every cycle would slow down the process. The following lines of code cause the GUI to be updated every 10 cycles:

```
update++;
if (update==10) {
  status.setText(
    "Cycles:" +
    prune.getCycles() +
    ",Hidden Neurons:" +
    prune.getHiddenNeuronCount() +
    ", Current Error=" + prune.getError() );
  update=0;
  }
}
```

Once the prune process has completed, we will display the final hidden neuron count. This allows the user to see how many neurons are to be used for the network.

```
status.setText("Best network found:" +
  prune.getHiddenNeuronCount() + ",error = " +
  prune.getError() );
```

Now that the neural prune process has completed, we will copy the current neural network from the prune class.

```
network = prune.getCurrentNetwork();
```

Next, we must set the run button to an enabled state. This will allow the user to test the neural network.

```
  btnRun.setEnabled(true);
}
```

In this section, you saw how the prune class was used to implement an incremental prune of a neural network. In the next section, you will see how to use the prune class for a selective prune of a neural network.

The Selective Prune Example

The selective prune example is also based on the XOR problem that was shown in Chapter 3. Because of this, the complete code to the selective prune example will not be shown here. Rather we will show you the additional code that was added to the XOR example in Chapter 3 to support selective pruning. You can see the output from the incremental prune example in Figure 11.4.

Figure 11.4: The Selective Prune Example

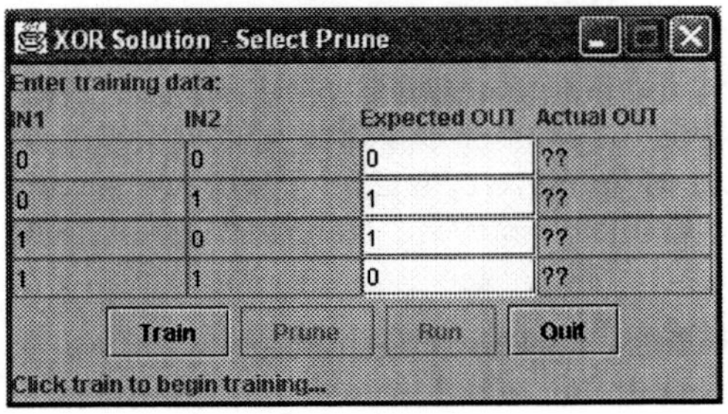

Because the selective prune example requires that a neural network already be present to prune, you should begin by clicking the "Train" button. This will train the neural network with the backpropagation method. The neural network being shown in this example initially contains ten neurons in the hidden layer. Clicking the "Prune" button will run a selective prune and attempt to remove some of the neurons from the hidden layer.

The code necessary to implement a selective prune is very simple. Because the selective prune executes very fast, there is no need for a background thread. This greatly simplifies the use of the selective prune. When the "Prune" button is clicked, the "prune" method is executed. The "prune" method is shown here:

```
public void prune()
{
  double xorData[][] = getGrid();
  double xorIdeal[][] = getIdeal();

  Prune prune = new Prune(network,xorData,xorIdeal);
  int count = prune.pruneSelective();
  network = prune.getCurrentNetwork();
  status.setText("Prune removed " + count + " neurons.");
  btnTrain.setEnabled(false);
}
```

As you can see from the above method, first, the training and ideal data are obtained from the components on the window. Next a "Prune" object is instantiated. The "pruneSelective" method is called which returns a count of the neurons that were removed during the prune. This value is displayed to the user and the new network is copied to the current network. The user may now run the network to see, first hand, how the performance of the neural network is. You will find that the selective prune algorithm is usually able to eliminate two or three neurons. While this leaves more neurons than the incremental algorithm, much less processor time is required, and there is no need to retrain the neural network.

Summary

As you learned in this chapter, it is possible to prune neural networks. Pruning a neural network removes connections and neurons to make the neural network more efficient. This allows the neural network to execute faster. The goal of pruning is not to make the neural network more effective at recognizing patterns, but to be more efficient. There are several different algorithms for pruning a neural network. In this chapter we examined two of these algorithms.

The first algorithm that we examined was called the incremental pruning algorithm. In this algorithm new neural networks are trained as the number of hidden neurons is increased. The incremental pruning algorithm eventually settles on the neural network that has the lowest number of neurons in the hidden layer, yet still maintains an acceptable error level. While the incremental algorithm will often find the ideal number of hidden neurons, it often takes a considerable amount of time to execute.

The second algorithm that we examined was called the selective pruning algorithm. The selective pruning algorithm begins with an already trained neural network. The algorithm will then remove hidden neurons, so long as the error stays below a specified level. Although the selective pruning algorithm will often not find as optimal a number of neurons as the incremental pruning algorithm, the selective pruning algorithm will execute considerably faster.

The primary goal of neural network pruning is efficiency. By pruning the neural network, you are able to create a neural network that will execute faster and require fewer processor cycles. If your neural network is already operating sufficiently fast, you must evaluate whether the pruning is justified. Even when efficiency is of great importance, you must weigh the trade-offs between efficiency and the decrease in effectiveness of your neural network.

Thus far, this book has focused primarily on neural networks and the algorithms to support those networks. In the next chapter, you will learn about fuzzy logic. Fuzzy logic allows programs to venture from the crisp world of "yes and no" to less precise definitions.

CHAPTER 12: FUZZY LOGIC

Chapter Highlights
- **What is Logic**
- **Understanding Crisp Logic**
- **Understanding Fuzzy Logic**
- **Fuzzy Determination of Hot and Cold**

In this chapter, we will examine fuzzy logic. Fuzzy logic is a branch of artificial intelligence that is not directly related to the neural networks that we have been examining so far. Fuzzy logic is often used to process data before it is fed to a neural network, or to process the outputs from the neural network. In this chapter, we will examine cases of how this can be done.

Before we begin using fuzzy logic, you must be aware of exactly what fuzzy logic is. Computer programs make extensive use of "logic". However, the program logic that you are likely accustomed to, is referred to as "crisp" logic. We will begin this chapter by examining the difference between fuzzy logic and "crisp" logic.

What is Logic

Merriam Webster's New Collegiate Dictionary defines logic as, "a science that deals with the principles and criteria of validity of inference and demonstration : the science of the formal principles of reasoning". Logic deals with reasoning. Reasoning is the method by which your program accepts input and makes decisions based on that input.

Most programs are designed to deal with crisp logic statements. We will begin by examining what exactly crisp logic is.

What is Crisp Logic

Crisp logic is likely the sort of logic that most programmers are familiar with. Crisp logic can be said to be either black or white. The programming logic that you are already familiar with from the Java programming language can be considered crisp. Such logic is often encapsulated in "if" statements in the Java programming language. You might construct a set of Java if statements to determine if the current temperature is considered cold, warm, or hot. Such a determination would like look something like this:

```java
double t = getCurrentTemperature();
if( t>0 && t<50 )
  System.out.println("It is cold");
else if(t>50 && t<80 )
```

```
    System.out.println("It is warm");
else if(t>80)
    System.out.println("It is hot");
```

As you can see from the above logic, the current temperature is either hot, warm or cold. There is no in between. While this form of "crisp" logic is very convenient for computer programs, it not how many human problems are thought of. In the next section, we will examine "fuzzy logic" and contrast it to the "crisp logic" just examined.

What is Fuzzy Logic

Fuzzy logic attempts to more closely emulate the way the human mind thinks of set membership. Given a particular human, you can ask him questions about the temperature sets given in the previous section. You may ask your human subject if 85 degrees Fahrenheit is hot. Your human subject answers yes. You may now ask the human subject if 85 degrees is warm. Your human subject also answers yes.

Fuzzy logic would treat the temperature statements of hot, cold and warm as individual sets. A given temperature could have membership in more than one set. In the next section, we will examine the specific means by which these class memberships are determined.

Understanding Fuzzy Logic

In this section we will examine exactly how fuzzy logic works. We will see how fuzzy set membership is determined. Fuzzy sets must be established that contain certain criteria for membership within that set. But because this is fuzzy, and not crisp, logic, membership in a fuzzy set is not absolute. One number may be a member of several fuzzy sets, or none at all. Additionally, an input number will have a membership value, which will determine the degree to which that input number is a member of the afore mentioned set.

Understanding Fuzzy Sets

A fuzzy set must have an established minimum and maximum value. It is the purpose of the fuzzy set algorithm to determine to what degree an input value belongs in this set. This is done by establishing a midpoint within the set. Usually, this mid point is the true midpoint, which is halfway between the minimum and maximum values. It will be at this midpoint that the degree to which an input value will have maximum membership in this set.

Understanding Fuzzy Set Calculation

We will now look at an example of the calculations that will be used to determine membership in a fuzzy set. For this example, we will assume a fuzzy set that has the following parameters. The upper bound of the fuzzy set will be 30. The lower bound for the fuzzy set will be 10. The midpoint will be a true midpoint with a value of 20. Finally, the value that will be returned from this set to indicate maximum membership will be 1. As a result, the value 1 will be returned at the midpoint. A zero value will be returned for any other value that is either equal to or outside of the minimum and maximum values. Plotting this fuzzy set would result in Figure 12.1.

Figure 12.1: A Fuzzy Set with a True Midpoint

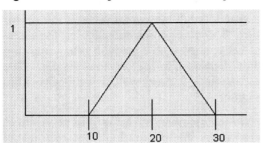

We will now see the process by which you determine the membership value for a specified input value. The input value that we will calculate the membership value for will be 15. The number 15 is clearly between the minimum values of 10 and 30, so the number 15 is a member of the fuzzy set. We must now calculate the membership value for 15.

Because we want the membership value to achieve its maximum value at the midpoint and reach a value of zero at either the minimum or the maximum we must calculate the amount of the membership value that will be lost for each unit of distance between the input number and the midpoint of the fuzzy set.

To calculate the amount by which the membership value decreases for each unit that the input number is from the midpoint we must calculate the distance between the midpoint and the minimum value. For this example, the distance between the midpoint and either the minimum or maximum is the same (this will not be the case in the next section). For this example we simply calculate the distance between the minimum and the midpoint. For this example this distance is 10. Now we will divide the membership value by 10 resulting in the value of .1.

To calculate the membership value for 15 we begin by determining the distance that the number 15 is from the midpoint. In this example the midpoint is 20, so the distance that our input number is from the mid point is 5.

We are now ready to calculate the membership value for the input value of 15. We take the previously calculate distance between 15 and the midpoint, which is 5. This value is the multiplied by the value of .1 that was calculated in the previous paragraph. This results in a membership value of .5.

This can be summarized as:

```
((20-10)/10) * 5
```

In this section we examined the simple case where the fuzzy set reaches its maximum membership value at the exact center between the minimum and maximum values. In the next section we will examine fuzzy sets where this is not the case.

Fuzzy Sets with Off-Center Midpoints

It is not always desirable to have a fuzzy set reach its full maximum value at the center point between the minimum and maximum values. The process for determining the membership value when the maximum membership value occurs at a position other than the midpoint, is only slightly different that the method discussed in the previous section. The algorithm that will be presented in this section will handle both cases well. It is this algorithm that we will implement, using Java, in the next section.

We will now look at an example where the maximum membership value does not occur at the midpoint between the minimum and maximum values. We will now look at an example of the calculations that will be used to determine membership in a fuzzy set. For this example we will assume a fuzzy set that has the following parameters. The upper bound of the fuzzy set will be 30, and the lower bound for the fuzzy set will be 10. The point at which the maximum membership value will be returned will be 17. Finally, the value that will be returned from this set to indicate maximum membership will be 1. As a result, the value 1 will be returned at the 17. A zero value will be returned for any other value that is either equal to or outside of the minimum and maximum values. Plotting this fuzzy set would result in Figure 12.2.

Figure 12.2: A Fuzzy Set with a Maximum Value not at the Midpoint

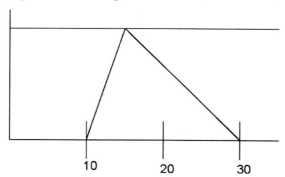

We will now examine this process for the input value of 22. The number 22 is clearly between the minimum values of 10 and 30, so the number 22 is a member of the fuzzy set. We must now calculate the membership value for 22.

Because the maximum membership value is not at the midpoint it now becomes very important to the calculation to determine if the input number is below or above 17. Because the value of 22 is above the number 17 we will use the distance between 17 and 30 to calculate the amount to decrease the membership value. The distance between 17 and 30 is 13. We will divide 1 by 13 to determine the amount that the membership value decreases per unit difference from 17. The input value of 22 is 5 units from 17, so we are left with 5 divided by 13, or a membership of 0.38.

Implementing Fuzzy Logic

We will now implement the fuzzy logic algorithms discussed in the previous section. To implement fuzzy logic in Java, we will create two classes. Each of these classes will be used to define and then process our fuzzy sets.

The first class that we will create will encapsulate a fuzzy logic set. This class will be named FuzzySet. These fuzzy sets will be added to a fuzzy logic processing class that will be named FuzzyLogic. In this section, we will examine both of these classes. We will begin by examining the FuzzySet class.

Fuzzy Sets

Fuzzy logic sets will be stored in the FuzzySet class. This class will hold the minimum and maximum values for this set. The FuzzySet will also be able to determine the degree to which a sample is a member of this set. The FuzzySet class is shown in Listing 12.1.

Listing 12.1: Fuzzy Sets (FuzzySet.java)

```java
public class FuzzySet {

  protected double min;
  protected double max;
  protected double mid;
  protected double midValue;

  /**
   * Create a new fuzzy set and let the mid value be
   * automatically calculated to be the midpoint between
   * the minimum and maximum values.
   *
   * @param min The minimum value to be part of this set.
   * @param max The maximum value to be part of this set.
   * @param midValue The midValue to be part of this set.
   */
  public FuzzySet(double min,double max,double midValue)
  {
    this(min,max,min+((max-min)/2),midValue);
  }

  /**
   * Create a new fuzzy set and specify the midpoint between
   * the minimum and maximum values.
   *
   * @param min The minimum value to be part of this set.
   * @param max The maximum value to be part of this set.
   * @param midValue The midValue to be part of this set.
   * @param mid The midpoint of the fuzzy set.
```

```java
   */
  public FuzzySet(double min,double max,double mid,double
    midValue)
  {
    this.min = min;
    this.max = max;
    this.mid = mid;
    this.midValue = midValue;
  }


  /**
   * Evaluate the input value and determine the membership
   * of that value in this set.
   *
   * @param in The input value to be evaluated.
   * @return Returns the membership value of the input value for
   * this set.
   */
  public double evaluate(double in)
  {
    if ( in<=min || in>=max )
      return 0;
    else if (in==mid)
      return midValue;
    else if (in<mid) {
      double step = midValue / (mid-min);
      double d = in-min;
      return d*step;
    } else {
      double step = midValue / (max-mid);
      double d = max-in;
      return d*step;
    }
  }


  /**
   * Determine if the specified input value is inside
   * of this set or not.
   *
   * @param in The input value to be checked.
   * @return Returns true if the specified input value is
   * contained in the set.
   */
  public boolean isMember(double in)
  {
    return evaluate(in)!=0;
```

```
}

/**
 * Get the minimum value that must be present for membership
 * in this set.
 *
 * @return Returns the minimum value that must be present
 * for membership
 * in this set.
 */
public double getMin()
{
  return mid;
}

/**
 * Get the maximum value that must be present for membership
 * in this set.
 *
 * @return Returns the maximum value that must be present
 * for membership
 * in this set.
 */
public double getMax()
{
  return max;
}

/**
 * Get the midpoint of this set.
 *
 * @return Returns the midpoint of this set.
 */
public double getMid()
{
  return mid;
}

/**
 * Get the value that should be returned when the midpoint
 * is reached.
 *
 * @return Returns the value that should be returned when
 * the midpoint
 * is reached.
 */
```

```
public double getMidValue()
{
  return midValue;
}
}
```

As you can see from the above code the several properties are used by the FuzzySet class. These variables are summarized in Table 12.1.

Table 12.1: Fuzzy Set Variables

Variable	Purpose
min	The minimum value to be part of this set.
max	The maximum value to be part of this set.
mid	The midpoint value of this set.
midValue	The value to be returned at the mid point. This would represent maximum membership in this set.

Most of the processing that will take place in the FuzzySet class will be preformed inside of the evaluate method. This is where the membership value for an input number will be calculated. This method implements the algorithm discussed in a previous section of this chapter. We will now review the process that is executed by the evaluate method.

First we will determine if the input number is outside of the minimum and maximum for this set. If this is the case we will return a value of zero.

```
if ( in<=min || in>=max )
  return 0;
```

Next, we will determine if the input number falls exactly on the midpoint. If this is the case we want to return the maximum membership value, which is stored in the property midValue.

```
else if (in==mid)
  return midValue;
```

Finally, if the input number is not directly on the midpoint or outside of the minimum and maximum values, we must calculate the membership value. First, we check to see if the input number is above or below the midpoint.

```
else if (in<mid) {
```

If the input number is below the midpoint, we will calculate the membership value using the following algorithm. The first step is to determine a variable called step. This variable will hold the amount by which the maximum membership variable is decreased for each unit that the input number is from the midpoint. This is done by dividing the maximum membership value by the difference between the midpoint and the maximum.

```
double step = midValue / (mid-min);
```

Next, we will calculate the distance between the input number and the minimum.

```
double d = in-min;
```

Finally this distance is multiplied by the step value. It is this calculation that is returned as the set membership.

```
    return d*step;
} else {
```

If the input number is above the mid point we will calculate the membership values using the following algorithm. The first step is to determine a variable called step. As in the previous case, this variable will hold the amount by which the maximum membership variable is decreased by for each unit that the input number is from the mid point. This is done by dividing the maximum membership value by the difference between the midpoint and the maximum.

```
double step = midValue / (max-mid);
```

Next we will calculate the distance between the maximum and the input number.

```
double d = max-in;
```

Finally this distance is multiplied by the step value. It is this calculation that is returned as the set membership.

```
    return d*step;
```

There are other methods in the FuzzySet class than the evaluate method. Most of the other methods are simply getters and setters that allow the user to interact with the minimum, maximum and other properties.

You have now seen how the FuzzySet class was implemented. In the next section, you will be introduced to the FuzzyLogic class which allows many different FuzzySet objects to be used together.

Fuzzy Logic Processing

In this section, you will be shown how the FuzzyLogic class is done. While the FuzzySet class, does contain the logic to determine set membership, you will not usually be using a single fuzzy set. Using the FuzzyLogic class, you will be able to work with several fuzzy sets at one time. The FuzzyLogic class can be seen in Listing 12.2.

Listing 12.2: Fuzzy Logic Processing (FuzzyLogic.java)

```java
import java.util.*;

public class FuzzyLogic {

  /**
   * A list of all fuzzy logic sets that are associated with
   * this class.
   */
  protected ArrayList list = new ArrayList();
  /**
   * Add a fuzzy set to this fuzzy logic processor.
   *
   * @param set The fuzzy logic set to be added.
   */

  public void add(FuzzySet set)
  {
    list.add(set);
  }

  /**
   * Clear all fuzzy logic sets from this processor.
   */
  public void clear()
  {
    list.clear();
  }

  /**
   * This method is called to evaluate an input variable against
   * all fuzzy logic sets that are contained by this processor.
   * This method will return the membership that is held by
   * each fuzzy logic set given the input value.
   *
   * @param in An input parameter that should be checked against
   * all of the
   * fuzzy sets that are contained by this processor.
   * @return An array of doubles that contains the degree to
```

```
  * which each of the
  * fuzzy sets matched with the input parameter.
  */
 public double []evaluate(double in)
 {
   double result[] = new double[list.size()];
   Iterator itr = list.iterator();
   int i = 0;
   while (itr.hasNext()) {
     FuzzySet set = (FuzzySet)itr.next();
     result[i++] = set.evaluate(in);
   }
   return result;
 }
}
```

As you can see from the above code, the FuzzyLogic class manages a list of FuzzySet objects. These FuzzySet objects are contained in an ArrayList which is, simply, named "list". The FuzzyLogic class provides two methods that are used to manage this list. The first method, which is named "clear," can be used to clear all FuzzySet objects from the Fuzzy-Logic object's list. This returns the FuzzySet object to the state that it was in just after being instantiated. The second method, which is named add, is used to add FuzzySet objects to this FuzzyLogic object. There is no method provided that removes a single FuzzySet object from a FuzzyLogic object. This is because it is rare that you would add and remove fuzzy sets dynamically. If you do need to routinely process with different fuzzy sets, you should instanciate multiple FuzzyLogic classes to cover the number of possible outcomes.

The last remaining method in the FuzzyLogic class, is named "evaluate". The "evaluate" method accepts a double as input. The "evaluate" method will then return an array of doubles that corresponds to the membership value obtained from each of the fuzzy sets. To do this, the evaluate method begins by allocating an array of doubles that is large enough to hold one value for each element in this list.

```
   double result[] = new double[list.size()];
```

Next the "evaluate" method must loop through all of the fuzzy sets.

```
   Iterator itr = list.iterator();
   int i = 0;
   while (itr.hasNext()) {
     FuzzySet set = (FuzzySet)itr.next();
```

For each fuzzy set, the membership value will be stored inside of the array.

```
     result[i++] = set.evaluate(in);
```

Finally, the "evaluate" method must return the array of membership values that was collected.

```
return result;
```

In the previous sections you saw how the fuzzy logic classes were constructed. Now it is time to put this knowledge to use. In the next section, we will examine two example programs that make use of fuzzy logic.

Fuzzy Logic Examples

In this section, we will examine two programs that make use of the fuzzy logic classes that we developed in previous sections. First, we will examine a program that is capable of graphing the boundaries between fuzzy sets. Second, we will look at a program that checks the current temperature to see if it is hot, cold or warm. We will begin by reviewing the graphing program.

Graphing Fuzzy Sets

In this section, we will examine a program that can graph fuzzy logic sets. This program will make use the same fuzzy logic sets that we just reviewed. The fuzzy sets that will be used with this program will be the temperature sets of warm, cool and hot. The output from this program is shown in Figure 12.3.

Figure 12.3: Graphing Fuzzy Sets

The source code to this example program is contained entirely in the file Graph.java. The listing for this source file is shown in Listing 12.3;

Listing 12.3: Graphing Fuzzy Sets (Graph.java)

```java
import javax.swing.*;
import java.awt.*;

public class Graph extends JFrame {

  public static final int WIDTH = 200;
  public static final int HEIGHT = 200;
  protected FuzzyLogic fuzzyLogic;
  protected FuzzySet cold;
  protected FuzzySet warm;
  protected FuzzySet hot;

  Graph()
  {
    // setup fuzzy sets

    fuzzyLogic = new FuzzyLogic();
    fuzzyLogic.clear();

    cold = new FuzzySet(-20,59,1);
    warm = new FuzzySet(45,90,1);
    hot = new FuzzySet(75,120,1);

    fuzzyLogic.add(cold);
    fuzzyLogic.add(warm);
    fuzzyLogic.add(hot);



    // setup window
    setTitle("Fuzzy Graph");
    setSize(WIDTH,HEIGHT);
  }

  /**
   * Paint the graph.
   *
   * @param g A graphics object.
   */
  public void paint(Graphics g)
  {
    int last[] = new int[3];
```

```
        g.setColor(Color.black);
        g.fillRect(0,0,HEIGHT,WIDTH);
        for (int i=-20;i<=120;i++) {
          double array[] = fuzzyLogic.evaluate(i);
          for (int j=0;j<array.length;j++) {
            switch (j) {
            case 0:g.setColor(Color.green);break;
            case 1:g.setColor(Color.yellow);break;
            case 2:g.setColor(Color.red);break;
            }

            if (array[j]!=0) {
              if (last[j]!=0)
                g.drawLine(
                          i+20,
                          last[j],
                          i+20,
                          HEIGHT-(int)((HEIGHT-20)*array[j]));
              last[j]=HEIGHT-(int)((HEIGHT-20)*array[j]);
            }
          }
        }
      }
      /**
       * The main method.
       *
       * @param args Arguments to main are not used.
       */
      public static void main(String args[])
      {
        (new Graph()).show();
      }
    }
```

As you can see the Graph class defines several properties that are used to display the graph. These variables are summarized in Table 12.2.

Table 12.2: Graph Variables

Variable	Purpose
WIDTH	The desired width of the window.
HEIGHT	The desired height of the window.
fuzzyLogic	The FuzzyLogic class that will hold and process all of the FuzzySet objects.
cold	The FuzzySet that will recognize cold temperatures.
warm	The FuzzySet that will recognize warm temperatures.
hot	The FuzzySet that will recognize hot temperatures.

As the application begins, the constructor is called to setup the fuzzy sets. First, a FuzzyLogic object is allocated to hold the fuzzy sets.

```
fuzzyLogic = new FuzzyLogic();
fuzzyLogic.clear();
```

Next, the fuzzy sets will be created for cold, warm and hot. You can see the temperature ranges below. The maximum membership value for each of these sets is 1.

```
cold = new FuzzySet(-20,59,1);
warm = new FuzzySet(45,90,1);
hot = new FuzzySet(75,120,1);
```

Once the fuzzy sets have been created, we will add them to the fuzzy logic class so that they can be processed.

```
fuzzyLogic.add(cold);
fuzzyLogic.add(warm);
fuzzyLogic.add(hot);
```

Finally, we setup the window.

```
// setup window
setTitle("Fuzzy Graph");
setSize(WIDTH,HEIGHT);
```

Nearly all of the work done by this application is done inside of the paint method. We will now examine how the paint method works. As the graph is plotted, we must track where the last point plotted was. This will allow us to draw lines that connect the points. The last points will be stored int the "last" array that is declared here.

```
int last[] = new int[3];
```

Because there are three fuzzy sets, we must allocate an array of three integers. Next we clear the entire window to a black background.

```
g.setColor(Color.black);
g.fillRect(0,0,HEIGHT,WIDTH);
```

We are now ready to loop through temperature values and plot the graph. To plot these values we will loop through the temperature range from -20 to 120 degrees Fahrenheit.

```
for (int i=-20;i<=120;i++) {
```

Next we present the current temperature to the evaluate method. We will receive an array of the membership values for the current temperature for each of the fuzzy sets.

```
double array[] = fuzzyLogic.evaluate(i);
```

These membership values will now be plotted using a different color for each of the fuzzy sets.

```
for (int j=0;j<array.length;j++) {
  switch (j) {
  case 0:g.setColor(Color.green);break;
  case 1:g.setColor(Color.yellow);break;
  case 2:g.setColor(Color.red);break;
  }
```

Now, each of the lines must be drawn. We will draw the lines from the last position to the current position.

```
if (array[j]!=0) {
  if (last[j]!=0)
    g.drawLine(
            i+20,
            last[j],
            i+20,
            HEIGHT-(int)((HEIGHT-20)*
            array[j]));
```

Finally we update the last value to the current point.

```
last[j]=HEIGHT-(int)((HEIGHT-20)*array[j]);
```

This program allows you to see visually how the different fuzzy sets overlap. Now that we have examined this program, we will see an example that allows you to present user inputted data to the fuzzy logic processor.

Fuzzy Logic Temperature Sets

The program that will be presented in this section will allow the user to input temperatures into the program and see the membership values that will be produced for each of the fuzzy sets. This program is implemented as a console application. You can see the output from this program in Figure 12.4.

Figure 12.4: Temperature Set Determination with Fuzzy Logic

As you can see, this program allows the user to input temperatures. When the user submits a temperature, the membership value for each of the fuzzy sets is displayed. This program creates a relatively simple layer over the fuzzy logic classes that were created earlier in this chapter. We will now examine how the temperature example is constructed. The complete source code for the temperature application is shown in Listing 12.4.

Listing 12.4: Temperature Fuzzy Sets (Temperature.java)

```java
public class Temperature {

/**
 * Read a single line from the console.
 *
 * @return The line that the user typed.
 */
  static String getline()
  {
    String str="";
    char ch;
    try {
      do {
        ch = (char)System.in.read();
        if ( (ch!='\n') && (ch!='\r') )
          str+=ch;
      } while (ch!='\n');
    } catch (Exception e) {
```

```java
      System.out.println("Error: " + e.getMessage());
    }
    return str;
  }
  /**
   * The main method.
   *
   * @param args This program does not use arguments to main.
   */


  public static void main(String args[])
  {
    // prepare the fuzzy logic processor
    FuzzyLogic fuzzyLogic = new FuzzyLogic();
    fuzzyLogic.clear();

    FuzzySet cold = new FuzzySet(-20,59,1);
    FuzzySet warm = new FuzzySet(45,90,1);
    FuzzySet hot = new FuzzySet(75,120,1);

    fuzzyLogic.add(cold);
    fuzzyLogic.add(warm);
    fuzzyLogic.add(hot);
    // present
    String str = "*";

    while (!str.equals("")) {
      System.out.print(
       "Enter a temperature(between -20 and 120 deg f)? ");
      str = getline();
      double temp = 0;
      try {
        if (!str.equals(""))
          temp = Double.parseDouble(str);
      } catch (NumberFormatException e) {
        System.out.println(
"***Please enter a valid temperature or a blank line to exit");
      }

      double array[] = fuzzyLogic.evaluate(temp);
      System.out.println("Cold:" + array[0] );
      System.out.println("Warm:" + array[1] );
      System.out.println("Hot :" + array[2] );
    }
  }
```

```
}
```

There are two methods that are presented in the temperature application. The first method is named "getline". The "getline" method is designed to read a single line of user input from the console. The other method is the Java "main" method. In this simple application, all of the processing is done inside of the main method. We will now examine how the main method is constructed.

The first step that is carried out by the "main" method, is to allocate a FuzzyLogic object and prepare to add new fuzzy sets to it.

```
FuzzyLogic fuzzyLogic = new FuzzyLogic();
```

Next, the three fuzzy sets must be allocated. In the statements below you can see the temperature ranges. The maximum membership value for all three sets is one.

```
FuzzySet cold = new FuzzySet(-20,59,1);
FuzzySet warm = new FuzzySet(45,90,1);
FuzzySet hot = new FuzzySet(75,120,1);
```

Once the fuzzy sets have been allocated, they must be added to the FuzzyLogic object.

```
fuzzyLogic.add(cold);
fuzzyLogic.add(warm);
fuzzyLogic.add(hot);
```

We are now ready to begin looping until the user enters a blank line.

```
String str = "*";

while (!str.equals("")) {
  System.out.print(
    "Enter a temperature(between -20 and 120 deg f)? ");
  str = getline();
  double temp = 0;
  try {
    if (!str.equals(""))
```

The string that the user enters is converted into a double.

```
    temp = Double.parseDouble(str);
  } catch (NumberFormatException e) {
    System.out.println(
```

```
"***Please enter a valid temperature or a blank line to exit");
    }
```

The double is then presented to the FuzzyLogic processor and the results are displayed.

```
    double array[] = fuzzyLogic.evaluate(temp);
    System.out.println("Cold:" + array[0] );
    System.out.println("Warm:" + array[1] );
    System.out.println("Hot :" + array[2] );
  }
}
```

You have now seen two examples of fuzzy logic. Fuzzy logic can also be used in conjunction with neural networks and allow you to prepare incoming data for recognition by a neural network.

Summary

In this chapter, we examined fuzzy logic. Fuzzy logic is very different from the crisp logic that most programs use. Crisp logic is absolute. The result of crisp logic is either true or false, or one precise value. Fuzzy logic is not so precise. Fuzzy logic can return multiple answers, each with a degree of certainty.

A good example of fuzzy logic is temperatures. Consider a human subject. The human will be asked if certain temperatures are considered warm, cold or hot. When asked if the temperature 80 degrees Fahrenheit is hot, the human will respond yes. When asked if the temperature 80 degrees is warm, the human will also reply yes. This would not work so well with crisp logic. Fuzzy logic is needed, because a single temperature can be both warm and hot.

The concepts of warm and hot can be thought of as sets. Each of these sets has many temperatures that belong to that set. Though a human may put a temperature into more than one set, that same human could most likely tell you which set he feels stronger about. This is facilitated in fuzzy logic by using a membership value. This value is returned by the fuzzy set to indicate the degree to which the sampled data belongs in this set. Therefore, when asked if 85 degrees Fahrenheit is either warm or hot, the human would most likely reply with the set that 85 hold the largest membership value for.

In this chapter, we examined two example programs. Both examples dealt with the issue of determining if a temperature were cold, hot or warm. The first one was a graphical Java program that plotted the set membership of data. Using this example program, you were able to clearly see the linear separation between the sets.

The second program was more interactive, in that it allowed you to enter temperatures, and the program would respond back telling you the membership value that the inputted temperature had in each of the sets of warm, hot and cold. The program did this by displaying the set membership value for each of the three fuzzy sets that were used in this example program.

This completes our introduction to neural networks in Java. Be sure to check out the Heaton Research website, http://www.heatonresearch.com, for more artificial intelligence books and articles.

APPENDIX A: JOONE REFERENCE

Many of the examples in this book make use of JOONE. JOONE can be downloaded from http://www.jooneworld.com. What exactly, is JOONE? The following was taken from the JOONE website.

Joone is a FREE neural net framework to create, train and test neural nets. (What is a neural network?)

The aim is to create a powerful environment both for enthusiastic and professional users, based on the newest Java technologies.

Joone is composed by a central engine that is the fulcrum of all applications that already exist or will be developed with Joone.

Joone's neural networks can be built on a local machine, be trained on a distributed environment and run on whatever device. Everyone can write new modules to implement new algorithms or new architectures starting from the simple components distributed with the core engine .

The main idea is to create the basis to promote a zillion of AI applications that revolve around the core framework.

APPENDIX B. MATHEMATICAL BACKGROUND

Neural network programming is deeply rooted in mathematics. One of the most common forms of mathematics used in Neural Network study is the Matrix. In this appendix I will present some of the math skills needed for this book, and show you where you can find more information.

Why Matrixes?

Why are matrixes so important to Neural Networks? It is because a matrix is generally used to store the Neuron weights. Consider a 2-layer neural network with two neurons in each layer. A weight exists between each neuron, in each layer. The neurons within a single layer are not connected. This results in two connections. The two neurons in the first layer each have a connection to the two in the other layer.

But wait! There are more than just the two neurons. Each connection is two way. This results in four total connections. This can be written as the following weight matrix.

$$\begin{bmatrix} 1 & 2 \\ 3 & 4 \end{bmatrix}$$

Matrix Operations

There are many operations that can be performed on Matrixes. In AI, the most common are:

Matrix Multiplication
Matrix Inverse
Matrix Dot Product

These topics are covered, in detail, at the following site. This site is operated by the makers of MathCAD.

http://mathworld.wolfram.com/topics/MatrixOperations.html

Sigma Notation

Many programmers, without a mathematical background, are intimidated by sigma notation. Its actually VERY simple. In programming, it relates very much to a for loop. Consider the following:

$$\sum_{y=1}^{10} (y+1)$$

Sigma is used to sum something, in a loop. Think of the above sigma-equation as a for loop that counts from 1 to 10, using y as the index. Each time through the (y+1) part is summed and the result is placed into x. The following Java program does the same thing.

```
int x = 0;
for( int y = 0; y<=10; y++ )
{
        x+= (y+1);
}
```

APPENDIX C: COMPILING EXAMPLES UNDER WINDOWS

All program source code can be downloaded from:

http://www.heatonresearch.com/

This book contains many examples that illustrate the use of neural networks. These examples can be downloaded from Heaton Research. The individual chapters do not describe how to compile and execute each example. Instead, this appendix is given to show you how to compile and execute the example programs under the Windows platform. If you are trying to compile examples under a UNIX environment, refer to Appendix D, "Compiling Examples under UNIX/Linux".

Java Environment

The examples contained in this book were all tested using Sun's JDK 1.4. You must have JDK 1.4 installed. Installing JDK is pretty straight forward. You download the "exe" from Sun (http://java.sun.com) and double click the "exe", usually named j2sdk-1_4_0-win.exe, to begin the installation process. This will install the JDK into the directory c:\j2sdk1.4.0\ or similar.

Installing JOONE

Many of the example programs contained in this book use the Java Objected Oriented Neural Engine (JOONE). To correctly execute these examples you must install JOONE. JOONE consists of a series of JAR files that must be added to your Java CLASSPATH. The JAR files necessary to run JOONE are included in a directory named "jar" on the companion download for this book. The JAR files included in this directory are summarized as follows:

JAR File	Purpose
crimson.jar	Part of the Sun XML parser. Note: this file is not needed if you are using JDK 1.4 or higher.
jhotdraw.jar	JHotDraw is a two-dimensional graphics framework for structured drawing editors that are written in Java. It is used internally by JOONE's editor. For more information on jhotdraw see http://sourceforge.net/projects/jhotdraw.
joone-editor.jar	The JOONE editor. This is Java application that lets you graphically edit neural networks.
joone-engine.jar	The JOONE engine. This JAR file must be included with programs use the JOONE engine. This contains the core routines and not the editor.
junit.jar	Used internally by JOONE.
log4j.jar	This is a logging API developed by Apache. JOONE uses this internally. For more information on Log4J see http://jakarta.apache.org/log4j/.
ppi.jar	Used internally by JOONE.
xalan.jar	Part of the Sun XML parser. Note: this file is not needed if you are using JDK 1.4 or higher.

In order to use JOONE, and the examples that require JOONE, these files must be accessible on the CLASSPATH. Two of these JARs are now included as part of JDK 1.4. If you are using JDK 1.4, you will most likely use a CLASSPATH such as:

```
./;c:\jar\joone-editor.jar;c:\jar\joone-engine.jar;c:\jar\jhot-
draw.jar;c:\jar\junit.jar; c:\jar\ppi.jar;c:\jar\log4j.jar
```

If you are using a version of the JDK that is lower than JDK 1.4 you will need a longer CLASSPATH that includes all of the previously mentioned JARs.

```
./;c:\jar\joone-editor.jar;c:\jar\joone-engine.jar;c:\jar\crimson.
jar;c:\jar\jhotdraw.jar; c:\jar\junit.jar;c:\jar\xalan.jar;c:\jar\
ppi.jar;c:\jar\log4j.jar
```

To add these to your CLASSPATH, you must modify your system's environmental variables. In addition to setting the CLASSPATH, you must also modify your path environmental to make the JDK part of your system path. By making JDK part of the system path you can invoke the Java commands, such as javac and java, from any directory. Additionally, you must also set the environmental variable JAVA_HOME to point to this directory. JDK_HOME is used by various Apache tools to locate Java. In this book we will be using Apache ANT. ANT will be discussed later in this appendix. The exact directions for setting your environmental variables are different, depending on which version of Windows you are using.

Setting the Environmental Variables in Windows XP/2000 Professional

To set environmental variables under the professional Editions of Microsoft Windows, you must use the System Properties panel. The System Properties panel can be found under the "Control Panel" option on the Windows Start Menu. The System Properties Panel is shown in Figure C.1. Once the System Properties panel is open you should click the advanced tab.

Figure C.1: The System Properties Panel

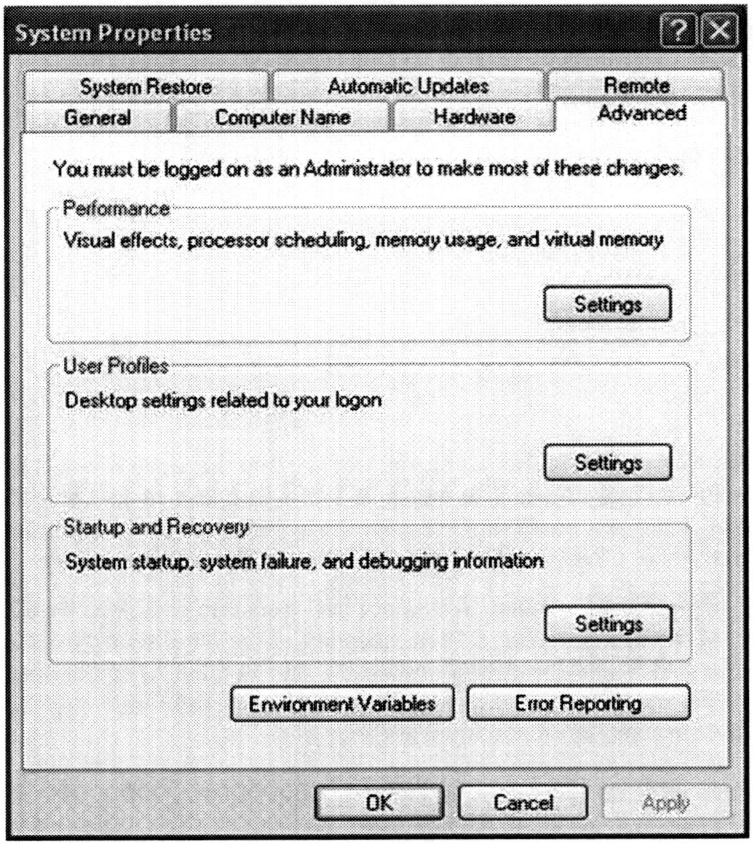

From the System Properties panel you can access the Environmental Variables panel. This window contains a number of tabs. First, you should click the tab labeled "Advanced". Next. click the button labeled "Environmental Variables" near the bottom of the System Properties panel. Your screen should now resemble Figure C.2, which shows these settings in the System Properties dialog box under Windows XP Professional Edition.

Figure C.2: The Environmental Variables Panel

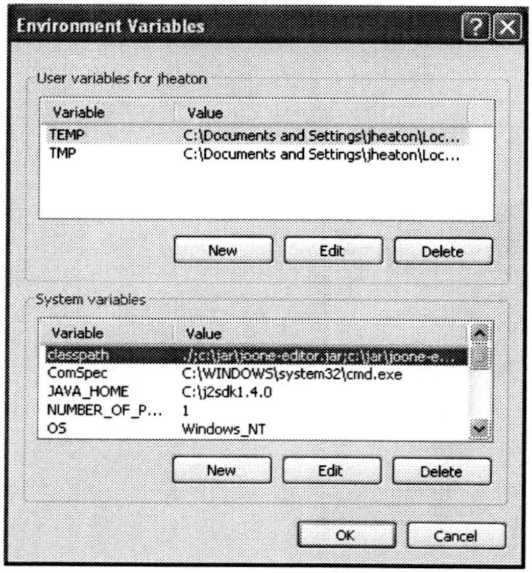

When you enter the Environmental Variables panel, you will see that there are two sets of environmental variables (shown in Figure C.2). The top set is for the current user. The bottom set is for the entire system. I suggest modifying them for the system because this seems to be where most systems modify the CLASSPATH setting. To do so, follow these steps:

1. Find the path setting. If your JDK installation was not in the system path, you would have to add its bin directory to the system path. Add the location of the bin directory (usually C:\ j2sdk1.4.0\bin\) to the PATH environmental variable. This is done by appending your bin directory to whatever currently exists in the PATH variable. Do not forget to put a semicolon (;) at the end of the current path if you must add on.

2. Create an environmental variable named JAVA_HOME. The value of JAVA_HOME should be set to the root of your JDK installation. For most systems this is C:\j2sdk1.4.0\ bin\

3. Either create or append to the CLASSPATH setting the complete location of the required jars which were discussed in the previous section. Note that each path setting is delimited by a semicolon (;). If there already is a CLASSPATH, simply append the required JARs to the end, if there is no CLASSPATH, you must click New, to create a CLASSPATH.

4. Click OK to accept your changes. This completes the process.

Make sure you include the dot slash (./) portion of your CLASSPATH. If you do not include the dot-slash (./), which represents the current directory, many Java programs will not execute properly.

Setting Environmental Variables in Windows 95/98/ME

To modify the system path and CLASSPATH under these versions of Windows, the autoexec.bat file must be modified. Your autoexec.bat file may look like the one shown in Figure C.3, but also may not. It all depends on which system you use. However, no matter what your autoexec.bat looks like, you should be able to follow these steps to execute it regardless of which system you use.

1. Locate the autoexec.bat file in the root of your C drive. Open the file with Notepad. You may want to save a copy of your current autoexec.bat file to a backup, such as autoexec. bak.

2. Create an environmental variable named JAVA_HOME. The value of JAVA_HOME should be set to the root of your JDK installation. For most systems line will be "set JAVA_ HOME = C:\j2sdk1.4.0\".

3. Locate the set classpath command. If you cannot find this command, type it in (as it is shown in Figure C.3). Add the bot.jar to the CLASSPATH by appending a "SET CLASSPATH = " line to the end of the autoexec.bat file.

4. Locate the path statement, and add the location of your bin directory. Figure C.3 shows a properly modified autoexec.bat file.

Your autoexec.bat file will look slightly different than this example. This example is shown primarily to give you an idea of how it should look. Always make sure that the current directory—represented by a dot-slash (./)—is part of the CLASSPATH. Without the current directory as part of the CLASSPATH, most Java programs will not correctly execute.

The information provided here is meant to give you a general idea of how Java should be set up. To completely describe how to configure the Java environment would is beyond the scope of this book. For more information on CLASSPATHs and installing JDK, please refer to the JDK installation instructions or a book about the Java programming language. A book that provides an introduction to Java, such as "Java2 Complete, (Sybex, 1999)", ISBN 0782124682 , would provide more information.

Figure C.3: An autoexec.bat File

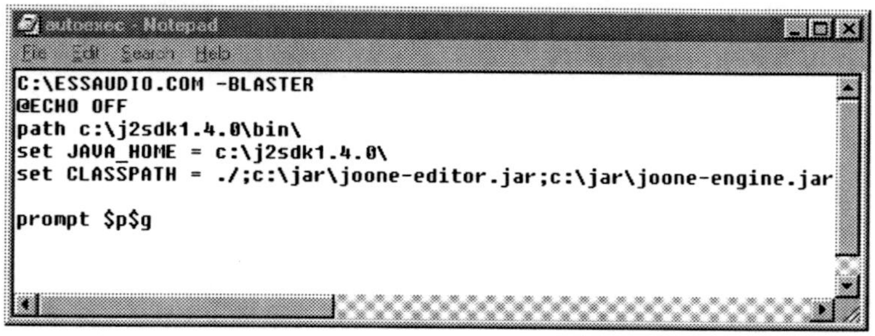

```
C:\ESSAUDIO.COM -BLASTER
@ECHO OFF
path c:\j2sdk1.4.0\bin\
set JAVA_HOME = c:\j2sdk1.4.0\
set CLASSPATH = ./;c:\jar\joone-editor.jar;c:\jar\joone-engine.jar

prompt $p$g
```

Testing Your Environment

You should now have both JDK and JOONE properly installed. To test these configurations, try the following command from a DOS or command prompt window. The directory you are in is unimportant.

```
java org.joone.edit.JoonEdit c:\jar\layers.xml
```

For convenience, I have included a copy of the layers.xml file in stored in the JAR directory. For more information about the layers file, refer to Chapter 3, "Using Multilayer Neural Networks". The layers file does not need to be in the JAR directory and could be stored anywhere, so long as a complete path is given to the JOONE Editor. If you have properly installed your environment, you should see the JOONE editor, as shown in Figure C.4.

Figure C.4: The JOONE Editor

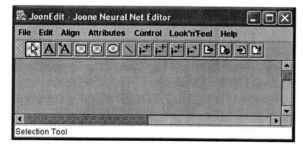

If you get an error message instead of the window shown in Figure C.4, recheck the steps in the previous sections. If you are getting an error, it most likely means that either your system path or CLASSPATH are configured incorrectly.

Compiling and Executing Examples

This book contains many example programs to illustrate neural networks. This section shows you how to compile and execute these examples. Before you can compile and execute the examples, you must properly configure your system as described in the previous section.

The examples contain build scripts that use ANT. ANT is a utility that was created by Apache to allow cross-platform build scripts to be created for Java programs. For more information about ANT, refer to http://jakarta.apache.org/ant/.

Installing Ant

ANT is distributed as a simple ZIP file that must be extracted to a directory on your system. The copy of ANT that I am currently using is installed in the directory c:\jakarta-ant-1.4.1. To properly use ANT, you must include its bin directory (c:\jakarta-ant-1.4.1\bin\) as part of your system path. Refer to the previous section to see how to do this. To test to see if you have properly installed ANT, just enter the command "ant" from the command prompt. You should get output as follows:

```
C:\>ant
Buildfile: build.xml does not exist!
Build failed
C:\>
```

Do not worry about the build failed; at this point we just wanted to see if ANT could be found. The next section shows you how to properly specify a script.

Compiling an Example

In order to compile an example, it is necessary to execute the build script with ANT. All of the examples in this book have a build file named build.xml. The build file will be stored in that example's directory on the companion download.

To begin the build process you should enter the following command.

```
ant -buildfile build.xml
```

For this example, we are using the Hopfield example from Chapter 2. If the build is successful, you will see the following output.

```
Buildfile: build.xml

init:
    [mkdir] Created dir: C:\NeuralNetworks\examples\Ch2\Hopfield\
```

```
build

compile:
    [javac] Compiling 3 source files to C:\NeuralNetworks\exam-
ples\Ch2\Hopfield\build

dist:
    [mkdir] Created dir: C:\NeuralNetworks\examples\Ch2\Hopfield\
dist\lib
      [jar] Building jar: C:\NeuralNetworks\examples\Ch2\Hopfield\
dist\lib\Hopfield.jar

BUILD SUCCESSFUL

Total time: 2 seconds
```

Executing an Example

If the build is successful, a JAR file will be created that contains the example. For Chapter 2's Hopfield example, the JAR file created is Hopfield.jar. You should be able to execute the JAR file simply by double clicking it. If this fails you will have to run the JAR by going to its directory (dist\lib) and entering the following command.

```
java -jar Hopfield.jar
```

If the Hopfield example executes correctly, you should see a window like Figure C.5.

Figure C.5: The Hopfield Example

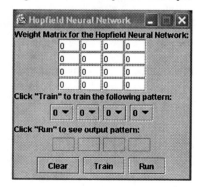

Using an IDE Such as Eclipse

Using an IDE, such as Eclipse or Borland JBuilder can often speed development and debugging times. Every example in this book also comes with a Eclipse project file. This allows you to open the project in Visual Cafe. Once the project is opened, you might have to reconfigure the project directories. Currently every project file is configured to assume that the JOONE JAR files are stored in c:\jar\. If you have installed these files elsewhere, you will have to change the directory setting for the projects.

APPENDIX D. COMPILING EXAMPLES UNDER LINUX/UNIX

All program source code can be downloaded from:

http://www.heatonresearch.com/

This book contains many examples that illustrate the use of neural networks. These examples are contained on the companion download. The individual chapters do not describe how to compile and execute each example. Instead, this appendix is given to show you how to compile and execute the example programs under a UNIX platform. The examples given in this appendix were tried under Red Hat Linux 7.2; other UNIX environments should be similar. If you are trying to compile examples under a Windows environment, refer to Appendix C, "Compiling Examples under Windows".

Java Environment

The examples contained in this book were all tested using Sun's JDK 1.4. A copy of JDK1.4 is included on the companion download. You must have JDK 1.4 installed. Installing JDK is pretty straight forward. You download the BIN file from Sun (http://java.sun.com). This BIN file is actually just a wrapper around an RPM file. This is done so that you accept the Sun agreement before receiving the RPM file. To extract the RPM from the bin file, you should execute the BIN file. Once you have your RPM file, you should switch to the root user, by using the su command, to complete the installation. To install the RPM file, use the following command.

```
rpm - i j2sdk-1_4_0-fcs-linux-i386.rpm
```

This should install the JDK to the directory /usr/java/j2sdk1.4.0.

Installing JOONE

Many of the example programs contained in this book use the Java Objected Oriented Neural Engine (JOONE). To correctly execute these examples, you must install JOONE. JOONE consists of a series of JAR files that must be added to your Java CLASSPATH. The JAR files necessary to run JOONE are included in a directory named "jar" on the companion download for this book. The JAR files included in this directory are summarized as follows:

JAR File	Purpose
crimson.jar	Part of the Sun XML parser. Note: This file is not needed if you are using JDK 1.4 or higher.
jhotdraw.jar	JHotDraw is a two-dimensional graphics framework for structured drawing editors that are written in Java. It is used internally by JOONE's editor. For more information on jhotdraw see http://sourceforge.net/projects/jhotdraw.
joone-editor.jar	The JOONE editor. This Java application that lets you graphically edit neural networks.
joone-engine.jar	The JOONE engine. This JAR file must be included with programs that use the JOONE engine. This contains the core routines and not the editor.
junit.jar	Used internally by JOONE.
log4j.jar	This is a logging API developed by Apache. JOONE uses this internally. For more information on Log4J see http://jakarta.apache.org/log4j/.
ppi.jar	Used internally by JOONE.
xalan.jar	Part of the Sun XML parser. Note: This file is not needed if you are using JDK 1.4 or higher.

In order to use JOONE and the examples that require JOONE, these files must be accessible on the CLASSPATH. Two of these JARs are now included as part of JDK 1.4. If you are using JDK 1.4, you will most likely use a CLASSPATH such as:

```
./:/usr/jar/joone-editor.jar:/usr/jar/joone-engine.jar:/usr/jar/
jhotdraw.jar:/jar/junit.jar: /usr/jar/ppi.jar:/usr/jar/log4j.jar
```

If you are using a version of the JDK that is lower than JDK 1.4, you will need a longer CLASSPATH that includes all of the previously mentioned JARs.

```
./:/usr/jar/joone-editor.jar:/usr/jar/joone-engine.jar:/usr/jar/
crimson.jar: /usr/jar/jhotdraw.jar:/jar/junit.jar:/usr/jar/xalan.
jar:/usr/jar/ppi.jar:/usr/jar/log4j.jar
```

To add these to your CLASSPATH, you must modify your system's environmental variables. In addition to setting the CLASSPATH, you must also modify your path environmental variable to make the JDK part of your system path. By making JDK part of the system path you can invoke the Java commands, such as javac and java, from any directory. Additionally you must also set the environmental variable JAVA_HOME to point to this directory.

JDK_HOME is used by various Apache tools to locate Java. In this book we will be using Apache ANT. ANT will be discussed later in this appendix. The exact directions for setting your environmental variables are different, depending on which version of Linux/UNIX you are using.

This is done by modifying your login profile. The exact name of this file depends on what shell you are using. If you are using a default Red Hat installation, then you will be using the bash shell. To change environmental variables under bash, you must modify the .bash_profile file. This file is shown in Figure D.1.

Figure D.1: Editing the .bash_profile File

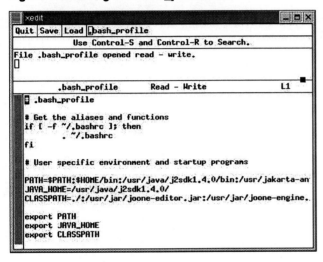

To edit your ".bash_profile" file, make sure you are in your home directory and use xedit to open the file. This can be done as follows:

```
cd ~
xedit .bash_profile
```

Once you are editing your profile file, you must make several changes to this file.

1.   Find the path setting. If your JDK installation was not in the system path, you would have to add its bin directory to the system path. Add the location of the bin directory (usually /usr/java/j2sdk1.4.0/) to the PATH environmental variable. This is done by appending your bin directory to whatever currently exists in the PATH variable. Do not forget to put a colon (:) at the end of the current path if you must add on.

2.   Create an environmental variable named JAVA_HOME. The value of JAVA_HOME should be set to the root of your JDK installation. For most systems this is /usr/java/j2sdk1.4.0/.

3.   Either create or append to the CLASSPATH, setting the complete location of the required jars which were discussed in the previous section. Note that each path setting is delimited by a colon (:). If there already is a CLASSPATH, simply append the required JARs to the end, if there is no CLASSPATH, you must click New, to create a CLASSPATH.

4.   Make sure that these environmental variables are exported. There should be an export line for each of these variables, as seen in Figure D.1.

5.   Click SAVE to accept your changes. This completes the process.

Make sure you include the dot slash (./) portion of your CLASSPATH. If you do not include the dot-slash (./), which represents the current directory, many Java programs will execute properly.

Testing Your Environment

You should now have both JDK and JOONE properly installed. To test these configurations, try the following command from a DOS or command prompt window. The directory you are in is unimportant.

java org.joone.edit.JoonEdit /usr/jar/layers.xml

For convenience, I have included a copy of the layers.xml file in stored in the JAR directory. For more information about the layers file refer to Chapter 3, "Using Multilayer Neural Networks". The layers file does not need to be in the JAR directory and could be stored anywhere, so long as a complete path is given to the JOONE Editor. If you have properly installed your environment, you should see the JOONE editor as shown in Figure D.2.

Figure D.2: The JOONE Editor

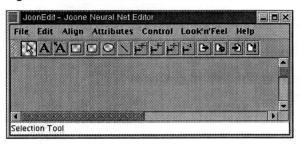

If you get an error message instead of the window shown in Figure D.2, recheck the steps in the previous sections. If you are getting an error, it most likely means that either your system path or CLASSPATH are configured incorrectly.

Compiling and Executing Examples

This book contains many example programs to illustrate neural networks. This section shows you how to compile and execute these examples. Before you can compile and execute the examples, you must properly configure your system as described in the previous section.

The examples contain build scripts that use ANT. ANT is a utility that was created by Apache to allow cross-platform build scripts to be created for Java programs.   For more information about ANT refer to http://jakarta.apache.org/ant/.

Installing Ant

ANT is distributed as a simple ZIP file that must be extracted to a directory on your system. The copy of ANT that I am currently using is installed in the directory /usr/jakarta-ant-1.4.1. To properly use ANT you must include its bin directory (/usr/jakarta-ant-1.4.1/bin/) as part of your system path. Refer to the previous section to see how to do this. To test to see if you have properly installed ANT just enter the command "ant" from the command prompt. You should get output as follows:

```
>ant
Buildfile: build.xml does not exist!
Build failed
```

Do not worry about the build failed; at this point we just wanted to see if ANT could be found. The next section shows you how to properly specify a script.

Compiling an Example

In order to compile an example, it is necessary to execute the build script with ANT. All of the examples in this book have a build file named build.xml. The build file will be stored in that example's directory on the companion.

To begin the build process you should enter the following command.

```
ant -buildfile build.xml
```

For this example, we are using the Hopfield example from Chapter 2. If the build is successful you will see the following output.

```
[jheaton@localhost Hopfield]$ ant
Buildfile: build.xml

init:
    [mkdir] Created dir: /home/jheaton/cdrom/examples/Ch2/Hopfield/build

compile:
    [javac] Compiling 3 source files to /home/jheaton/cdrom/examples/Ch2/Hopfield/
build

dist:
    [mkdir] Created dir: /home/jheaton/cdrom/examples/Ch2/Hopfield/dist/lib
      [jar] Building jar: /home/jheaton/cdrom/examples/Ch2/Hopfield/dist/lib/Hop-
field.jar

BUILD SUCCESSFUL

Total time: 9 seconds
[jheaton@localhost Hopfield]$
```

One possible error that you might get is the "bad interpreter" error shown below.

```
bash: /usr/jakarta-ant-1.4.1/bin/antRun: bad interpreter: Permis-
sion denied
```

If you are getting this error, then it means that the main ant script file does not have execute permission. To fix this, you must change into a super user then set the permission on the ant file in the bin directory. This is done with the "chmod 777 ant" command.

Executing an Example

If the build is successful, a JAR file will be created that contains the example. For Chapter 2's Hopfield example, the JAR file created is Hopfield.jar. You should be able to execute the JAR file simply by double clicking it. If this fails, you will have to run the JAR by going to its directory (dist/lib) and entering the following command.

```
java -jar Hopfield.jar
```

If the Hopfield example executes correctly you should see a window like Figure D.3.

Figure D.3: The Hopfield Example

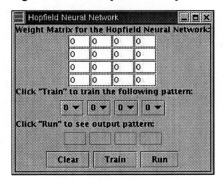

INDEX

U

UML. *See* uniform modeling language
underfitting 129
Uniform Modeling Language 78
United States Postal Service 193
unsupervised training 36, 107, 108, 115, 123
URLInputSynapse 79

V

validation 45
vector length 158, 162-163, 169, 175
Von Neumann computer 42, 43, 44

W

weight matrix 50-57, 64, 69
winner 155, 176-178, 181-185, 190, 195, 206, 207

X

XOR 39-41, 80-91, 94-96, 101, 103, 104, 107, 109, 138-148, 269-318, 321

Z

zip codes 193

OTHER BOOKS FROM HEATON RESEARCH

Introduction to Neural Networks with Java
by Jeff Heaton
ISBN:0-9773206-0-X

Introduction to Neural Networks with Java teaches the reader to solve a variety of problems using neural networks. The reader is introduced to the open source JOONE neural engine, as well as a simple Optical Character Recognition (OCR) program, the traveling salesman problem and the feedfoward backpropagation neural network.

Build a Computer from Scratch
by Jeff Heaton
ISBN: 0-9773206-2-6

Building a computer is not as hard as you might think. This book shows how to select the best parts and build your very own computer. Knowing how to build your computer saves money and gets you the computer you really want. A computer you build yourself is one that YOU can always upgrade and repair.

Java for the Beginning Programmer
by Jeff Heaton
ISBN: 0-9773206-1-8

If you would like to learn to program in Java but have never attempted programming before, this book takes it from the beginning. This book focuses on the fundamentals of Java programming, such as loops, functions, classes and methods. Emphasis is placed on learning core programming techniques and rather than using an IDE to generate code for you.

To purchase any of these books visit:

http://www.heatonresearch.com/book/

Visit http://www.HeatonResearch.com

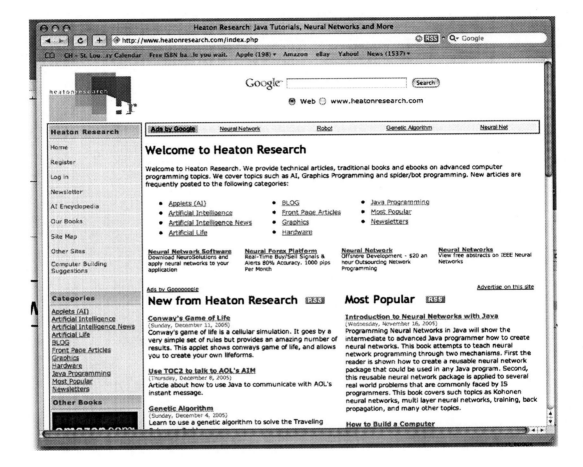

Visit www.HeatonResearch.com for our latest articles and books.

To download the source code to this book visit:

http://www.heatonresearch.com/book/

Printed in the United States
72230LV00006B/179-188